BROAD SIDES

One Woman's Clash with a Corrupt Culture

Ilana Mercer

Books can be ordered from Amazon.com, BN.com, other online bookstores and:

www.bytechservices.com
1500A East College Way #554
Mount Vernon, WA 98273

www.ilanamercer.com

Library of Congress Cataloging-in-Publication data

Mercer, Ilana

Broad sides: one woman's clash with a corrupt culture / Ilana Mercer

Includes bibliographical references and index.

ISBN: 0-9741039-0-X

1. Social history – 21st century. 2. Social values. 3. Popular culture.

4. United States – Social conditions – 21st century.

5. United States – Politics and government – 21st century.

LC Control No.:   2004271417

Printed in the United States of America

Photography by Gordan Dumka

Cover by Stephen Symons Design

Second Edition

Visit us online at www.ilanamercer.com

Contents

Acknowledgments

These are acknowledgments with a difference—appropriate, I think, since they flow from a brief writing trajectory that itself has been different.

Both personal experience and example account for the libertarian principles of individual rights, limited government, and free markets that coalesce in *Broad Sides*.

As for the experience, I've seen the impact of moral and political ideas on many cultures torn by strife. I'm an ex-Israeli and ex-South African who eventually found her way to America by way of Canada. From this, dare I say, "multicultural" background, I learned basic lessons about the nefarious influence of government power on individual life—lessons that crystallized while I endured life in the Canadian Welfare State.

After immigrating to Canada in 1995, I fully intended to pursue work in psychology, in which I have degrees. But I discovered that field had, for the most part, gone pop. Ruminations about the corrosive effects on society of the therapeutic culture, and of the cult of the victim, soon led me to other realizations as well. Whether it was promoting official multiculturalism, radical feminist orthodoxy, critical race theory, affirmative action policies or literary deconstruction—I saw that the state was everywhere a destructive presence.

I observed how citizens—neatly factioned into warring special interests—lined up to cheer the state's every assault on basic liberties. To them, "freedom" had become synonymous with receiving some government entitlement. Private charity was flagging, usurped by welfare programs. "Equality" was to be achieved through newly minted "human rights," institutionalized by the state's divide-and-rule, wealth-confiscation-and-distribution activities.

Government was eroding private property not only by redistributing it, but by regulating how its rightful owners could use it.

In short, while the *state* was waxing, *society* was waning.

Up until then, I was a stay-at-home mom to a daughter, now 20 years old, whom I had at a relatively young age. (I had made the decision to be a full-time mom before it became a fashionable annoyance for unmarried, "conservative" career women to harangue less fortunate females about the obvious merits of the practice.)

But around 1998, incensed by the political and cultural degeneration around me, I began writing editorials. Except for an early dose of Randianism, I knew nothing about the libertarian political philosophy. Yet, unbeknown to me, I was espousing it.

That describes the "experience." As for the "example," I cite my father, Rabbi Ben Isaacson, a South African anti-apartheid activist who fled to Israel, where I grew up. From him I learned an unwavering commitment to one's beliefs.

He also established for me an attractive role model of idealism. Mother Teresa had firm convictions, too, but—and no disrespect is intended—I'm not sure I'd have chosen to spend an afternoon with her. By contrast, what does one say about a father (and a Rabbi to boot) who once, transported by the sounds of music, whispered in his young daughter's ear: "Don't tell anyone, Ilana, but Bach is really God." Knowing him, he was paying The Almighty the highest compliment.

So for imparting to me his sense of life, irreverence and contrariness, tempered always by a dedication to timeless standards and verities, I thank my father.

Within a year of my first editorializing efforts, I had a regular weekly column with a gem of a Vancouver-based newspaper, the *North Shore News.* I am indebted to its then-editor, Timothy Renshaw, and former proprietor, Peter Speck. These gentlemen gave me my first break.

A stint with the conservative—and exceptional—*Calgary Herald* followed. A doff of the hat to the debonair Peter Stockland, now editor-in-chief of the *Montreal Gazette*, for getting excited about my early and rather raw fare; to Larry Solomon of the prestigious Canadian *Financial Post,* who also took note and proceeded to publish pieces of which I am very proud; and to the editors at the libertarian *Ottawa Citizen*, the paleoconservative *Report Newsmagazine*, the *Vancouver Sun*, *Insight* magazine, the *Colorado Gazette,* and the *Orange County Register.*

Special appreciation goes to the splendid editorialists at the *Globe and Mail*, Canada's national newspaper, who continue to call on me for commentary contributions.

The Internet presented an opportunity to reach a vast readership. I owe gratitude to Sam Karnick of the Hudson Institute, and to Jeffrey Tucker of the Ludwig von Mises Institute, for their ongoing interest in posting my essays. And, of course, to Joseph Farah for making me a featured columnist for WorldNetDaily.com in 2002. About Mr. Farah's pluck, not enough can ever be said.

I gratefully acknowledge Professor Walter Block for bringing me into the libertarian fold, and for introducing me to his remarkable corpus of work, as well as to the writings of economists Ludwig von Mises, Murray N. Rothbard, and other seminal libertarian thinkers. Also, Thomas DiLorenzo and Paul Gottfried, for many joyous conversations, invaluable friendship, and steady support; the multitalented Robert Bidinotto, publisher of ecoNOT.com, for the gift of his guidance, professional and personal; and a consummate Southern gentleman, my proofreader Paul Wicks, for his skills and commitment.

From the bottom of my heart I thank Peter Brimelow who found the time to write the book's Foreword, despite his many important commitments and daunting challenges.

Above all, a debt of gratitude is owed to my sweet mother, Ann-Wendy Cumes, for her love and support, and to my husband, Sean Russell Mercer. This book was his brainchild—without his patience and pragmatism none of this would have been possible.

—ILANA MERCER

Foreword

"Yes – but she's a handful!"

This was the reaction of one of the leaders of American libertarianism when I called to consult him about the blazing arrival on the media scene of Ilana Mercer, ground zero in Washington State after a meteoric transit through Canada. (And before that, Israel—and before that South Africa…)

My attention had been instantly commanded by Ilana's columns, circulated by her many admirers by email and now appearing every Friday on WorldNetDaily. And also, I admit, by pictures of her lovely face. (Ditto). The combination of brains and beauty is rare. But I am old enough to know that it does happen and has to be taken very seriously when it occurs.

Still, looking again at Ilana's columns, now collected in this volume, I have to admit: she *is* a handful!

It is one thing to advocate libertarianism in a political culture that is still basically dominated by statist liberals. It is another to be willing to address the problems of mass legal and illegal immigration—a government policy, of course, and a logical subject for analysis, but absolutely ruled out of court by the libertarian establishment, what the late and much-missed Murray Rothbard called the "Kochtopus" after a major donor. It is yet another thing to be a proud Zionist *and* fiercely opposed to America's Iraq invasion (*and* critical of Pat Buchanan's criticisms of the neoconservative "cabal" in the Bush Administration, albeit fairly moderately by Mercer standards … for what that's worth!)

I don't know what this is doing for Ilana's career. But it's great for her readers—although they must be prepared, as they turn these pages, for her furious eye to fall on one or other of their own favorite causes.

This volume appears at a moment of peculiar crisis for libertarians in general and for Ilana in particular. The normal patriotic reaction to the 9/11 terrorist attacks has been translated by the Bush Administration and its cheerleaders into a general war in the Middle East.

Ilana supported going after al-Qaida in Afghanistan—she characteristically describes it as "a legitimate act of retaliation and defense, accommodated within St. Augustine's teachings." But she is appalled by the invasion of Iraq. The measure of her distress can be gauged by a fact that she notes grimly: despite massive U.S. media coverage, audiences are getting a more balanced picture of the complexities, and of the carnage, from the Canadian Broadcasting Corporation.

You have to have reached the U.S. after a prolonged passage through Canada, as both Ilana and I did, to appreciate what it takes to say that.

Ilana's experience of Canada's combination of parochial political correctness and complacency—now that must have been an epic confrontation!—came after her experience of living in two countries at the center of world attention, and in constant danger: South Africa and Israel.

Reflecting on the mounting costs of the Iraq War, she writes:

> These days, I think a lot about Avshalom. The Avshalom I knew was as beautiful as his biblical namesake, King David's son. Avshalom had dimples to die for, big brown eyes, and blond, sun-streaked curls. The vision of him, topless, on a red Ferguson tractor, as he ploughed the fields of the kibbutz, was very fetching.
>
> Avshalom was 19 or 20 when he died. Like all Israeli boys, he was conscripted and he fell in some or other maneuver. My class lost another boy. There may have been others since, but I lost touch.

Yet, somewhat to my surprise, it is actually quite rare for this most emotionally intense of columnists to draw on such personal experiences. What seem to motivate Ilana, ultimately, are ideas.

Thus at a time when the entire American punditocracy, liberal and "conservative" (and, emphatically, libertarian), had turned on Senate Majority leader Trent Lott for his momentary excess of enthusiasm at Strom Thurmond's 100th birthday party, Ilana raises her elegantly manicured (I imagine) hand to say that

(a) Lott obviously had no intention whatever of restoring segregation (or doing much of anything else, she might have added);

(b) Quite apart from segregation, Thurmond's presidential run in 1948 did have a worthwhile point: states' rights.

The autonomy of the states, Ilana points out, indeed is—was—a barrier to tyranny.

"States' rights," she notes,

> are an obstacle to ridding the nation of racism only in as much as the First Amendment is such a barrier. So long as property rights and free speech are respected, individuals are bound to exhibit preferences or express tastes that others will find displeasing....Abolish states' rights and one does away with a measure of freedom and property rights, not racism.

Then, being Ilana, she goes on to add:

> A fact that was not lost on Abraham Lincoln and Adolf Hitler; both were great centralizers. Lincoln hagiographers would protest to the contrary, but it isn't remotely incendiary to point out that he and Hitler shared very similar views on states' rights—Lincoln's unfavorable views of such rights are seconded by Hitler in *Mein Kampf*.

It *is* incendiary to point this out, of course. But it also displays a mind fearlessly in pursuit of analytical truth—as does the fact that Ilana wasn't even born until long after 1948, and grew up in countries with no real tradition of federalism at all. She has figured this out all by herself, in the teeth of the conventional wisdom.

Very much the same is true of Ilana's writing's on immigration policy. Mass immigration is actually a new phenomenon in the U.S.—it was triggered by the Great Society's disastrous 1965 Immigration and Nationality Act, before which there had been 40 years with very little immigration, one of many such pauses in U.S. history. As a result, because most people are incapable of absorbing new ideas after 18 or so, most of the current generation of politicians and pundits just haven't gotten the message.

Ilana appears to have gotten the message in part because of empirical evidence proving current policy's paradoxical consequences—she cites Harvard economist George Borjas on the deteriorating relative skill levels of the post-1965 influx. But, also, characteristically, she is fascinated by Hans-Herman Hoppe's argument—in his *Natural Order, The State And The Immigration Problem*—that immigration is ultimately an issue of the host community's private property rights, systematically violated by the modern welfare/ transfer/ managerial state.

And this is just the trivial stuff. Reading Ilana, I learn that Halle Berry "sells" because she is "...a sepia-tinted Charlize Theron: a hollow-eyed, marshmallow-cheeked, toothy, Theron-type looker." And that

> the true finger-blistering, almighty fender-benders [this seems to be something to do with guitar playing] remain in the musical closet...Tony MacAlpine, Yngwie Malmsteen, Eric Johnson, Vinnie Moore, Steve Morse and, of course, Sean Mercer. Recordings of their furious licks will be missing from the stores and the airwaves so long as consumers are willing to pay for stuff that sounds as if it was produced after three lessons with a bad tutor.

Wow!

For me, the single most arresting, and illuminating passage in this book was Ilana's analysis of the "spasms of no-fault forgiveness" that caused some citizens of Littleton, Colorado, to applaud the erection of crosses for the Columbine high school killers alongside those for their victims. (The two crosses were destroyed by a father still bearing the unimaginable burden of grief for a murdered son.)

Ilana succinctly describes this as "the first sign of people adrift in a moral twilight zone" and "showing religious doctrinal failure."

In contrast, she writes:

> The Jewish perspective pivots on the 'passion for justice,' wrote my father, Rabbi B. Isaacson, in the *International Jewish Encyclopedia*. Justice always precedes and is a perquisite for mercy...mercy without justice is no mercy at all.

In Ilana Mercer, the passion for justice lives on.

—Peter Brimelow

President of the Center for American Unity, Senior Fellow at the Pacific Research Institute, Editor, VDARE.com, columnist for CBS MarketWatch, and best-selling author of *Alien Nation: Common Sense About America's Immigration Disaster*, and *The Worm In The Apple: How The Teacher Unions Are Destroying American Education*

Introduction

In post-September-11 America, the one emotion dominating the culture is anxiety—a vague, amorphous uneasiness about the future.

It's not only that Americans worry and war over foreign threats to their lives and liberties. They also sense a vague uneasiness about the health of their own society, about what many believe is the steady erosion of their nation's moral and cultural infrastructure.

I, for one, believe that this cultural degeneration is the more fundamental cause for concern. The greatest menace to our free civil society comes not from without, but from within.

I also believe that when the state—backed by the force of law and power of police—comes to foster and manage this social deconstruction, the demise of civil society is near guaranteed and nearer at hand than we think.

As I write, our society revels in a drunken orgy of self-indulgence and self-abasement. We live in an era in which all rational standards are mocked and dismissed as irrelevant and impotent. The quest for moral reputation has been supplanted by an obsession for instant notoriety—a ferocious competition in attention-seeking that elevates shameless degenerates. "Reality" TV lifts from well-deserved obscurity a procession of vacuous narcissists who flaunt their neuroses and intimacies before millions of video voyeurs, themselves desperate to fill dull mornings and empty evenings with the solace of vicarious titillation.

These, the unsightly, untidy flotsam within today's sea of moral relativism, are the reigning role models for our children.

But it doesn't end there. All cultural products—from news, to film, to art, to literature—now compete to reject reasonable decorum and reflect emotional extremes, to exalt gross exhibitionism and encourage all forms of grotesquerie. It's not just that "nothing is sacred" anymore: the very notion of sanctity—or of virtue, of character, of any form of moral aspiration or standard—is dismissed indignantly, as an affront to our "sophistication," as a gross imposition on our "freedom," as an anachronistic impediment to our urgent rush toward the next sensation.

This cultural chaos has left many feeling adrift, and seeking the anchor of some sort of moral principle. But with the collapse of traditional standards, more than a few have turned in desperation to mysticism, New Age beliefs, or the solace of communitarianism— what one wag called "the warm smell of the herd." Such placebos have now all but replaced the principles that fostered the triumphant rise of our civilization.

The great and singular achievements of the West—from ancient Greece, through the Enlightenment, to the industrial and scientific revolutions of modern times—were products of a historically unprecedented union of rationality, morality, objectivity, and passion. These premises, combined with the freedom of individuals to actualize their potential, propelled man forward into modern civilization.

But despite the stunning achievements of modernity, the ancient specters of mindless irrationality, primitive superstition, and tribal warfare are returning to haunt us. In a time of computer chips and satellite dishes, religious fanatics fly airplanes into buildings, tribal terrorists blow themselves up to butcher ethnic enemies, scruffy activists vandalize research labs and violently protest material wealth…while millions, trying to make sense of it all, turn for guidance to gurus and horoscopes.

Small wonder. Ideas govern behavior; and consider which ideas we have rejected, and which we have embraced. The legacy of American thought—reason, objectivity, individualism, self-responsibility, liberty—has been expunged from our institutions. In its place we have elevated irrationalism, subjectivity, collectivism, self-indulgence, and statism.

This intellectual reversion began in universities here and abroad, and was intentionally anti-American in its roots and agenda. The influence of anti-Enlightenment intellectuals soon penetrated and captured all cultural institutions. Consider some examples. Our schools, from primary to university, now preach the subjective and tout the non-analytical. The media, posturing as champions of objectivity, wallow in rank emotionalism and flagrant subjectivity. Religious institutions, supposed compasses of our moral course, junk their core doctrines and standards for trendy feel-goodism—in essence, timidly following rather than leading their flocks. One consequence of this last can be found in public discourse, where what passes for compassion these days is little more than sappy sentimentality and whining victimology.

Worst of all, the state—reflexively rather than as a matter of collusion and conspiracy—presides over this disintegration of traditional Western values and standards, for its minions have a vested interest in our cultural corruption. To inflate their spheres of control, statists must chip away at our individual rights to life, liberty, and property. And to suppress popular resistance to Leviathan's unchecked growth at home and abroad, they must foster a pliable, emasculated, infantile, morally weak, and terminally dependent populace.

How, then, do we combat these ominous trends?

A free society requires, above all, a thinking people. To protect our liberty—the liberty bequeathed to us by the Enlightenment classical-liberal Founders—and to restore a healthy culture, we must return to reason.

And as a first step, we must free our minds from the popular myths and corrosive dogmas that have led us to this sorry state.

That's my mission in *Broad Sides*.

Whether I'm reviewing a film, critiquing art and music, or discussing the collapse of boundaries between private and public life—whether I'm defending creative social benefactors such as Bill Gates and Martha Stewart, or off-shore tax havens, or the deregulation of commerce and trade—my goal in these pages is to goad, prod, and otherwise motivate people to think in fresh ways about the issues of the day, to look beyond the corrupting clichés that have dragged our society to the brink.

Because of its central role as stage manager of our social disintegration, I necessarily devote much time to criticizing the state—that Thing Sir Humphrey Applebee of the British TV satire *Yes, Prime Minister* called "a disorganized criminal organization." But I frequently aim the arrows in my quiver at targets other than government and its policies. In addition to political economy, the topics in this book include popular culture, pseudo-science, and in particular pop-psychology. From sex, music, trade and terrorism to Microsoft, Medicare and Eminem, it's all here—basted with plenty of sauce, mercifully absent the bland, unpalatable pabulum served in mainstream media.

Chapter I introduces some basics principles. The inalienable rights of life, liberty, and property are meaningless unless we understand what individual rights are. Ayn Rand said it best: "Rights are conditions of existence required by man's nature for his proper survival." Once authentic rights are distinguished from bogus rights, it also becomes clear how essential are the principles of self-defense (including national defense), absolute property rights, American republicanism, and sound money to our well-being—in fact, to the preservation of human life itself.

Chapter II flows from its predecessor. Since recognition of individual rights is so vital to our lives and happiness, why are we up to the gills in coercive regulations? When it is not disposing of a good portion of our incomes, or deciding if and how we may do business, the federal government—or rather the many unaccountable federal bureaucrats—is interfering with what and how much we may consume. Though it's abundantly clear that economic freedom is commensurate with prosperity for all, there's more to economic freedom than market efficiency. When it molests you for engaging in peaceful capitalistic acts—be it accruing and exchanging information others don't have ("insider trading"), or making an excessively popular product ("market monopoly")—

government is tampering with your liberty and livelihood, and thus threatening your very existence.

Chapter III directs attention to a judiciary which is more eager to shape society than to safeguard its individual members. The law was supposed to protect the individual from "the two potential violators of man's rights: the criminals and the government." The judiciary, however, now chronically favors the criminal classes over their victims, and systematically enshrines the collectivist idea of the "Common Good."

Chapter IV: It doesn't take a village to raise well-adjusted children, and it certainly doesn't take state-sponsored day care. But it does take traditional morality, etiquette, and family. Here topics such as sexual exhibitionism, schoolyard slayings, family life and feminism, even blogging, serve to illustrate what happens when private life goes public.

Chapter V emphasizes the indispensable value of objective standards for assessing all cultural products. I temper racy film reviews with pieces on art, music, the media, and Things that go bump in the night...like Monica Lewinsky. Today the ethical and aesthetic order has been inverted. Good stuff—Bach—is uncool. Bad stuff—"Piss art"—is hip. But maddening as it is, documenting the decay of the *Zeitgeist* can be a lot of fun.

As Friedrich A. Hayek observed, "Liberty and responsibility are inseparable." A free society cannot function unless its members assume or are made to assume full responsibility for their actions. So Chapter VI's main theme is responsibility. What has that to do with "the psychiatric articles of faith" this section attacks? Simply this: Backed by junk science, contemporary "healers" are doing away with right and wrong and with civil society's ability to give its irresponsible members a good corrective kick.

Chapter VII traces "The War for Western Values" from ancient Egypt and the pyramids' modern raiders, to the "Noble Savage" that roamed the Americas, to the taverns of terrorism in Afghanistan, Israel, and Montgomery County. The survey terminates, fittingly, in the United States of America. "The War for Western Values" must be waged at home, because it is here that the last remnants of reason and liberty are under siege.

Speaking of war, there's nothing like a good one to whet the political palate. Wars, be they against drugs or terrorism, allow our overlords to manufacture ideological excuses to tax and legislate. And so the state's wars are invariably framed as battles between good and bad, demanding ever-increasing central power. Unfortunately, while bureaucrats thrive during such crusades, you and I may find ourselves among their many casualties.

In that regard, Chapter VIII traces the ramp-up to the war in Iraq. The predictive value of the columns is indisputable. Controversial, even heretical, when first penned, they expressed opinions absent at the time from mainstream media. That these views on the war—its prosecutors, their propaganda, and those they persecuted—are now, belatedly, being echoed in the mainstream press is vindicating.

In sum, this is a personal manifesto, on one level aimed at rolling back the modern Leviathan State and reclaiming civil society. More fundamentally, however, it's a wide-ranging exploration of contemporary life through the filter of timeless principles— principles that led to the West's ascendancy, and whose neglect has led to its disastrous decline.

Notes

Ayn Rand, *Capitalism: The Unknown Ideal* (New York, 1967), p. 323.

Friedrich A. Hayek, *The Constitution of Liberty* (Chicago, 1960), p. 71.

I. First Principles

1. DEMOCRACY IS FOR THE DOGS

November 6, 2002

A succinct distinction between a republic and a democracy shows that the American republic rests in peace and that voting in the United States is undeniably democratic, not republican. In "Does Democracy Promote Peace," legal scholar James Ostrowski does just that:

> Democracy is nothing more than the numerous and their manipulators bullying the less numerous. It is an elaborate and deceptive rationalization for the strong in numbers to impose their will on the electorally weak by means of centralized state coercion ... Both forms of government feature voting by the people to select officials. The primary difference between them is that while republican voting is done for the purpose of choosing officials to administer the government in the pursuit of its narrowly defined functions, democratic voting is done, not only to select officials but also to determine the functions and goals and powers of the government ... The guiding principle of republics is that they exercise narrow powers delegated to them by the people, who themselves, as individuals, possess such powers.

The allusion to "narrow powers" is far removed from the realities of the American social democracy, particularly in light of the welter of new powers Washington has grabbed since September 11. With

1

the governed exerting so few controls over those doing the governing, the original notion of the people having the same powers as their elected officials is now positively quaint.

The powers available to power wielders in a democracy are, by definition, exceedingly broad and broaden with almost every bit of legislation passed. That we were once a republic and are now a social democracy makes clear that the Constitution has not halted this progression. The Constitution has, for all intents and purposes, been destroyed.

"The process of mutilation" libertarian writer Frank Chodorov dated to the Jackson Administration, but put the Constitution's final expiration down to the ratification of the 16th Amendment. "The income tax," wrote Chodorov in "Imperium in Imperio," "insinuated a theory of government quite unknown to the Founding Fathers, holding that the function of government is to act as *pater familias* to society as a whole. To perform that role, the government must have access to all that is produced, as a matter of right, just as a feudal baron might lay claim to the fruits of his vassals' labor."

Successive Supreme Courts have contributed to the "mutilation" by interpreting the Constitution so that it no longer reflects the eternal verities the framers spoke to, but the prevailing egalitarian redistributionist credo.

With individual rights being held hostage to the "greater good," the vote in a democracy is not to select people who would protect the inviolability of the rights the founders wanted to instantiate—the right to life, liberty and property. At best, the vote is a toss-up between a candidate who would loot for welfare and the candidate whose preference is to pillage for warfare.

The one fellow will ransack the taxpayer in order to secure prescription medication for those who think their health is the collective's responsibility; the other "virtuous" chap thinks nothing of a shakedown to impose democracy on far-flung nations, never with *their* democratic consent.

The vote in a democracy is about the coerced distribution James Madison, the Father of the Constitution, eschewed in his 1792 disquisition entitled "Property": "What a man has honestly acquired is absolutely his own, which he may freely give, but cannot be taken from him without his consent."

In a democracy, "even the individuals who voted and who managed to pick a winner are not actually ruling themselves in any sense of the word," say Linda and Morris Tannehill, in *The Market for Liberty*. They voted for a man, not for the specific laws that govern them." And the laws that man and his faceless bureaucrats usher in have their own momentum.

Who among the traditional support base of George W. Bush would have foreseen his protectionist policies for the steel, softwood lumber and agriculture industries? Or for legislation like the McCain-Feingold campaign finance regulation bill? Who would have predicted his newfound dedication to rights infringing anti-discrimination laws, not least the support for affirmative action in higher education and gender-based quotas in college athletics? What of this president's approval of a whopping wealth transfer to seniors in the form of a prescription drug entitlement? All of these reflect presidential pandering in a democracy to the real constituency: the special interest group.

This voracious voter forms the largest and most powerful constituency. He is the backbone of the system, and possesses the greatest political pull, because the tax burden in a democracy rests on a minority—the majority of taxpayers in the modern-day social democracy pays very little tax but receives myriad government benefits anyway.

Oddly enough, conservatives continue to stubbornly associate Republican candidates with the no-longer extant republican principles, believing that systemic ills can be remedied at the ballot box: Get the right—Republican—guy in and all will be swell.

Their confusion is understandable. Republicans are the drag queens of politics. While the Democrat is open about his devilishness—he finds the idea of a constitutional government with narrowly delimited powers as repellant as Dracula finds garlic—

modern-day conservatives are subtle about their aversion to a Jeffersonian republic.

Peel away the pules for family, faith, and fetuses and one discovers either what economist and political philosopher Hans-Hermann Hoppe calls "neoconservative welfare-warfare statists and global social democrats"—or, conversely, national socialists of sorts, who fuse economic protectionism, populism and support for the very welfare infrastructure which is at the root of the social rot they decry.

In a word, the social democratic *bona fides* of the Republican are beyond reproach. "Contrary to popular myth," demurs Ostrowski, "every Republican president since and including Herbert Hoover has increased the federal government's size, scope or power—and usually all three. Include regulations and foreign policy, as well as budgets approved by a Republican Congress, and a picture begins to emerge of the Republican Party as a reliable engine of government growth."

Mr. Bush has certainly earned his Great Society Democrat credentials!

Ultimately, the vote in a democracy is for the social democrat who thinks nothing of mob rule as a moral philosophy. Erik von Kuehnelt-Leddihn almost got it right when he said, "Fifty-one percent of a nation can establish a totalitarian regime, suppress minorities and still remain democratic." Correction: All that can be achieved with *only* 51 percent of the *vote*, making the slogan "freedom begins at the ballot box" a very cruel hoax indeed.

2. CREEPING STATISM BY STATIST CREEPS

July 27, 2000

His trip to the United States inspired Alexis de Tocqueville to write the famous 1835 book entitled *Democracy in America*. In it he warned "of the dangers of a nurturing government extending its arm over the whole community," and he contemplated presciently how "a democratic state of society, similar to that of the Americans, might offer singular facilities for the establishment of despotism".

Never before, in Tocqueville's estimation, had a rule undertaken without force to direct and bring all its subjects into uniformity. For all their brutality, even the Roman emperors left the "details of social and private occupations" to their subjects. Not so this benevolent American tyranny, which seemed capable of degrading men without tormenting them. In its mission to eradicate the natural inequalities of men, Tocqueville feared this "administrative despotism" would also diminish their imagination and their passions.

The outsized infants of the contemporary victim movement, who can bring to its knees an entire industry with the aid of benevolent public health bureaucrats, lobbyists, and sycophants of the law, would have Tocqueville gasping, "I told you so." For he warned, not of tyrants, but of the ruler as guardian. Unlike a parent, this guardian would not be "preparing men for manhood," but seeking to keep them in perpetual childhood by sparing them the trouble of thinking and living.

What would Tocqueville have said about the "free agency" of an individual whose demand for a risk-free society is met with a safety militia so intent on saving him from himself that it compels him to coddle his spineless frame with an ergonomic seat at his place of work; it fits his aspirin bottle with a cap only the jaws of life can pry open; it monitors the supplements he takes, and even promises to find a way to teach him to leave off the fries he so adores eating. Most frightening is that, as this benevolent power robs him of his ability to make full use of himself, the enfeebled individual will paradoxically see the robber as benefactor and the losses as benefits.

This governance "does not destroy, but prevents existence; it does not tyrannize, but it compresses, enervates, extinguishes, and stupefies a people, till each nation is reduced to be nothing better than a flock of timid and industrious animals, of which the government is shepherd." According to Tocqueville, it would be futile to call on a people "which has been rendered so dependent on the central power, to choose from time to time the representatives of that power." When people sink "below the level of humanity," even voting—ostensibly an act of free will—is meaningless.

It is a perverse irony that people are more concerned with the insane ramblings of Nostradamus than with the coming full circle of Tocqueville's prophetic words. The effect of the creeping statism he foresaw, however, fails to give pause, because the minds and hearts of people have been conquered. For a large portion of the population, government has become a source of wealth through its redistribution of money, benefits, services, contracts, franchises, and licenses. Over 50 percent of the Canadian population receives more money in benefits than it pays in taxes. In addition to directly employing approximately 20 million American civilians, the American government allots half of its spending to social welfare. For expropriating and then redistributing some people's wealth, citizens reward governments with the power to continue doing the same in perpetuity.

American rugged individualism is indeed in retreat. A survey conducted for the First Amendment Center in New York revealed that the Amendment is facing a veritable onslaught from the American public, a majority of whom would happily restrict the kind of public speech certain groups find offensive. Those surveyed applauded government involvement in rating television shows, as did they feel that while campaign contributions are a form of free speech, they should be restricted. Fully 51 percent of the sizeable sample surveyed felt the press has too much freedom, and 20 percent feel government should be able to veto what newspapers publish.

Decades after Tocqueville, Lenin declared freedom to be no more than a "bourgeois prejudice," a credo Canadians have lived by. Their love for government they flaunt as a sign of civility, and their freedoms-limiting Constitution they flash with an air of smugness. Americans, on the other hand, are guilty of betraying their very souls. By relinquishing their proud, radical-libertarian roots,

Americans have confirmed the worst of Alexis de Tocqueville's premonitions.

3. LANCING THE LOTT

But Lot's wife looked back, and she became a pillar of salt. (Genesis 19:25-27)

December 25, 2002

It's all over now: Senator Trent Lott fleetingly looked back in time and turned to salt, much like the wife of the biblical Lot, who gazed behind her at Sodom and Gomorrah as "the Lord rained down burning sulfur" on the sinful cities, and was terminated for her disobedience.

For his disobedience, albeit to a different Ministry, Trent Lott was also terminated.

Only seasoned and cynical opportunists could suggest that it was for segregation that Lott was pining, when he praised Strom Thurmond's 1948 party platform at the octogenarian's 100th birthday bash. That the cries of "racism" from the nation's professional pointy-heads are so successful demonstrates the power of the race card. Leveled at innocent white Americans, race is like stigmata. The custodians of consensus have only to say the word and most whites obediently welt and bleed.

Or so Trent Lott discovered.

To express a yearning for barbaric lynchings and segregation is by any standard tacky and tasteless. Southerners, to paraphrase H.L. Mencken, may have been drained of their best blood by the War of Northern Aggression, but vestiges of good breeding, charm, and civility remain in many a Southern man. As a Gallup poll duly confirmed, most Americans believe Lott's praise for Thurmond did not indicate that he endorsed segregationist policies, "but rather that he made a poor choice of words."

A courageous individual might have summoned the strength to state openly what exactly he was praising. Instead, Lott dissolved into an apologetic puddle.

Admittedly the Many Ministries of Truth make truth telling a difficult task. In fiction, the Orwellian Ministry of Truth is a reified entity. In reality, there isn't one concrete ministry that decides how the nation thinks—there are many such entities. They've evolved over time, and they issue countless subliminal edicts.

One type of aversion treatment is to call the unhappy victim a racist. It's the contemporary version of fingering a witch during the Salem witchcraft trials. This treatment awaits any and all who fail to conform to the correct thinking, transmitted by the education system, the churches, and the intellectuals.

When the Many Ministries of Truth—the media, G.W. Bush, and phalanxes of politicians, stakeholders, and activists—say that Trent Lott's remarks were emblematic of the eternal Mark of Cain whites must bear, most accept culpability. After all, older folks excepted, not many remember what Strom Thurmond voters were voting for.

Again, Gallup to the rescue: A 1948 poll exposes the issue the Ministries labor to conceal. It was not race that was on the minds of Thurmond voters and the average American voter for that matter, but increasing federal involvement in states and, by extension, in individual affairs.

In 1948, Americans didn't want the government to be involved in general, Frank Newport of the Gallup Poll Tuesday Briefing told an unreceptive Jerry Nachman of MSNBC. When asked, the majority polled insisted, for instance, that issues revolving around employer "discrimination" be left to employers and the states. The same goes for the adjudication of lynching. Nothing in the poll suggests an approval of the crime. Rather, Americans were emphatic about keeping the federal government out of state affairs.

When Strom Thurmond went up against Harry S. Truman and Thomas E. Dewey in 1948, it was about states' rights. Dixiecrats was the derogatory name the Media Ministry gave to what was really the States Rights Democratic Party. Considering that the

Constitution consigns law enforcement to state and local governments, the position the Dixiecrats took was hardly subversive.

The issue of segregation or racism, moreover, is intellectually independent of states' rights. The reason for the mistaken conflation of states' rights and segregation resides with the same propagandists who successfully equate, for the purposes of discrediting, the right of secession with an alleged support for slavery.

States' rights are an obstacle to ridding the nation of racism only in as much as the First Amendment is such a barrier. So long as property rights and free speech are respected, individuals are bound to exhibit preferences or express tastes that others will find displeasing. At best, one can make the case that a support for states' rights correlates with an appreciation or love of freedom, perhaps even with a belief that otherwise peaceable people with unpopular beliefs should be left unmolested, at least on their own property. Abolish states' rights and one does away with a measure of freedom and property rights, not racism.

The point, of course, is moot—states' rights no longer exist in any meaningful way. The drive behind discrediting so much as a nostalgic yen for rights that existed for almost a hundred and fifty years before the Constitution has more to do with an aversion to freedom than to racism. For the doctrine of states' rights is synonymous with decentralization, devolution of power, and local sovereignty—it's antithetical to concentration of power in the central government.

A fact that was not lost on Abraham Lincoln and Adolf Hitler; both were great centralizers. Lincoln hagiographers would protest to the contrary, but it isn't incendiary to point out that he and Hitler shared very similar views on states' rights—Lincoln's unfavorable views of such rights are seconded by Hitler in *Mein Kampf.*[*] Both invented a constitutional theory which flew in the face of the natural law, and according to which pre-existing states were to be forcibly subordinated to Union. Both led violent political revolutions aimed at consolidation. The one got away with murder, at least in the historical sense; the other didn't.

Reinvigorating states' rights would require the federal government to cede much of its power, becoming no more than a night watchman in its inconspicuousness. Consider this and it becomes clear why a great deal is staked on blotting-out such rights. How willing, after all, would an empire be to downgrade to the status of a foreign ministry and a defense department?

Steeped as they were in the Lockean tradition of natural rights and individual liberty, the founders felt the inalienable rights to life, liberty, and property were best preserved within a federal system of divided sovereignty, where the central government was weak and where most powers devolved to the states, or to the people, respectively, as stated in the 10th Amendment. If a state became tyrannical, competition from other states, and the individual's ability to exit the political arrangement and switch loyalties, would create something of a free market in government. This was the framers' genius.

If anything, the racism and slavery-related libels are belated excuses for sundering states' rights and secession. And if anything, our poll reflects the views of a more enlightened population in whom, as recently as 1948, the flames of federalism—and freedom—still flickered.

*See Felix Morley's *Freedom and Federalism* (Indianapolis, 1981), pp. 142-147, as well as Thomas J. DiLorenzo's "Jaffa's Hitlerian Defense of Lincoln".

4. WHOSE PROPERTY IS IT ANYWAY?

June 5, 2002

Violation of property rights by government hardly raises objections. If it did, the appropriate reaction to the banning by John Magaw of firearms in the cockpit would be: "Whose property is it anyway?" American airlines are, ostensibly, privately owned. Why, then, is the transportation secretary's minion not allowing rightful owners to defend their property?

The dangers for commercial aviation of such a prohibition, arguably, have a lot to do with turning ownership—in this case airline ownership—into conditional tenure.

If things were as they ought to be, we wouldn't chafe about whether pilots should carry guns or not. Any tension would revolve around passengers choosing the airline that optimizes their peace of mind. Passenger X's reasons for taking airline A to his destination might be because the carrier's pilots are armed. Mrs. Y's overriding priority is to ensure her young daughters are not subjected to the mandatory pat downs—she chooses airline B, because its security personnel profile passengers.

In a word, true market competition would arise, and the consumer would be in a position to shape the delivery of security through his buying or his abstention from buying. This would be possible if airlines were not merely nominally private, as they are now, but were instead in a position to freely fine-tune their responses to consumer demand without interference from Congress and the regulators. It stands to reason that the stronger the proprietor's rights in his property, the better he is able to respond to the consumer.

Since regulation replaces consumer preferences with bureaucratic decision-making, it invariably instates the wrong standards or simply settles on lower standards than those of the consumer. While business will pay a steep price in the free market for misreading the consumer, a government-granted reprieve is always on hand in a regulated industry, especially one that is considered an essential part of the national infrastructure, as civil aviation is. On the heels of September 11, government handed the airline industry a multi-billion-dollar bailout, as well as immunity from lawsuits. Thus were the airlines released from responsibility for the security of their passengers.

Government-run airports were—and still are—responsible for further vitiating passenger safety. As explained by economist Robert Murphy in an article entitled "The Source of Air-Travel Insecurity":

> The federal government had established minimum-security guidelines and then forced the airlines to chip in their share to pay for them. Whatever their airline, passengers were funneled through a common security checkpoint, staffed by a third-party company. In such an environment, it would have been silly for an individual airline to spend millions of dollars to exceed the government's minimum standards by providing expert security personnel. Because of the setup of [government-run] airports, every other airline would have benefited too from this arrangement, so it is doubtful that such expenditure would have been rewarded by increased consumer patronage. Further, because the public naively believes the government when it 'guarantees' air safety, even if an individual airline could have realistically offered better security measures than its competitors, consumers would still have felt that rival carriers were 'safe.'

Only when an airline can undertake "curb-to-curb" handling of its passengers will it stand both to reap the benefits that arise from providing superior service, as well as incur full liability for forsaking passenger safety. This is possible only in a privatized airport, where freedom of association and freedom of contract aren't overridden or blurred by government, and where responsibility isn't collectivized.

Alas, the recent federalizing of airport security has removed even the limited involvement the airlines had in the protection of their passengers, leaving no doubts about the political commitment of this administration to full socialization of airline security. With civil servants-cum-political appointees now overseeing the industry, airlines have to get in line and wait to be assigned a federal marshal, if they want to defend their passengers and property.

Granting the airlines the right to arm employees—and the freedom to privately contract with on-board security providers—will obviate somewhat the inevitable security pitfalls of a nationalized airport.

Closer to home—and equally ominous—is the manner in which the Fair Housing Act erodes property rights, and, with them, the right to safeguard our homes.

According to the Act, a property owner cannot "discriminate against any person … in the sale or rental of a dwelling … because of race, color, religion … or national origin."

An essential attribute of ownership is the right to exclude, a right that could come in handy considering that apartment-building owners have been warned by the FBI (for what it's worth) about the possibility that al-Qaida operatives may rent suites and plant explosives in them.

5. CRADLE OF CORRUPTION

September 4, 2002

When he demanded, at the United Nation's World Summit on Sustainable Development (WSSD), that the world's poor be liberated from poverty, South African President Thabo Mbeki was not inviting the upliftment that results from voluntary and peaceful trade, but summoning the force of a centralized Global Government.

The WSSD's social engineers began by inking reams of paper with their odes to diversity, which is code for homosexuals, lesbians, and the gender-challenged, those living with the consequences of rampant sexuality, namely the HIV-inflicted, poor non-whites, women and witch doctors.

The problem, as these central planners see it, however, lies not with the culturally exotic, but with the differences that dare not speak their name—the natural inequalities between men which also happen to drive development and innovation.

This is the diversity they want to eradicate.

To end the variety that leads to "global apartheid," Mbeki and the stakeholders at the conference want to use the steamrollers of the "democratic system of global governance." The bluntness of global governance stems from its overarching nature—a global government constitutes the ultimate monopoly because it straddles all nations. Once subject to global enforcement, inhabitants of nation-states, whose leaders have betrayed them by becoming signatories to global wealth-distributing agreements, have no escape routes. They cannot contest UN policies by upping and leaving. Well aware of this, the UN is working diligently to homogenize laws the world over. Once the same laws and regulations blanket all nations alike, citizens will be trapped.

Shrewdly, Mbeki figures that a lunge for wallets not his own starts by counterfeiting "human rights" and compelling "global society" to slake them.

Contrary to and notwithstanding the UN's rights minting, the only rights of man are the rights to life, liberty, and property. These rights exist irrespective of governments. Rights always give rise to binding obligations. In the case of natural rights, the duty is merely a duty to refrain from doing.

My right to life means you must refrain from killing me. My right to liberty means you cannot enslave me. My right to property means you should not take what is mine, or stop me from taking the necessary action for my survival, so long as I, in turn, heed the same strictures.

If to exercise a right a person must violate someone's life, liberty and property, then the exercised right is not a right, but a violation thereof. Because my right to acquire property doesn't diminish your right to the same liberty, this right is known as a negative right. Negative rights are real or natural rights because they don't conscript me in the fulfillment of your needs and desires, and vice versa. They merely impel both of us to keep our mitts to ourselves.

Which brings me to a different set of rights; those manufactured by governments and interest groups, also known as positive rights. Still under construction, this list of rights is defined by Harvard scholar Richard Pipes as "the right to the necessities of life at public expense, i.e., the right to something that was not one's own."

Access to clean water, sanitation, health care, energy and "food security," as specified at the WSSD, don't just materialize. Someone must be made to work in order to provide for those who've been granted the right to live "healthy productive lives in harmony with nature." Equally, the right to have one's debt forgiven means that someone will be defrauded.

And it won't be the UN. Neither the UN nor any other government has wealth of its own. To deliver these "rights," the UN must steal from taxpayers. This is why the rights dreamed up at the WSSD by its many initiative-yielding conferences have no moral authority; they are predicated on forcibly taking property that is already spoken for, and thus on the violation of the individual rights of other human beings.

Some argue that making some people supply others with work, water, and medical care will increase overall liberty in society. At best, this is a dubious claim. Like all welfare programs, the UN's initiatives compound the problems they are supposed to cure. As economist Hans-Hermann Hoppe points out, taking from original owners and producers and giving to non-owners and non-producers discourages ownership and production, and encourages non-ownership and non-production. In short, while overriding the rights of its unwitting funders, the UN underwrites and perpetuates parasitism on a global scale.

Even if this were not the case, liberty is not an aggregate social project. Every individual has rights. And rights give rise to obligations between all men, including those who are in power. That men band in a collective called "government" doesn't give them license to violate rights. No politician has the right to enslave some for the benefit of others, not for any reason whatsoever.

Much less is it legitimate to claim, as the democracy demagogues do, that the democratic process licenses entitlement programs. (Despite being crowned at the WSSD as "the most universal and representative system in the world," the UN doesn't even pass the flawed democratic test.) The position that the law is always just because it was arrived at through majority vote is a species of legal positivism. In opposition to classical natural law theory, legal positivism equates justice with the law of the state. According to this reasoning, Hitler's actions must be considered legitimate. Did he not come to power democratically? Clearly, that over half of the voters voted for a government which then murders, launches unjust wars, and takes from some to give to others doesn't legitimize the immoral actions. Theft or murder at the behest of majorities is still theft and murder.

Neither will it do to resort to the Constitution for a license to steal. If I sign a contract giving, for evermore, a portion of my income to you, you do indeed have a positive right to this income because I've *voluntarily* consented to give it to you. Although it authorizes the levying of some income taxes, not one of us was consulted or got to personally ratify the Constitution. Taxes by constitutional fiat are thus theft. To the extent that the Constitution sanctifies the natural rights of man—those to life, liberty and property—it is legitimate. To the extent that it enlists generations of non-signatories in the fulfillment of the needs of others, it is illegitimate.

If anything, the Constitution is the thin edge of the wedge that has allowed U.S. governments to cede the rights of Americans to the UN. Specifically, the "Supremacy Clause" in Article VI states that all treaties made by government shall be "the supreme Law of the Land," and shall usurp state law. Article VI has thus further compounded the loss of individual rights in the U.S.

To recap, a right is a legally binding claim against other human beings. Recognize the rights of all people to a guaranteed income or to certain life conditions and you also recognize the right of a bureaucrat to garnish property and enslave its owner to fulfill these "rights." The rights the World Summit on Sustainable Development wants to fabricate are not genuine human rights, but a means through which the UN seeks to expand its control.

6. MONKEYING WITH THE MONEY

August 7, 2002

When The People hoist their pitchforks, government responds. The "Sarbanes-Oxley Act," signed into law by President Bush, is such a response. Also known as the Corporate Corruption Bill, it singles out a much-maligned minority for the kind of persecution that, if visited on women, blacks or Jews, would be considered actionable, hate-filled discrimination.

The consensus is that corporate leaders are to blame for the spate of corporate malinvestment, debt, and the attendant plunge in stock prices. And how better to further persecute this envied minority than with a bill that constitutes a preemptive assault on CEOs and CFOs, prior to the fact of a crime, something government has no right doing.

About this atavistic assault, led by the masses and their mentors, economist George Reisman is eviscerating:

> Their ignorance of economics combines with an underlying mentality of such primitiveness that it recalls that of the wretched people of the Dark Ages or that of members of savage tribes. In the Dark Ages and among savages, when calamities occurred, such as one's hut being washed away by a flood ... a typical response would be to blame the occurrence not on any natural phenomenon, operating according to scientifically lawful principles, but on the will of an evil spirit, and to seek relief not in the better understanding and application of scientific principles but in the greater power of a

benevolent spirit. The only difference between then and
now is that today's intellectuals substitute for the good
and evil spirits of savages and the Dark Ages, the great
gods 'State' and 'Government' and the Devil's 'Big
Business,' 'Capitalism,' and 'The Profit Motive.'

Like Professor Reisman, those of us who follow the Austrian
school of economics understand why signals in the market suddenly
become irreparably jumbled, and why men at the helm of fantastic
corporations such as Tyco, Global Crossing, WorldCom, Xerox,
Vivendi and Qwest suddenly make predictions that don't pan out.

In the peak of the boom period, these usually astute people
somehow come to believe that they can turn massive spending into
profit—an exuberant optimism that has, in some instances,
translated into aggressive bookkeeping. Do they have a death wish? A
reckless impulse to demolish their life's work?

Hardly.

The first hint to their downfall lies in the dirty secret of inflation.
The official line has it that inflation is a rise in prices. False! Inflation
is an increase in the money supply. The general rise in prices is but a
consequence of an increase in the money supply.

One way by which government finances its spending is through
taxation. Increasing taxes, however, is politically dangerous. A
subtler way to finance wars, welfare and vote-procuring patronage is
to print paper money—worthless, unredeemable, fiat money.

When a two-bit felon counterfeits money and rushes to spend it,
prices may rise in a few of his favorite stores. Imagine the damage
wreaked by a money monopoly that can turn on the printing press at
will! The Fed and the subsidized banking system—which is given
carte blanche to loan out the newly minted paper money—are such a
counterfeiting operation.

Flooding the market with paper money unbacked by gold or real
assets, while the supply of goods remains the same, pushes up the
prices of goods. While the cost of goods and wages keeps climbing,
the purchasing power of the money diminishes.

See how government leeches away our lifeblood, robbing each and every one of us of the value of our assets?

In the economic realm, To Save or To Spend is the equivalent of "To Be or Not To Be." The ability to postpone present consumption in favor of saving and re-investing is the essence of real economic growth. In an unhampered market, interest rates fall when people accumulate capital. But when government floods the market with cheap credit, this too lowers interest rates—deceptively, artificially, and with ruinous results.

Government's lowering of interest rates by inflating the money supply messes with people's decision making. All the cheap credit that floods the market causes large-scale malinvestment. Increased and unsustainable consumption ensues, as business throws caution to the air and invests in risky projects, giving little thought to savings and capital accumulation. Cheap credit is what led to the creation of those worthless dot-coms, now bankrupt. At the time, however, the political class and their gormless media groupies heralded the dot-com pie-in-the-sky as a new messianic era.

Like all highs, this one, too, ends with a down phase: A necessary contraction in the economy is now upon us.

Tears welled as I watched a diminutive, 78-year-old John Rigas, World War II veteran, former CEO of Adelphia Communications, and a benefactor of the community, handcuffed like a goon. The yahoos were winning: Rigas is in jail, but the real robbers, chief of whom is Alan Greenspan, remain at large.

7. SIXTEEN, THE NUMBER OF THE BEAST

The Congress shall have power to lay and collect taxes
on incomes from whatever source derived, without
apportionment among the several states, and without
regard to any census or enumeration.

—The 16th Amendment

November 20, 2002

What are we to make of the idea Washington is floating of
replacing tax on income with a national sales tax? The libertarian
Cato Institute has described it as "simpler, more efficient, pro-
growth and fairer to taxpayers." I must be missing something
because I thought we already paid taxes on products and services. In
addition to states where a sales tax already exists, sizeable portions of
the prices we pay are taxes. The quandary as to whether an indirect
consumption tax is better than taxes on income masks what's
probably in the offing.

Once a tax is pushed through it seldom disappears. Last I looked,
government at all levels was consuming close on 40 percent of the
national income and growing. A reversal of the trend is almost
unheard of among developed nations. To keep the state in style,
consumption taxes will have to go through the roof. On the plus
side, the consumer can opt out, something he can't do with a tax on
income. On the downside, should he "choose" not to purchase, the
consumer may be destined to a rather austere existence.

In all likelihood, "tax reform" will leave us with the income tax in
addition to more consumption taxes. Hopes realistically must be
more modest. Let the idea of a tax reform, for once, engender a
discussion about First Principles, the kind Americans of the 19th
century were capable of having.

However contemptible taxes on consumption are, the
aforementioned Frank Chodorov insisted that taxes on income and

inheritance were "different in principle from all other taxes." In the seminal work, *The Income Tax: Root of all Evil,* he elaborates:

> The government says to the citizen: 'Your earnings are not exclusively your own; we have a claim on them, and our claim precedes yours; we will allow you to keep some of it, because we recognize your need, not your right; but whatever we grant you for yourself is for us to decide.'

Fundamentally, taxes on income imply a complete denial of private property, which is what socialism is in all its permutations; it rejects man's absolute and natural right to his property and vests property rights in the political establishment. The 16th Amendment does just that. When they incorporated the Amendment into the Constitution, Americans said a resounding "yes" to socialism.

Make no mistake: What's staving off communism is not the Constitution. If it so chooses, Congress has constitutional imprimatur to raise taxes to 100 percent of income, an odd thing considering the Declaration of Independence vests the source of man's rights in the Creator, not in government.

Philosopher Ayn Rand, on the other hand, anchored man's rights in his nature. "Rights are conditions of existence required by man's nature for his survival," she wrote in *Atlas Shrugged*. In order to survive, man must—and it is in his nature to—transform the resources around him by mixing his labor with them and making them his own. Man's labor and property are extensions of himself. The right of *ownership* is thus an extension of the right to *life*. If ownership is not an absolute right but is instead subject to the vagaries of majority vote, then so is the right to life.

Whether one defers to divine law or natural law, rights must be independent of the will of man. Congressional law was never intended to be the source of man's rights. Congress is merely entrusted with upholding the rights with which man is imbued.

This arrangement, the 16th Amendment corrupted.

Statists will always counter by claiming that if not for the state, man would be unable to produce.

Rubbish!

That's like saying that the tick created the dog! Production predates government predation. Government doesn't produce wealth—it only consumes it. What, pray tell, would government have fed off if people were not hard at work well before the advent of the bureaucracy? As usual, the statists have it topsy-turvy. First came the individual—he is the basic unit of society, without which there can be no society. And without man's labor there is no wealth for government to siphon.

However you slice it, there is no moral difference between a lone burglar who steals stuff he doesn't own and an "organized society" that does the same. In a just society, the moral rules that apply to the individual must also apply to the collective. A society founded on natural rights must not finesse theft.

The founders intended for government to safeguard the natural rights of Americans. The 16th Amendment gave government a limitless lien on their property and, by extension, on their lives. The Amendment turned government into the almighty source—rather than the protector—of rights and Americans into indentured slaves.

8. THE INCOME TAX: TURNING VICE INTO VOTES

January 8, 2003

The countless individuals who are at the receiving end of irrational malice from their inferiors will agree that an experiment conducted at the Universities of Warwick and Oxford was more of a confirmation than an investigation of human nature.

Ingeniously operationalized by Professor Andrew Oswald and Dr. Daniel Zizzo, the experiment demonstrated the lengths to which people will go to destroy the wealth of others, even if, in the process, they knowingly wipe out their own funds.

The economists approximated reality by distributing cash unequally among the subjects, who were then told they could anonymously "burn away other people's money," with one caveat: in the process, they would be destroying some of their own. Naively, the researchers expected little "burning" to occur, and certainly for it to stop once the destruction of the opponent's money became too painful to the player's pocket. They were flummoxed when 62 percent of the subjects continued to "burn" the wealth of others even at crippling costs to themselves.

Laboratory-to-life extrapolations can be problematic, but this experiment transports effortlessly.

Fact: Whether or not they are aware of the indirect harm to themselves, a sizeable majority of people in society does indeed want to see the wealth of others burned. Social determinists always blame this on the corrupting effects of extraneous forces—on the state, if they are libertarians; on the free market, if they are socialists. But implicit in a worldview that recognizes free will is an understanding that the venal are responsible for their venality.

Perhaps this is too radical an espousal of personal responsibility, but I suggest that this president—any of the absolute autocrats of a social democracy—derives a great deal of his power from human nature. Indeed, a moral deterioration of the people has facilitated the gradual movement toward the acceptance of income taxation, culminating in the Faustian ratification of the 16th amendment.

Taxation, the progressive graduated income tax in particular, is where the implications of our experiment are most striking.

Granted, people no longer view income tax as having pulverized the natural and absolute right of private property, or as being, to paraphrase Alan Keyes, a form of slavery utterly incompatible with liberty. But they surely must realize that taxation reduces their own wealth and hampers their present and future plans and goals. As pleased as they are to see the "rich" zapped, is it not both more rational and righteous to hope that no one is robbed blind, and that rich and poor alike can dispose of or save their income as they please?

Evidently not, because, overall, the debate about income tax is dominated by the quest to burn the "rich" rather than enrich all burn victims.

Compounding the destruction of property rights inherent in taxation, the progression principle in the income tax—the more you have the more you hand over—destroys the right of equal treatment under the law. It isn't remotely just to punish people for their wealth or their ability to accrue it. How is it different from making them pay for goods and services in proportion to their income (although one can well imagine the socialistic shills for a law that would force Bill Gates to pay a million dollars for a loaf of bread)?

Aside penalizing productivity, tax progression—the kind the Democrats' assorted tax rebates and handouts further entrench—has stratified American society into castes.

The top 50 percent of income earners pay 96 percent of the taxes; the bottom 50 percent pay only four percent. With the nation neatly bifurcated into taxpayers and tax consumers, John C. Calhoun's predictions in *A Disquisition on Government* about the consequences of taxation in a democracy have come full circle. A sizeable majority of the people "receives in disbursements more than it pays in taxes." The minority funding the orgy "pays in taxes more than it receives back in disbursements."

To the blatant discrimination of the progressive tax, the socialist's contra is to weasel with words. "The top-earning 25 percent of U.S. taxpayers may pay 84 percent of federal individual income taxes, but they also earned two-thirds of the *nation's income*" (my emphasis). Of course, there's no such thing as the "nation's income." This disingenuous characterization implies that there is a delimited income pie from which a disproportionate amount of wealth is handed over to, or seized by, the rich. What dross! Wealth doesn't exist in nature, but is created when individuals apply their smarts and labor to raw materials and transform them into things that can satisfy human needs. Wealth is thus individually created and owned. For an electorally powerful majority that gets stuff for nothing, and doesn't bear the costs of government, voting for more taxes makes perfect sense.

Washington's intention to accelerate reductions in income tax rates is welcome. To the extent the cuts are tilted toward the most burdened and enslaved taxpayers, this too is good. Keep in mind though that all we have here is a parasite careful to sap but not kill the host. That is, the president's new tax cuts haven't meaningfully changed the steeply graduated and high levels of taxation, but they will probably keep the golden goose—the tax base—going.

Recommending the best income tax is like selecting a preferred malignancy. Nevertheless, the least toxic tax is probably a poll or head tax, where all are burdened equally. Let the poor set the rate. This will sever the blood supply to the metastasizing state like nothing else.

Less for the "federal Frankenstein" is also less with which it can facilitate human wickedness.

9. NO RIGHT OF SELF-DEFENSE IN BLAIR'S BARBARIC BRITAIN

August 6, 2003

A British *Times Literary Supplement* reviewer recently took a shot at tracing the "providential themes" in George Bush's political rhetoric. Indeed, the interminable war on "tyrants and terrorists" is laced with evangelical zeal. The American president, however, is not alone "in the redemption business."

British Prime Minister Tony Blair fancies himself every bit the redeemer of mankind. Etched all over Blair's address to Congress was the devotion to the "mystic [and, might I add, malevolent] idea of national destiny."

One particularly chilling dictate was this: "I know out there there's a guy getting on with his life, perfectly happily, minding his own business, saying to you, the political leaders of this country,

'Why me? And why us? And why America?' And the only answer is, 'Because destiny put you in this place in history, in this moment in time, and the task is yours to do.'"

The tyranny implied by Blair's maudlin grandiosity should be obvious.

First, the little guy back home ought to be the one calling the shots, not Messrs. Messiah and Company. Second, before Blair joins Bush in rousing the "visionless" middle-class American from his uninspired slumber—The Great Redeemer thinks it's below contempt to harbor a civilized desire to mind one's own business and live in peace—he ought to take a look at the little guy back in England.

Tony Martin, for one, is not having a terribly tranquil time of it. Blair's blather to Congress about "the spread of freedom" being "the best security for the free" must ring hollow to the law-abiding, English farmer, who would no more advocate the spread of British-style freedom than he would the bubonic plague.

Tony Martin was recently released from jail after being arrested for the crime of defending his home—he killed a career criminal by the name of Fred Barras and injured his accomplice, Brendon Fearon, when the two broke into the elderly man's homestead. Martin was convicted of murder and sentenced to life in prison, the court finding that he had no freedom to use force to defend his property or his life.

The traditional "Rights of Englishmen"—the inspiration for the American founders—are no longer cool in Cool Britannia. The great system of law that the English people have long held dear, including the 1689 English Bill of Rights, which entails the right to possess arms, is in tatters. The British elites, many of whom enjoy taxpayer-funded security details, have disarmed law-abiding Britons, who now defend themselves against the protected criminal class only at their own peril.

A right that can't be defended, however, is a right in name only. In Britain today there is, in effect, no real right to life or property.

In Blair's Britain, the law has been turned around to break and subdue proud and self-sufficient people like Tony Martin. The Crown rejected his self-defense plea, although his conviction for murder was commuted to manslaughter once Martin capitulated and agreed to accept a diagnosis of mental illness. In other words, to defend your home in Britain is to evince a paranoid personality disorder.

Martin's case, unfortunately, is far from unique, and the consequences of this policy have been appalling. According to a recent UN study, writes Historian Joyce L. Malcolm, author of *Guns and Violence: The English Experience*, "England and Wales have the highest crime rate and worst record for 'very serious' offences of the 18 industrial countries surveyed." Whereas violent crime in America has been plummeting for 10 consecutive years, criminal violence in Britain has been rising.

Since Blair's 1997 total ban on armed self-defense, things have gone from very bad to even worse. "You are now six times more likely to be mugged in London than New York," notes Malcolm. "Why? Because as common law appreciated, not only does an armed individual have the ability to protect himself or herself but criminals are less likely to attack them....A study found American burglars fear armed homeowners more than the police." The most dangerous burglaries—the kind that occur when people are at home—are much rarer in the United States, only 13 percent, than in Britain, where they constitute 53 percent of all such home invasions.

How far has British barbarism gone? Malcolm's evidently garden-variety accounts include the story of an elderly lady who fought off a gang of thugs "by firing a blank from a toy gun, only to be arrested for the crime of putting someone in fear with an imitation firearm."

Similarly, when Eric Butler was brutally assaulted in a subway, "he unsheathed a sword blade in his walking stick and slashed" at one of his assailants. Butler was added to the lineup—he "was tried and convicted of carrying an offensive weapon."

Tony Martin was almost denied parole because he failed to show sufficient contrition for killing one of the creatures that invaded what was supposed to be his castle. In the words of a probation officer, Martin continues to be "a danger to burglars." In a truly civilized country, of course, that would be a compliment.

To add insult to injury, after having been robbed of three years and five months of his life for the crime of self-defense, Martin's ordeal is still not over. The surviving ruffian, who has more than 30 convictions to his name, has been granted permission to sue his victim, even given legal aid to so do, for the injury he suffered on the "job."

In addition, the criminal protection and reinforcement program that is contemporary British justice also entails honoring career criminal Brendon Fearon's "right" to know where his victim, the old farmer, will reside now that he's been released.

Tony Blair has gone to great (and dubious) lengths to make a case for Britain's right to defend itself from perceived threats in the international arena. He ought to be reminded that self-defense, like charity, begins at home.

10. IN DEFENSE OF MICHAEL VICK

August 24, 2007

While ranting about NFL quarterback Michael Vick for his alleged dog fighting activities, CNN talker Nancy Grace added another charge to her brilliant "legal" brief: Vick's been rapin' on the bitches. By that she meant inseminating bitches that "refused" to breed. The exact crazy quote has Grace say the following to her equally indignant guest: "You left out the rape stand, where female dogs that don't want to breed are raped, essentially."

In Graceland, canines must consent before being bred, or is it "having sex." Nancy didn't indicate whether she was as passionate about the "violations" visited upon thoroughbred racehorses and artificially inseminated cows. The frightening thing is that judging by the frenzy over Vick's alleged infractions against our furry friends, I suspect all too many Americans agree with nutty Nancy.

Dog fighting, which has been outlawed in all 50 states, is certainly uncivilized and cruel (although not everything that is immoral ought to be illegal). But even more uncivilized than Vick's alleged dogfighting violations has been the zeal among media pack animals to convict him. Vick is not a thief, a murderer, or a rapist. Neither has he defrauded anyone. He is a gifted athlete—and an obviously aggressive young man, who may have channeled his abundant aggression into a blood sport, as men have done throughout time.

The English relished dog fighting for centuries. Fox hunting is still a much cherished way of life in rural England, and, some argue, beneficial to conservation "and a method of pest control." The same animal rights activists who've successfully lobbied to have dog fighters declared felons are gunning for hunters. These activists consider hunting a blood sport too. To them, the torero—the Spanish bullfighter—is worse than a terrorist.

Animal rights activists share a humanity-hating agenda with environmentalists. The first would like ultimately to see the State proceed against anyone who slaughters, markets, experiments on, or even eats and wears animals; the latter wish to subordinate man to nature through codified law.

Human beings ought to care for and be kind to animals. But a civilized society is one that never threatens a man's liberty because of the callousness with which he has treated the livestock he owns. Members of a society in which peace and liberty are valued above all would have settled for boycotting Vick's games and merchandize. They might have urged the NFL to discipline, even fire, him. But they would not have called for his incarceration.

Man's The Only Top Dog

Anthropomorphism is the practice of attributing human characteristics to an animal. Dogs have small brains, devoted mainly to smell and other instinct-driven behaviors. The love and loyalty dog lovers see in their mutt's eyes is a projection of the owner's large, cerebral cortex. (You'll learn more about sharks from Steven Spielberg's magnificent thriller "Jaws," than from our radically ideological "experts." When sharks feed on folks, it is not a case of "mistaken identity." The reason these powerful, flesh-eating animals with pointy teeth don't tuck in more frequently is because there are more fish in the sea than people.)

PETA's ethos has prevailed: Vick is being treated like an animal and his dogs like human beings. "People for the Ethical Treatment of Animals" is to animal rights what the Sierra Club (and Al Gore) is to the environmental movement. Both these radical-left organizations are bent upon using state power to further curb property and production. To be fair, PETA is philosophically more consistent than those who've hounded Vick for dogfighting, yet spare the manufacturers of *pâté de foie gras*.

As PETA sees it, all animals ought to have rights. Be it for beef or bloodsport, their "exploitation" should be prohibited. To PETA, man and beast exist along the same continuum, their faculties and feelings differing in degree, not in kind. In the words of PETA's founder: "When it comes to pain, love, joy, loneliness, and fear, a rat is a pig is a dog is a boy." To adapt Voltaire's quip to Rousseau, whom he hated (me too): One longs, in hearing PETA's rants against the human race, to walk on all fours.

Like PETA, I don't distinguish between the pig farmer and the dogfighter. Unlike PETA, I believe all animals are property. Man is the only top dog. Although people will go to great lengths to distinguish their preferred form of animal use from Vick's, the distinction is nebulous. One either owns a resource or one doesn't. Whether one kills animals for food or for fun, the naturally licit basis for large-scale pig farming or game hunting is the same: ownership of the resource.

Arguably, commercial pig farming is crueler than dispatching dogs, then-and-there, as Vick did. These "Babe" look-alikes wallow for ages in their own waste, in pig pens so cramped, the creature cannot even collapse when exhausted. The animal's skin often ulcerates and its muscles and bones atrophy. Food farming can involve practices such as tail docking, tooth-clipping, "castration, branding, debeaking, and other painful processes." I solve this ethical problem by patronizing farmers whose animals roam and graze, not by agitating for government to criminalize commercial farmers and hurt the multitudes they feed.

Contrary to PETA, there is a reason animals are ineligible for rights. Rights arise from man's unique nature. Man and man alone has moral agency—only man possesses free will, the capacity to tell right from wrong, and to reflect on his actions and beliefs.

"Given that non-human animals aren't moral agents—not in the general and fundamental sense that we take human beings to be—there is no conceptual basis for ascribing them the kind of rights human beings are said to possess," writes ethicist Tibor Machan. "Rights not founded on the moral agency of the rights holder are not the sorts of rights that ... require protection in a just legal order."

Animal-rights advocates counter by claiming that not all human beings have the capacity for moral agency. They don't mean Michael Moore, but poor Terri Schiavo, RIP. Remember how far-left (and far-gone) liberals fought like rabid dogs to slowly starve and dehydrate her? One philosophical argument they deployed to justify Terri's torture was that she had lost what made her uniquely human.

But, as Machan emphasizes, "To complain that moral agency is lacking while someone is in a coma or asleep is to misunderstand the point of a definition, a statement about the nature of something." An elk doesn't stop being an elk if without antlers. The criminal Carranza consciously used his capacities in choosing to kill. And while a baby doesn't have moral agency, it will develop it in time. However damaged or depraved, a human being is still a human being.

Easily the most salient aspect about human beings is that they live in moral communities. When the lunatic left and a few "Crunchy Cons" abandoned the weak and the enfeebled Terri Schiavo, others (Sean Hannity, Thomas Szasz, Alan Dershowitz, WND, and this column, etc.,) stepped in to fight for her rights. This is not the case

with animals. Members of the canine community have yet to deliver
disquisitions against dog fighting. However, when the day arrives
and Fido fights tooth and nail for more than Kibbles 'n Bits, he will
indeed have earned his rights.

While animals are still regarded as property under the law, if
heavily circumscribed, the trend in tort law cases is, increasingly,
toward treating them as PETA prescribes. Given the public and
popular press's sentimental slobbering over Vick's dogs, this lobby's
power is sure to increase.

Rights give rise to legal claims. Ultimately, the more rights
animals are granted, the greater the legal lien exercised on their
behalf against the liberty and property of people. As it is, deputized
agents of the Humane Society and the SPCA have the power to turn
you into a felon for "the crime of a skinny dog."

So far, public pressure, not the law, has brought about the
termination of Vick's lucrative, promising career. Civil society is
clearly quite capable of censuring Vick. The law should have left him
be.

11. 'HONEST ABE'S' LEGACY OF CORRUPTION

February 12, 2002

Enron is not the topic of this column—Lincoln is. So why
mention Enron in the same breath? Well, the system of subsidies and
corporate welfare exemplified by the government-Enron incest is
one of the pillars of policy that Lincoln—whose birth is celebrated
today by some—dedicated his life to realizing.

Cretinous commentary in the media notwithstanding, Enron's
entanglement with the state has nothing to do with genuine
capitalism. True capitalism ropes entrepreneurs into the service of
only one master: the consumer. It allows no grants of government
privilege, and it banishes corrupting interference by the political
class.

Enron's collapse relates to capitalism as Lincoln relates to liberty: not in the least. There is, however, a direct historical link between Abraham Lincoln and the phenomenon epitomized by the Enron fiasco. It is this link, among others, that Thomas J. DiLorenzo's book, *The Real Lincoln: A New Look at Abraham Lincoln, His Agenda, and an Unnecessary War*, painstakingly traces.

Professor DiLorenzo documents Lincoln's consummate and unrelenting devotion to the cause of "protectionist tariffs, taxpayer subsidies...for corporations," and the nationalization of the money supply, so that governments could "simply print paper money in order to finance their special-interest subsidies." At once, it becomes clear that Lincoln's legacy lives on in the ugly specter of a Congress that uses the Export-Import Bank and the Overseas Private Investment Corporation as a routine money-laundering scheme, to hand over taxpayer-funded subsidies and grants to politically connected corporations.

This is Lincoln's legacy in action.

As DiLorenzo shows, Lincoln's political career was guided by "The American System," the brainchild of his Whig idol, Henry Clay. Lincoln wanted to extend to politically favored industries in the north "legal protection from international competition through trade tariffs and quotas." There is no better example of special-interest politics than protectionism and the corporate welfare schemes that Lincoln championed, where the force of the law is used to benefit a select group of politicians and their cronies, at the cost of limited choice and high prices for the consumer at large.

Lincoln was single-minded in this pursuit.

"The American System" had at its core a massive consolidation of power in the hands of a central government. The powers Lincoln sought were inimical to the Constitution of the founders. To realize his expansionist dream, Lincoln would have to crush any notion of the Union as a voluntary pact between sovereign states. The entire American political history, including the fact that America was born of secession, would have to be expunged, and secession tarnished as treason. Lincoln then would proceed to fabricate the notion that the federal government created the states, when the opposite was true.

Wait a sec, what about slavery?

No serious historian, says DiLorenzo, would claim that Lincoln invaded the South to free slaves. In Lincoln's own famous 1862 words: "If I could save the Union without freeing any slave I would do it." Here too, DiLorenzo exposes the Lincoln who could speak of the natural right to liberty from one corner of his mouth, and from the other corner express opposition to citizenship for blacks. Or the Lincoln who never once lent his legendary legal skills to a runaway slave, but did plead the case of a slave owner. Or the Lincoln who was devoted to—and attempted to implement—Henry Clay's colonization ideas, namely the plan to send blacks packing back to Africa.

If anti-slavery sentiments were his muse, the dissembling Lincoln never let on until 1854, which is when he began getting religion on slavery.

Stripped of double-talk, Lincoln's proclaimed primary objective was to destroy federalism and states' rights. His victory included much more than waging a war that killed 620,000 young men. Lincoln's "achievement" went beyond murdering roughly 50,000 Southern civilians, blacks included. His conquest transcended the destruction of the Southern economy, and lives on in the unconstitutional, violent and mob-dominated institution over which President Bush now smirkingly presides.

Having exposed every dank nook and cranny in Lincoln's putrid pedigree, DiLorenzo understandably expresses sadness that the loss of states' sovereignty—and by extension, individual sovereignty over the state—seems not to matter to most Americans.

As fine a Lincoln scholar as he is, DiLorenzo the economist is as valuable a presence throughout, dissecting for the reader the perverse incentives and consequent ruinous economic outcomes that Lincoln's economic plank of nationalization and nepotism wreaked.

DiLorenzo has harnessed his passion for liberty and truth to give us a tightly argued, wonderful work.

12. A TOAST TO WESTERN SEPARATISM AND
CANADA'S GOOD HEALTH

January 3, 2001

Canadian Western alienation is a good-news story, and it is doubtless one of the signs of well being in the Canadian polity. Much like the low-grade fever a healthy body might develop in response to an ailment, a revival of Western separatism is a sign of vitality.

Judging from the public flap over any hint of a threat to national unity, however, I'm in a rejoicing minority. News anchors on the Canadian Broadcasting Corporation always grow grimmer than usual when broaching the topic. Never shy about privileging his own values, Mr. Jean Chrétien, Canada's prime minster, is fond of doing his utmost to deepen the "us" versus "them" divide, repeatedly referring to Westerners as "they." "They think we are too centrist," he correctly claimed about Westerners, and "they like to have right-wing governments."

Well, here's a scary thought for Mr. Chrétien: According to the results of an election study published in the *Globe and Mail*, the PM and his patriciate may not be that different from those rube hicks in the West. In fact, the substantive ideological differences between Westerners and Ontarians are few.

On immigration, tougher juvenile sentencing, the death penalty, and race-based preferential policies, the gap in opinion between the regions is narrow. The right to bear arms is an exception. But, even on this issue, the differences are likely rooted in urban/rural—more than regional—distinctions.

Same thing with the economy: Canadians, West and East, share a predilection for *dirigisme*. Unaware as they are that government make-work schemes are predicated on taxing, borrowing or inflating the money supply, Canadians believe government has a role in job creation. Neither are tax cuts a top priority.

If Canadians are not divided over The Issues, why the regional fault lines? The leftist Liberals, you recall, won most of the seats in

Ontario but very few Western seats. The conservative Canadian
Alliance, on the other hand, took most of the seats in the West and
hardly any in Ontario.

Some Western commentators explained the election outcome by
alluding to characteristic Western rugged individualism; a preference
for self-government and direct democracy over the administrative
leviathan ensconced in Ottawa.

True, there are scattered islands of individualism in the West,
predominantly in Alberta and in rural areas. But, in general, the
survey doesn't support this romantic portrayal. Here in British
Columbia, we bleat like any Easterner at the hint that individuals
should be permitted to spend their money on purchasing health care.
We applaud discriminating affirmative action laws, and we generally
frame government inroads into our lives as the mark of a civilized
society.

There were the pundits who identified the source of
disenfranchisement in our first-past-the-post system of election. The
regional gap narrows when votes—not seats—are considered.

This tack serves to obscure a more prosaic truth. In as much as
democracy is the tyranny of the majority, it is always a disgrace, and
it is certainly not the thing that protects individual freedoms. If you
belong to the 40.8 percent of Canadian voters who chose the
Liberals, then democracy becomes you. If you are among the 59.2
percent of voters who did not elect the Liberals, then majority rule
has little to recommend it.

Indeed, democracy can easily descend into tyranny if not
accompanied by strict limitations on the power and size of the
central government. The American Founding Fathers knew this.
Thomas Jefferson viewed extreme decentralization as the bulwark of
the liberty and rights of man. Consequently, the United States was
created as a pact between sovereign states with which the ultimate
power lay. Sadly, it has progressed from a decentralized republic
into a highly consolidated one.

Canada, on the other hand, was born of a highly-centralized
regime, and has always cleaved to an expansionist national policy.

Yet, paradoxically, Canada has outstripped the United States in spurring powerful regional movements. This blessing may, in part, be due to the once-sensible courts, which, until 1949, interpreted the Constitution Act, 1867, in a manner favorable to provincial power.

Western welfare states these days have mixed economies, large portions of which are nationalized, regulated, or subject to government monopoly and cartelization. Governments—federal, provincial, and municipal—in the United States, Canada and Britain, now consume almost half of the national income. Wealth in Alberta is being created despite Mr. Chrétien's government, not because of it.

Western Canadians sense that the more power bureaucrats subsume, the less power they themselves retain. They ask themselves, how did the PM come to threaten them with "tough love"? Why can he punish their province for making decisions on health care? A Western province elects a senator; The All-Powerful One dismisses him. Above all, the PM gets to handpick the Supreme Court of Canada. Shielded from the popular vote, and with Charter imprimatur, these oligarchs are rapidly usurping the rights of locals to shape their communities.

The discontent Westerners experience lies not in the substance of the issues, but in the process itself. The pathology caused by an overreaching federal government is fuelling the low-grade fever of freedom, and all hail to that.

13. UNNATURAL LAWLESSNESS

May 7, 2003

When The Germans come to stay at *Fawlty Towers*, Basil Fawlty, the quirky hotel manager in the classic British comedy, is adamant to put his best foot forward and not to mention The War. Basil being Basil, this is not to be. The caustic anti-hero suffers a concussion, and spends a good deal of the episode goose-stepping around his poor guests, reducing them to tears.

I'd have preferred not to mention The War during a talk I recently gave at a Libertarian Party convention. To further commandeer the *Fawlty Towers* script: We know who started it! Still, it's been personally important for me to keep processing it because there are certain things about this war that make it unprecedented. And so, I spoke at length about how it came to be that Americans, by and large, took the war, its prosecutors and their propaganda to their hearts. Needless to say, the effect I had on some in the audience was as intense as the effect Basil Fawlty had on his German guests.

This is a testament to the administration's achievements. In mere months, Washington has radically transformed the way most Americans—including some libertarians—think. True to their Trotskyist roots, the ideologues in this administration have been catalysts for a consciousness *lowering*—not *raising*—among most Americans, breaking down and even inverting certain civilizing precepts which only a short while ago united us.

Commentator Eric S. Margolis offered up a quote by U.S. Supreme Court Justice Robert H. Jackson, America's senior representative at the 1945 Nuremberg war crimes trials, and the tribunal's chief prosecutor. It highlights all the more the gaping moral void that has opened up in American society:

"We must make clear to the Germans," said Jackson, "that the wrong for which their leaders are on trial is not that they lost the war, but that they started it. And we must not allow ourselves to be drawn into a trial of the causes of the war, for our position is that no grievances or policies will justify resort to aggressive war. It is utterly renounced and condemned as an instrument of policy."

Justice Jackson was articulating not a temporary but a timeless truth—the principles of the natural law are indisputably correct. To wage aggressive wars violates a universally accepted verity. It violates the paramount laws that children manage to internalize at a tender age: "…one child must not, without just cause, strike or otherwise hurt, another; that one child must not assume any arbitrary control or domination over another; that one child must not, either by force, deceit, or stealth, obtain possession of anything that belongs to another," spelled out Lysander Spooner.

To the 19th-century libertarian natural rights theorist this may have been child's play, but it has become a chore for most Americans. How they square their adoption of Bush's New Morality (preemptively lying one's way to war) with their commitment to a higher authority is outside my purview. I do know that the state ought not to come between a libertarian and the natural law.

A vehement letter I received from a conference attendee reveals sadly that many "libertarians" see the law of the state as the ultimate arbiter of right and wrong. Or as the man blasted, "Get your facts straight, the president has the power to declare war under the War Powers Act—like it or not, that is the law."

The inference here is that what the law says is inviolably just.

The writer got one thing straight: War was declared by executive order! Flouting his obligation to get "the consent of the governed," to quote the Declaration of Independence, Mr. Bush bullied a corrupt Congress into authorizing war against Iraq before the November midterm elections. Congress's vote was no more than a formality.

The writer, however, proves ignorant both of the U.S Constitution and the libertarian duty to reject the law of the state when it is at odds with natural justice.

Over to James Madison: "Those who are to conduct a war cannot in the nature of things, be proper or safe judges, whether a war ought to be commenced, continued, or concluded." Thus it is Congress that declares a war. The U.S. government is beholden to the Constitution, which prohibits the president from declaring war. Explains Louis Fisher, senior specialist in separation of powers at the Congressional Research Service of the Library of Congress: "Keeping the power to commit the country to war—and to all the costs of war—in separate hands from the power to wage war once declared was a bedrock principle for the framers."

Modern statutes like the War Powers Resolution, the Iraq Resolution, and the Use of Force Act do not displace the constitutional text and the framers' intent.

But even if the Constitution approved of Bush and Congress' subterfuge, the natural law does not. Because it is rational and rooted in the very nature of man, natural justice is immutably true; it is the ultimate guide to what is right or wrong. It may no longer guide most Americans, but it must never cease to inform libertarians.

14. WHEN THE LEFT STEALS THE RIGHT WORDS

June 8, 2000

Never underestimate a progressive's penchant for perverted prolix! Honest English words are continually hijacked by "the forces of socialism, statism…and political correctness," rendering them unfit for use by those outside this camp. Considering that language mediates thoughts and actions, and hence public debate and policy, vigilance about co-opted semantics can seldom be overemphasized.

An especially nasty misnomer is "progressive taxation," although it has a benevolent connotation and sounds like a splendid idea. True, it's meant to denote not progressivity in the sense of forward and onward moving, but rather a scheme in the spirit of, "From each according to his ability, to each according to their need": The more you earn the more you forfeit. (That this is the communist credo is evidently not sufficient to make people run for their lives.) Still, progressives piggyback on the double *entendre*.

Ever hear anyone question why taking from some more than from others is a good thing? Or why failing to treat individuals equally under the law is progressive rather than very backward? Much less does anyone ask why the confiscation of the property of citizens by force and without consent should be called anything other than barbaric. Or what will be done once "progressive taxation" places so many disincentives in the path of the most productive members of society that they cut back wealth-creating activities.

Is our compliance with taxation in general and taxation structure in particular all due to upbeat language? Of course not, but locutional lies help.

Government inhabits a moral penumbra; its actions are often the actions of a bandit who incurs no criminal liability. To this habitual—and legally immune—burglar, the superiority of a "progressive tax" scheme is more than apparent. If the object is to cram the get-away car to its fullest capacity, then hit on the mansion, don't shake down the shack. If the object is to sustain power through appeasing the majority, then, as George Bernard Shaw put it, "A government which robs Peter to pay Paul can always depend on the support of Paul."

How does a contradiction in terms like "redistributive justice" grab you? How does one distribute justly what has been seized unjustly? And to whom is left the definition of just, to those who steal?

Perhaps, you say, we ought to look beyond the immoral act of "legalized plunder." Perhaps robbing Peter to pay Paul is a noble end if Paul is in dire need—If it fulfills a duty of beneficence, you say, let's turn a blind eye to government's political predation.

On purely utilitarian grounds this fails. When a private charity like the Salvation Army collects for the poor, almost all of its funds reach their destiny. Little of the wealth appropriated by the Welfare State actually reaches the needy, going instead toward the funding of an ever-growing bureaucracy that perpetuates the very problems it claims to ameliorate. The Welfare State doesn't promote the well being of its inhabitants. The opposite is true: its policies are to their detriment.

Indeed, for an entity that impoverishes in its own right, the Welfare State is curiously named. A form of price control such as minimum wage laws actually creates poverty by creating unemployment among the poor and unskilled. Fixing the price of labor above the market rate or the productivity of the employee as the minimum wage does causes surpluses of labor. The jobs exist, only government has legislated them out of the reach of those who need them.

When it turns to control prices of electricity, medical services, and housing units, as in the case of rent control, the state sets prices below market value, causing rampant overuse. Without fail, endemic shortages of the resource ensue. In New York, where government has drastically reduced incentives to supply low cost rental housing, there are apparently as many boarded up buildings as there are homeless.

With its tariffs, quotas and both international and intranational barriers to trade, the Welfare State weighs on the average consumer, filching his funds and handing these over to protected industries and special interests. It also helps pauperize undeveloped nations by making it difficult for them to peddle their wares in our markets. Above all, interventions that veto our choice of who to patronize with our trade violate the right of freedom of association. Clearly, not only does it fail to do what it purports to do, but the Welfare State is antithetical to all but the well-being of the bureaucrats and politicians who administer it and the sectional interests who feed off it.

Sadly, merely reclaiming lost linguistic territory will not turn the tide, although it may help. Freedom is reclaimed by a change in hearts and minds.

15. THE STATE SWELLS, OUR WEALTH SHRINKS

August 21, 2002

Using data from the Congressional Budget Office, Jeff Tucker of the Mises Institute provides an account of the Bush administration's orgiastic outlays:

From October 2001 to March 2002, federal outlays
were up by $60 billion over the same period the previous
year. In this time period, the federal government...has
somehow managed to burn through fully $1 trillion in
wealth formerly owned by the private sector. As for
revenue, it is down from last year by $44 billion, netting
a deficit of $129 billion. All told, annual government
spending is growing right now at an astonishing 8
percent rate.

In keeping with the trend, the president has doubled funding for
homeland security to almost $38 billion, describing this profligacy as
"money to train and equip firefighters, police officers and emergency
medical personnel; money for the Coast Guard, to protect our ports
and coasts; money to keep our water treatment plants and nuclear
facilities safe."

What amounts to a multi-billion-dollar government job creation
program is never a good thing, especially during a recession. For
one, government workers are covered by rigid, "prevailing wage"
legislation: The jobs created in the realm of homeland security are
well paid irrespective of efficiency and productivity. This precludes
the necessary flexibility in wage structure, so essential during an
economic downturn.

If not through the theft of taxation or borrowing, jobs for federal
employees are financed by printing money. Government employees
are the first in line for newly minted funny money. This means that
governmental job creation schemes are causal factors in the inflation
of the money supply and in the further dilution of privately owned
wealth.

As is the reality with a government job, the money appropriated
goes to support a large bureaucracy that will do little to secure
person or property in a rational, effective manner. Why? Because it's
the nature of a monopoly to supply a service that is more expensive
and less efficient than one which would arise in a competitive
market.

A government work force is largely divorced from market standards: government employees have no incentives to heed consumer-dictated needs. There is neither demand nor tolerance in the real job market for security personnel who fondle the scar tissue on the mastectomy-ravaged chest of a (white) woman before they will allow her to board an airplane. There are no jobs outside government for goons who strip (white) old ladies down to their "Depends" before allowing them to use a service for which the women have paid. Needless to say, the only security in this is the job security availed to the public-sector worker.

An increase in the number of jobs for federal employees will invariably come at the cost of real, sustainable jobs in the private sector. Government borrowing, taxing, or printing money, some— or all—of which are required to finance this program, serve to reduce capital available to the private sector, making investors less likely to take employment-generating risks with their capital. Private economic activity is crowded out because of government confiscation. For every job "created" by government, an unidentifiable job will thus be destroyed in the private sector. The multitudes thrown out of work because of this, however, remain invisible.

Invisible too are the thriving consumer-driven, private security industries that might have arisen had resources not been funneled to the Homeland Security patronage playground. (Legislation secures monopoly: where government monopolizes security, private security is prohibited.) Such industries would not only be more efficient, but would have enjoyed an ethical dimension absent from a government-created industry. Whereas government jobs involve bureaucrat and job recipient in a beneficial and voluntary exchange, they leave out of the loop those who pay for the programs through taxes or through unemployment in their neck of the woods.

As a share of GDP, the United States government's spending has been rising steadily over the decades. In a paper entitled "The Scope of Government and The Wealth of Nations," economists James Gwartney, Randall Holcombe, and Robert Lawson demonstrate that, on average, Organization for Economic Co-operation and Development governments, the U.S. included, now spend 48 percent of GDP. "In 1960, government expenditures in this group averaged 27 percent of GDP."

Governments in high-income developed economies have been steadily accreting for decades. The evidence culled from numerous studies tracking this trend goes to show that government growth as a share of GDP coincides with a decline in GDP growth. The decline in prosperity or in real growth rates in these nations is measurable. "A 10 percent increase in government expenditure as a share of GDP results in a 1 percent point reduction in GDP growth." As government share of the GDP rises, so has GDP in the OECD nations declined.

The plundering class' momentum is intractable. Once the political parasites acquire confiscatory power, they seldom relinquish it and toil diligently to expand it. In only three cases among OECD and 60 other nations surveyed was there a decline in government growth during the last decade or so. Most notable has been the rapid growth Ireland underwent, after government expenditure in the 1987-96 period was curtailed. New Zealand's politicians loosened the chokehold in 1996, with the result that substantial economic growth followed. "While shrinking government has been rare in the past few decades, evidence from places where government has shrunk is consistent with the hypothesis that larger government lowers economic growth," write Gwartney, Holcombe, and Lawson.

Even if government pelf caused plenty, it would still be immoral. Citizens, however, can be hostile to moral arguments, because theft by bureaucratic bandits is often to their immediate advantage. Where morals fail to impress, numbers come in handy. The negative relationship between the size of government and prosperity is sufficiently compelling to convince the average individual to stop salivating for the state.

16. SON OF UNCLE SAM

April 9, 2003

William Rusher of the Claremont Institute is right. There is an ideological war between Bush's social democrats, known as neoconservatives, and those of us who stand on the Old Right, namely paleoconservatives and paleolibertarians.

Rusher, however, is not about to tell his readers what it is about the set of policies neoconservatives support that makes them global social democrats or rank leftists. It's probably more accurate to speak both of modern-day liberals and neoconservatives as proponents of a highly centralized—and hence dictatorial—managerial form of government, except that the neoconservatives are proving to be far more dangerous to life, liberty, and livelihoods.

Nor is Rusher writing to sound the alarm, as paleos are, about an administration that is using war and manufacturing crisis to grow government to unprecedented levels, unseen since Lyndon Johnson. The neoconservatives' aggrandizing zeal to make the world safe for democracy is making, to paraphrase Felix Morley in *Freedom and Federalism*, a constitutional government unsafe in the U.S.

Not a sound from Rusher about these paleo observations, nor a reminder that neoconservatives are more the sons and daughters of an FDR than of Ronald Reagan.

What Rusher does inform his readers of is that his buddy, neoconservative David Frum, has written an essay entitled "Unpatriotic Conservatives," and that the thing constitutes a profound condemnation of paleoconservatives. So profound is Frum's indictment that Rusher can't quite bring himself to summarize it.

I'll do the honors.

Having read it, I can say that Frum hasn't got a "De Profundis" (Oscar Wilde's really profound essay) in him. He lacks the necessary depth.

In the praised essay, Frum remains faithful to the gossipy style of his tittle-tattle tome, and produces a series of vignettes designed to "prove" that paleoconservatives, whom he slothfully lumps with paleolibertarians, developed an ideology in order to compensate for alleged career failure.

Contrary to Frum and Rusher's ad libs, Murray N. Rothbard traced the American Old Right's inception to a reaction against the New Deal and its crushing of the old republic's classical-liberal foundations. Members of the original Right wanted to abolish the Welfare State ushered in by the New Deal and return to the traditional American foreign policy. Anyone remember George Washington's wisdom about aiming at extensive commercial but no political foreign entanglements?

Rusher and Frum share the same debating habits. They both bog down in gossip and name dropping to build a political pedigree, mentioning the many retreaded communists that make up their neoconservative movement. It's thus hard to see how Frum warrants such superlatives if he never deals with the substance of paleo ideas.

Once he gets past Frum's tall tales about allegedly belligerent paleo personalities and their putative professional failures, the reader might just have wanted to know that paleolibertarians care first about the effects of the state on civil society.

Everything flows from the passion for "the Old Republic of property rights, freedom of association, and radical political decentralization," as Lew Rockwell has written. The main point of contention between paleos and neocons is thus the role arrogated to the state. Yet the main "profundity" Rusher and Frum are able to parrot is to charge paleos with racism.

The paleolibertarian beef, of course, is with the coercive distribution by the state of wealth from those who create it to those who consume it. Even Frum must be cognizant of discernible trends in wealth creation and wealth consumption. Ditto where crime is concerned: Certain populations are more likely to be perpetrators, others more likely to be victims. To the extent that it is a relevant variable in crime and welfare, paleos comment honestly about demographics. This may not be politically correct, but it's hardly racist. If so "profound," why does Frum's silly screed not factor in the state, considering it's such a crucial construct here?

Clearly, it isn't flattering to have to admit that the force of the Frum faction comes from its endorsement of the state, while the tenacity of the paleolibertarian team comes from its enduring commitment to natural rights, to justice, and to society, not to the state.

Frum and Rusher's attempt to cast these paleo ideas as new and discontinuous is clearly ignorant of the history of the ideas.

Don't wait, then, for neocons to tell you that, had they been catapulted by a time machine into the U.S. of the 21st century, the Founding Fathers would be called libertarians and would be firmly ensconced on the Old Right, in the paleo camp.

The founders, moreover, would be leading an armed revolution against this dictatorial anti-republican centralization of power promoted by both parties, but especially escalated under Bush's neoconservatives.

17. NEOCON ARTISTS

April 24, 2002

In a world where rank bipartisan politics is held up as a paragon of principle, attention to ideology is nothing to sneeze at. But before examining why the "conservative" label has become a liability to some men and women of the Right, a brief mention is in order of a landmark linguistic loss that mars the history of the Right.

The word "liberal" belonged to the Old Right. It stood for "classical liberalism" which blossomed in the 18th and 19th centuries. In the words of David Conway, author of *Classical Liberalism: The Unvanquished Ideal,* classical liberalism is a form of polity that grants to its adult members "the liberty to do whatever they want, provided no one but, at most, themselves is harmed by their doing it." Government is constrained constitutionally and ethically to the defense of life, liberty, and property alone.

Subsequent to the looting of the term by The Left, "liberal" came to denote a social democrat who champions the Welfare State and government omnipotence. It goes without saying that the "liberal" appellation includes most Republicans; establishment politicians are social democrats of one or another variety.

In the wonderfully conciliatory 1992 essay "A Strategy for The Right," Murray N. Rothbard traced the original American Right to a reaction against the New Deal and the manner in which it obliterated the old republic's classical-liberal foundations. Members of the original Right wanted to abolish the Welfare State ushered in by the New Deal and return to the foreign policy of George Washington or Thomas Jefferson, enunciated in his First Inaugural Address, in March 1801: "Peace, commerce, and honest friendship with all nations, entangling alliances with none." Avoiding the metropole status our imposter conservatives or neoconservatives are currently cultivating was crucial to an America First foreign affairs position.

By no means a monolith, the Old Right sported nuanced opinions in matters of philosophy and policy. Sadly, it petered out politically, only to be usurped by the W. F. Buckley, big-government "conservatives."

So who are these "conservative" social democrats, and what do they stand for?

Behind the current administration there is a cadre of people working to help President Bush unleash his inner Caligula. Smitten with their "National Greatness" agenda, President Bush has prosecuted an aggressive war on Iraq, and may have his eyes on Iran and North Korea. This particular neoconservative ideological putsch is fueled by William Kristol's *Weekly Standard* faction, to which many members of the current administration trace their political family tree. And there are the advocates of what can only be described as the quintessential Trotskyist permanent revolution, like neocon academic Michael Ledeen and Richard Perle of the American Enterprise Institute.

The *National Review* has also spawned its share of Beltway Buckleyites, tagged ferociously by historian Paul Gottfried. Particularly pique-making is the claim by a prominent *National Review* scribe to be writing in defense of the "West." As Gottfried points out, the denuded and emasculated West that neocons typically defend is a "post-Christian and post-conservative phenomenon run by retread communists and supranational social-engineering bureaucracies." These "crypto-leftists" uphold a "vast managerial state" and support every bit of encroachment on liberty rejected by the Old Right and its authentic modern adherents.

From anti-discrimination legislative attacks on private property and First Amendment rights to the promotion of "large-scale Third World immigration" that displaces "Western core populations by groups that are culturally different and, in some cases, openly antagonistic"—the neocons are in philosophical tandem with The Left.

This may shed some light on why these "illiterate leftists posturing as conservatives," as Gottfried calls them, have been partial to—even complicit in—the historical elevation of Martin Luther King Jr. above the Founding Fathers. Neocons are always eager to conflate the messages of the two solitudes, even though the founders' liberty is related to King's egalitarianism as neoconservatism is related to traditional Republicanism—never the twain shall mix.

It is thus futile to suggest to neocons that the correct foreign affairs position is the isolationism of the traditional Republican, Robert A. Taft. He may be historically less distant than the classical liberal founders, but to neocons, his memory is as unhip. At their core, neocons are simply deeply hostile to proponents of authentic constitutional regimes.

The affinity for Israel is another contentious issue in the neocon worldview.

To the extent that this affinity—not necessarily its policy prescriptions—is based on the coherent recognition that Israel stands in stark contrast to the region's totalitarian, purely socialistic chieftains, it has clarity. To the extent that neocon cheerleading for

Israel is rooted in the idea of Israel as a U.S.-compatible, postmodern social democracy, it is confused.

The *de facto* state of Israel is nothing of the kind.

Israel is an attempt at an ethnically homogeneous nation-state. In order to survive as well as defend its identity, Israel must practice ethnic—not racial—exclusion. The justification for Israel is rooted in the right of an ethnically homogeneous, voluntary association of people to defend and preserve its distinct identity, even if it entails exclusion based on the preserved characteristics, something our neocon champions of multiculturalism disavow. Like their leftist compatriots, neocons believe that the health of the state is best served by dissolving national distinctiveness with the aid of identity politics and multiculturalism.

Neocon nirvana is thus a U.S.-supervised world where Afghani, Israeli and Iraqi alike are fashioned into global democrats, citizens of the universe. This caricature of freedom helps explain why neoconservatives are convinced that their sojourn in Iraq will have a happy ending.

That Somalia-type native impulses are missing from their Hollywood-inspired script is because neocons are ignorant of history in general, and Arab history in particular. Economist Ludwig von Mises, for instance, didn't go so far as to say that the "Mohammedan countries" were barbaric, but he did genteelly point out that there was a reason the East—far and near—had not contributed anything to "the intellectual effort of mankind" for centuries. You cannot force the culture of freedom and individual rights, reasoned Mises, where it never arose, and where the legal framework that would protect private wealth and guard against confiscation by the rulers is missing.

Considering their progenitors, it's no surprise that neocons easily slip into Marxoid consciousness-raising talk. Iraqis might have expressed a desire to be left to their devices but, as the neocons see it, they don't really know their minds and must be led to the truth—to American-style democracy—even if delivered with daisy cutters. Those of us who are on the receiving end of the neocons' Stalinist name-calling will verify that, when it comes to besmirching their opponents, they are faithful to the tactics perfected by their brutish muses.

Any nattering neocons do about American national sovereignty vis-à-vis the United Nations fails to explain why the UN should be condemned for impeding U.S. sovereignty, while American global hegemony must be praised as benign and beneficent. It is patently obvious that the real beef neocons had with the UN, leading up to the assault on Iraq, was that, for a short while, it stood between the administration and its grand designs for the Middle East.

Like good leftists, neocons support the meddlesome expansion of the "Managerial State" at home. When it comes to extending the intrusive crusade abroad, they go beyond The Left's call of duty: What defines Bush's neoconservative administration is energetic social engineering both at home and abroad.

Needless to say, the political recrudescence of the Real Right is still a long way away.

18. LIBERTARIANS WHO LOATHE ISRAEL

August 13, 2003

Admittedly, there is a lot about the Israeli side of the Palestinian-Israeli dispute to be critical of. For one, demolishing the homes of a terrorist's family isn't just or prudent. But it's hard to make sense of a perspective that sees everything Israel does as arch-evil, as is the case with those libertarians who religiously and robotically depict Israel as the devil incarnate.

So, how about it? Is Israel always wrong? Is there nothing redeeming about a people that revived a desolate land and a long-dead biblical language just over 100 years ago? Can nothing good be said about the thriving cities that have sprung up on what was, only a century ago, swampland and desert?

Evidently not.

True, Israel's founding fathers were socialists (although there's something to be said for voluntary forms of socialism like the kibbutz, in contrast to politically imposed socialism). Born of a collectivist political philosophy, Israel has been progressing, albeit slowly, toward greater economic freedom. Trade liberalization, financial market reforms, increased privatization and decreased regulation have been part of this historical retreat from socialism. But the steady abolition of state subsidies and the enhancement of competition supported by Sharon's Thatcherite Finance Minister (Bibi Netanyahu) cannot easily offset the effects of endemic violence. Coupled with the slowdown in the U.S. economy, terrorism is one of the main reasons for the slump in the Israeli economy.

Although Israel's economy is by no means ideal, it is not much different from Western Europe's Third-Way, mixed economies. Still, many libertarians find Israel particularly repugnant. With a respectable per capita GDP of roughly $18,440, compared to the Palestinian Authority's $1,000, Israel apparently has nothing to recommend her.

The PA, on the other hand, with no economy, no free speech and press, no independent courts, no sound contract laws, and no individual—including property—rights, wins the sympathies of legions of freedom lovers hands down. That hundreds of millions of dollars in foreign aid have done nothing to change this bleak reality bothers anti-Israel libertarians only in so far as to point out that Israel is to blame.

If this seems a little harsh, it is to be expected—irrational hatred is harsh.

Consider the Israeli fence now inspiring hyperbolic hysteria among libertarians. What can a leadership do to stop its people from being blown up in the streets as they go about their daily lives? (That is, besides following the libertarian prescription propounded by Stephen P. Halbrook in "The Alienation of a Homeland: How Palestine Became Israel," and turn Israel into a multicultural potage with a Right of Return for any self-styled, United Nations Relief and Works Agency-sponsored "Palestinian" agitator.)

If you are the United States of America, you commit to frisking old ladies on airplanes and reducing far-away, unrelated nations to rubble. At the same time, you leave your own borders as porous as possible, while working to disarm and dispossess your people.

That's the American way.

Israel has a different idea. She defends her own turf aggressively. In a last-ditch attempt to physically stop attacks on its civilian population—terrorists have killed more than 800 Israelis in the past three years, and maimed and injured nearly 6,000—Israel began erecting a security fence along the West Bank, from where most terror attacks inside Israel proper are launched.

Yet a mechanical barrier is construed by one libertarian writer, Justin Raimondo, as "an act of aggression…a land grab of huge proportions…" What most reasonable people would view as a desperate defensive measure is to Raimondo a symbol of Israeli sadism.

The comparisons between the Israeli fence and the wall between East and West Berlin are theatrically invoked: "Mr. Sharon, tear down that wall," rings Raimondo's cleverly adapted Reagan classic. (An equally plaintive plea from Israelis went unheard. So I'll make it for them: "Mahmoud Abbas, alias Abu Mazen, aka Yasser Arafat, stop blowing up Israelis.")

Raimondo thereafter follows with an idealized description (omitting opportunity costs) of the wonders the wall can't thwart: "Markets conquer all; they leap over walls, over oceans, to create the most complex, interconnected, international division of labor possible …"

I too love free markets. But open borders are not a prerequisite for free trade. People can trade goods very well without trading places. Moreover, the hate so many libertarians have for Israel leads them to periodically forget that her comparative and competitive advantage is in knowledge-based hi-tech industries. Israel's natural trading partners are the U.S. and the European Union. With all due respect, Israel needs the economic powerhouse that is the PA like China needs trade with a tribe of rain-forest-dwelling pygmies. The theory of free trade, which is always a positive-sum game, ought not to be compared with the dubious "benefits" of the unfettered movement of people across borders (especially ones with bombs strapped beneath their clothing).

Notwithstanding that libertarians, very plainly, believe that the Palestinians have a universal right to Israeli labor markets, it's worth noting that just as the U.S. can do without the hordes of Mexicans streaming across the borders, so too can Israel do without Palestinian cheap labor if the dangers of an open border exceed the benefits. If Israel (and the U.S. for that matter) eliminated her socialistic minimum-wage laws, which prohibit agriculture from hiring Israelis at a true market price, namely below minimum wage, Israelis—Jews and Arabs alike—would do farm work.

Indeed, irrational hatred for "an isolated Sparta, bristling with weaponry and little else" even prompts libertarians to forget their welfare economics. Without American aid, Raimondo menacingly warns, Israel will cease to exist.

Come again?

First off, aid is just a fraction of Israeli GDP, so the point is laughable. More significantly, foreign aid, like welfare, exacerbates the problems it is supposed to ameliorate. As a government-to-government transfer, foreign aid serves to entrench and grow the bureaucracy and the public sector in general at the expense of the taxpayer and the private productive economy.

An ardent defender of the free market ought to know that American aid, if anything, retards Israel's progress. Cut Israel loose—it'll be for the best. In the absence of U.S. loans and cash grants, she would be forced to economize. Capital, including the billions in private donor dollars, will be channeled to its best use and will flow to where it is most productive.

Unlike her neighbors, Israel has what Peter Bauer, author of the seminal *Dissent on Development*, called "the faculties, attitudes and institutions favorable to material progress." Without foreign aid, she would gallop toward a freer economy.

I understand that libertarians like Sheldon Richman (and the Holocaust-denying Institute for Historical Review[*]) believe, mistakenly, that all "the land" belongs to the Arabs.[†]

And no doubt, American libertarians do speak with the authority that comes from having the finest fathers a nation could wish for. How then can Israel's humble, evidently uninspiring, ideological beginnings compare with founders who fought for their freedom and their land?

But let me ask my fellow libertarians this: When last did an American man fight honorably for *his* land, *his* home, *his* women, and *his* children? The men of the South circa 1861?

I thought so.

As much as libertarians hate them, Israelis, at least, defend what they perceive to be *their* land, *their* homes, and *their* freedoms.

---

[*]Mr. Richman took umbrage at my deployment of a perfectly legitimate literary device to illustrate his extremist position on Israel, claiming that other than to smear him and call him a Holocaust denier, there was no reason to invoke the IHR. However, I said that Mr. Richman's views on the "land," not the Holocaust, conjure theirs. In retrospect, I should have also listed the Aztlan "freedom fighters," Islamists, and radical leftists. These groups would also warm to Mr. Richman's position on the land of Israel. Would he then still have gone on to complain that I had labeled him an Islamist, a radical leftist, or a "La Raza" liberationalist? I somehow doubt it. All the same, I note Mr. Richman's objection but I still think the same.

[†]"In candid moments," wrote Mr. Richman in "Cant and the Middle East," "Israeli military leaders acknowledged that the land belonged to the Arabs."

19. *TAKING AMERICA BACK* MEANS TAKING LINCOLN DOWN

February 12, 2003

If Americans want to reclaim their moral character as a nation, they will have to confront and denounce "The Real Lincoln," who carried out a violent unconstitutional revolution (instead of pursuing peaceful emancipation like every other nation did), a revolution, which, in turn, sired the modern imperialist, interventionist, and highly centralized American State.

This moral reckoning will be an uphill battle, not least because of the "Church of Lincoln." The moral and intellectual nurturers of Lincoln's legacy have carved careers out of denying that the soul of the American federal system is state sovereignty. And state sovereignty, as author Thomas J. DiLorenzo points out, is gutless in its power to check the federal government *sans* the right of secession.

The constitutional casuistry of the "Church of Lincoln" only underscores its moral decay.

Let's imagine, as Lincoln lovers claim, that the Constitution ratified in 1788 forbade peaceful secession and authorized the federal government, which was supposed to have limited powers delegated to it by the people, to invade and occupy any seceding state, declare martial law, subdue the secessionists by force, burn and ransack entire cities, and then establish a military dictatorship over those states for a dozen years.

Let's pretend that it was constitutional to intentionally wage war on civilians—blacks included—to imprison without trial thousands of Northern citizens, jail—even execute—people who refused to take a loyalty oath to Lord Lincoln, shut down hundreds of opposition newspapers, incarcerating editors and owners, and generally suspend the Bill of Rights, the writ of habeas corpus, and international law.

If it endorsed—or even accommodated—what Lincoln did, including his ignoring of the Ninth and 10th amendments, and his violating of the Second, then the Constitution is categorically evil and self-contradictory.

The other more plausible option is that the "Church of Lincoln" is lying: In 1861, Lincoln kidnapped and killed the Constitution! The Jacobin Jackals who defend Lincoln's actions (by referring to his beguiling words) have been covering up his crimes and ignoring the consequences of this *coup* ever since.

The nation's popular war lore must also take a moral turn.

In the film *Gettysburg*, the effects of moral relativism moderate the usual outright condemnation of the South. That's not an achievement worth celebrating. Filmmakers are never shy of underdog endorsement. Yet the battle for "Little Round Top" is filmed from one angle only; never once does the lens stray to the Confederates' side. Militarily—certainly visually—the Confederates charging up the hill in unrelenting waves form the suicide mission. The film, however, fails miserably to bring alive the implications of the David/Goliath power differential in the War of Northern Aggression.

The film's prominent unionists get to deliver all the impassioned speeches. The over-represented abolitionist rhetoric comes from no other than Colonel Joshua Lawrence Chamberlain, who was not even an abolitionist. In the South's corner, an inarticulate oaf, sniggered at by his compatriots, is charged with presenting the Jeffersonian ideas of states' rights, liberty, and self-government.

This is inexcusable when you consider that Lord Acton, "the great historian of liberty," wrote poignantly to Robert E. Lee in person to praise the General for fighting to preserve "the only availing check upon the absolutism of the sovereign will": states' rights and secession.

The great Lee's defining features in *Gettysburg* are a southern drawl and a doddering demeanor. He certainly didn't get to orate his inspired reply to Lord Acton:

> ...I believe that the maintenance of the rights and
> authority reserved to the states and to the people...are

the safeguard to the continuance of a free government...
whereas the consolidation of the states into one vast
republic, *sure to be aggressive abroad and despotic at home*,
[my emphasis], will be the certain precursor of that ruin
which has overwhelmed all those that have preceded it.

Gettysburg does portray the obscene and tragic result of Lincoln's
fratricidal war in which 620,000 soldiers died, and 50,000 Southern
civilians perished as a result of the war the hands-on Lincoln waged
on non-combatants.

Predictably, the apologists for these atrocities are the same people
who quiver like post-coital Court Courtesans (Peggy Noonan comes
to mind) every time George Bush promises to forcibly uproot evil
from all corners of the globe. Like Bush, they probably believe that
invading a nation that has not attacked the U.S. is just another faith-
based initiative.

If director and producer Ronald F. Maxwell brings the *Gettysburg*
moral incoherence to his sequel film *Gods and Generals*, I'll keep my
distance, no matter how much praying goes on in the film. Piety is
not to be equated with the kind of goodness Americans must regain.

20. JUDGE MOORE AND THE GODLESS 14TH AMENDMENT

August 27, 2003

Alabama Supreme Court Chief Justice Roy Moore paid for and
placed a granite monument inscribed with the Ten Commandments
in the Alabama judicial building, where he presides. This was two
years ago. Predictably, the American Civil Liberties Union (ACLU)
could not tolerate the sight of a moral code displayed on taxpayer-
funded property. Together with Americans United for Separation of
Church and State, the ACLU alleged the justice had violated the
Establishment Clause of the First Amendment.

A district judge by the name of Myron Thompson then ordered the removal of the Decalogue. Moore appealed to the U.S. Supreme Court for an emergency stay. When this was denied, a nine-member state tribunal suspended him with pay. If the monument is not removed, the plaintiffs want Moore held in contempt and fines levied against the state.

First Amendment jurisprudence has tended to see the injunction against the establishment of a state religion as an injunction against the expression of faith—especially discriminating against the founding Judeo-Christian faith—in taxpayer-supported spheres. The end result has been the expulsion of religion from the public square and the suppression therein of freedom of religion.

Thomas Jefferson was prolific on the topic of religious freedom—the Virginia Statute for Religious Freedom was a crowning achievement for which he wished to be remembered, along with the Declaration of Independence and the founding of the University of Virginia.

With "Congress shall make no law respecting the establishment of religion, or prohibiting the exercise thereof," Jefferson intended, according to David N. Meyer, author of *Jefferson's Constitutional Thought*, to guarantee both "an absolute free exercise of religion and an absolute prohibition of an establishment of religion."

It's difficult to see how the display of the Decalogue constitutes an establishment of a state religion or why Moore should be forbidden to so express his faith. The Ten Commandments are a civilizing moral code. Fine, the first few Commandments, among which are Commandments that exhort against idolatry and pantheism, do pertain to ethical monotheism. But other than those, why would anyone (bar the ACLU) object to "thou shall not kill," or to "thou shall not commit adultery, steal, or covet?" The Ten Commandments can hardly be perceived as an instrument for state proselytization.

However obvious, this is not the soul of the subject in the case of Justice Moore.

Back to Jefferson: "I consider the government of the U.S. as interdicted by the Constitution from intermeddling with religious institutions, their doctrines, discipline, or exercise," Jefferson expatiated. He then gets to the essence of the issue: "This results not only from the provision that no law shall be made respecting the establishment, or free exercise of religion but also from the Tenth Amendment, which reserves to the states [or to the people] the powers not delegated to the U.S."

That was true until the ratification of the 14th Amendment!

Prior to that, the federal government had no authority to enforce the Bill of Rights in the states, religious freedoms included. The Bill of Rights, very plainly, did not grant the federal government any powers, but was intended to place limits on the federal government's actions. Ratified illegally after the War Between the States, the 14th Amendment overrode, to all intents and purposes, the doctrine of states' rights, to which Jefferson looked for the preservation of freedoms.

The particular portion of the miscellany that is the 14th states: "No State shall make or enforce any law which shall abridge the privileges and immunities of citizens of the United States; nor shall any state deprive any person of life, liberty, or property without due process of law; nor deny to any person within its jurisdiction the equal protection of the laws." The gargantuan grant of power to the federal government is thus sealed: "The Congress shall have power to enforce, by appropriate legislation, the provisions of this article."

In American federalism, the rights of the individual are secured through the strict limits imposed on the power of the central government by a Bill of Rights and the division of authority between autonomous states and a federal government. As Frank Chodorov wrote, states' rights are "an essential Americanism. The Founding Fathers and the opponents of the Constitution agreed on the principle of divided authority as a safeguard to the rights of the individual."

If the Bill of Rights was intended to place strict limits on federal power and protect the individual from government, the 14th, in effect, defeated that purpose. What it did was to put the power to enforce the Bill of Rights in federal hands, where it was never intended to be.

Naturally, states can just as well violate individual rights. But, as Chodorov highlighted, there is no monopoly power behind a state's action. If a state wants to outlaw alcohol, then one can move to a state that doesn't. (That's one way for state legislators to ensure that their states will be as densely populated as the moon.) If a state wants to establish a religion, and its own constitution doesn't prohibit this, one can move to a state with a different constitution. Competition in government puts the brakes on folly and abuse and preserves freedom.

The 14th Amendment violated this balance, or as Felix Morley observed in *Freedom and Federalism*, it nullified "the original purpose of the Bill of Rights, by vesting its enforcement in the national rather than in the state governments." This just about renders asunder the Ninth and 10th amendments—what powers do the states retain if the federal government has gobbled them all up?

When the federal government became the arbiter of individual rights—freedom of religion included—the doctrine of limitation of powers was badly damaged, if not destroyed. In the real world, as opposed to the wasteland of pure theory, government—especially centralized government—is the natural enemy of natural rights. Putting the central government in exclusive charge of protecting natural rights is the height of folly.

Judge Moore rightly proclaimed his innocence in the *Wall Street Journal*. "The First Amendment says that 'Congress shall make no law respecting the establishment of religion, or prohibiting the free exercise thereof.' It does not take a constitutional scholar to recognize that I am not Congress, and no law has been passed," he protests.

However, when the Justice proclaims, "The Ninth Amendment secured our right as a people. The 10th guaranteed our right as a sovereign state," he is neglecting that along came the 14th and did away with all that.

Justice Roy Moore has more on his hands than he bargained for, although his passions are well suited to begin the necessary groundswell that'll see the repeal of the 14th Amendment.

II. To Control and to Plunder

21. DEFICIT DISORDERS

May 14, 2003

The guy on one of those policy-bereft-of-principle debates plaguing television had me confused. He was saying that the dot-com bust of the 1990s is a big factor in the deficits. As I pondered what he meant, it occurred to me that he was putting the cashless cart before the horse.

The process began with the Chairman of the Fed, also the most revered government lackey, Alan Greenspan. With policies of cheap money and credit, which are, invariably, accompanied by boom and bust cycles, Greenspan, his Federal Reserve System, and the consecutive governments they've served created the "irrational exuberance" that typified the times—in cahoots, this cartel created the conditions for the speculative glut that was the dot-com era.

Still, the dot-com bust saw the private sector bite the bullet and undergo the necessary downsizing. Gone are the annoying "wonder kids." When their business plans proved to be without substance, they, presumably, sold the Porsches and moved back with mom and pop.

How then did this rational, post-hangover, private-sector sobriety contribute to government deficits?

Well, guess who didn't shrink operations to fit the emptying coffers? When you and I fall on hard times, often due to the policies of plunder, we economize or face the legal and economic ramifications of our excesses. When the parasites who feed upon us exhaust our resources, what do they do?

Answers Rep. Ron Paul: "Congress almost always spends more each year than the treasury collects in revenues." The budget passed in 2003, says Paul, is 22 percent higher than two years ago, and encompasses all federal programs, not only those concerned with homeland security. In the face of faltering revenues, government has continued to expand, and federal spending to rise.

Because of the oil-and-water relationship governments have cultivated between ethics and politics, speaking in plain terms— spelling it out as it is—has become foreign to the public. So here goes: When government sports a "surplus," this implies that the political pickpockets have stolen more funds than they can possibly dream of spending. The property is not theirs to keep! Conversely, when "deficits" are reported, this means that the kleptomaniacs have not been able to steal sufficient funds to cover their profligacy.

The tax cut, which is an agreement by the plundering class to pilfer less, has become a red herring, used for political hay on both sides. Democrats say that reduced revenues will contribute to the deficit, hence tax cuts are bad. Republicans, as unflinching about fleecing the people, say that tax rate cuts will ultimately increase their revenues by stimulating the economy. Each of the morally bankrupt parties has used the tax cut as a decoy to avoid addressing the cause of the deficit: government's spending more than it steals.

In fact, not only has Congress failed to show the kind of restraint you and I exercise in tough times, it has "magnanimously" raised its debt ceiling by one trillion dollars. Over and above a staggering national debt that now stands at 6.4 trillion dollars, Congress, reports Ron Paul, has also provided in the 2004 budget for an annual increase in the debt limit to 12 trillion over the next ten years!

Figures from the Bureau of Economic Analysis confirm that federal spending under Mr. Bush has indeed reached historic levels, with years of record deficits looming ahead. Our politicians have saddled every American with a debt of $22,000, reserving the option to double that burden.

At best, Bush's tax cut will see him siphon approximately $35 billion per year less from taxpayers, over a period of 10 years, while simultaneously accelerating federal spending. At worst, the tax cut Bush proposes to phase in over the course of a decade will be repealed by a future Congress after his departure, thus never taking effect. Bush gets to claim he cut taxes without implementing the cut, but all the while spending like there is no tomorrow—for every dollar that may or may not remain with its rightful owner, the president will have blown tens of non-existent bucks on brand-new spending.

How will Bush make the money materialize? There're a few easy options, chief of which is a tax infinitely more dastardly and damaging than all others: Alan Greenspan has been faithful, as he has been promiscuous, about inflating the money supply. To feed the deficit, government will pressure the Fed to print money. This practice—inflation—raises prices and depreciates the value of the currency. Politicians, first to feast on the new money, get richer; you and I get poorer.

Here's another simple truth: A decrease of a $100 billion in government spending would, according to professors Richard Vedder and Lowell Gallaway, authors of *Out of Work: Unemployment and Government in Twentieth Century America*, lift three million children out of poverty!

In their work on "The Scope of Government and the Wealth of Nations," for the Joint Economic Committee of Congress, James Gwartney, Randall Holcombe, and Robert Lawson have demonstrated that as government expenditures grow—a trend the United States has adopted for the past several decades—so does the national income shrivel, point for painful point.

Larger government, be it through welfare or warfare programs, spells slower economic growth. Sustained job creation and economic prosperity hinge on slashing federal spending. The degree of economic stagnation currently reached indicates that The Beast has eaten away at the flesh and is now biting at the bone...our bones.

22. THE WAR ON TAX HAVENS

September 4, 2001

Despite a din of protests from the *New York Times* and the *Washington Post*, the Bush administration refused to support an attempt by the Organization for Economic Co-operation and Development (OECD) to clamp down on tax havens. Fronting for about 30 high-tax governments, the Paris-based organization has been leaning on jurisdictions like the Cayman Islands, Bermuda, and the Isle of Man. If the junta of high-tax governments has its way, not only will there be no place left to run to, but by eliminating what tax havens offer, these governments will have eliminated tax competition, and with it the imperative to downsize their fiefdoms.

In a paper deceptively entitled "Promoting Tax Competition," OECD überbureaucrats Jeffrey Owens and Richard M. Hammer of Fiscal Affairs build their case against the tax haven. Their starting point is, of course, the implicit understanding that laws regulating how people use their rightful capital are just laws. Our authors grant that property owners ought to be allowed to do that which they do naturally—namely, invest their capital where it will yield the best returns. But this must be done "without impeding the aim of national governments to meet the legitimate expectations of their citizens." Freedom to make economic decisions must be tempered by the OECD governments' ongoing confiscatory agenda.

The OECD skillfully adopts the language of the anti-globalization camp to agitate against tax havens. Globalization is good, say the writers, but not when the benefits are unequally shared. The OECD frames an alleged "world-wide reduction in welfare" as the consequences of "… tax-induced distortions in capital and financial flows." This anti-globalization choice of rhetoric is understandable. If anything, the OECD's efforts are in keeping with government globalization. In advancing the aims of an accretive bureaucracy, what better ally to court than the anti-globalization crowd, with its equal enthusiasm for unbounded state powers? Business, of course, needs no co-opting. Historically, it has always been on the side of government taxation and regulations, because these hamper nascent competition.

This official line omits that wealth in the hands of its rightful owners enriches all sectors of the population more than funds in the sticky paws of officials. Using a sample of 92 countries, David Dollar and Aart Kraay, authors of a study entitled "Growth is Good for the Poor," offer evidence that when average incomes rise, the average income of the poorest fifth of society rise proportionately. The study spans four decades, and yields results that hold across regions, periods, income levels and growth rates. By extension, the same effect must hold good whether the reason for a rise in real income is higher earnings or less taxation. Clearly, keeping more of one's income is not "harmful" to the rightful owners of capital, or to the beneficiaries of its investment, which include any and all bar the taxman.

Although the OECD's meddling gives an impression to the contrary, a tax haven is a sovereign territory that does not levy taxes, or levies them at non-punitive rates. Sometimes these countries opt to tax only domestic—but not foreign—income. The economy of the tax haven depends to a large degree on the banking and financial sectors. With this come imperatives such as financial privacy and secrecy.

Hell-bent on forcing low—or no—tax nations to suspend their financial privacy laws, and impelling them, through the threat of sanctions, to provide information to foreign tax collectors, the OECD has set about framing their practices as harmful, if not criminal. With the aid of the media, tax havens have been depicted as cauldrons of counterfeiting and money laundering (a strange accusation coming from governments whose national banks regularly inflate the money supply and dilute with fiat money the value of people's assets).

To be guilty of "harmful tax practices," says the OECD, a country must be an area of "no or nominal effective tax rates." The OECD further suggests that a haven transgresses when it is bereft of "transparency" and "effective exchange of information." By demanding information exchange when this defies a tax haven's own laws, the OECD disregards the comity of nations in international law—the courtesy by which one nation respects and recognizes the laws of another. This principle implies deference and goodwill towards the legislative, judicial, and executive acts of another country. It is uncivil, not to mention coercive, for the OECD to force tax havens to prostrate their laws before those of the aggressor governments.

Another weapon in the OECD's bullyboy arsenal is its hit list, entitled "List of Uncooperative Tax Havens." So far the OECD is gunning for only "35 jurisdictions identified as meeting the tax haven criteria," but fully 45 jurisdictions are deemed sufficiently irksome to the OECD as to warrant the term "potentially harmful." Of course, these jurisdictions are manifestly not "harmful" to their inhabitants and clients. Nevertheless, they are now the objects of assorted cold war tactics called the "common framework of defensive measures."

Having sidelined sovereignty and international law, and having all but criminalized certain financial practices, the OECD proceeds to demand that these practices be "rolled back" and eliminated. Sanctuaries such as Bermuda, the Cayman Islands, Cyprus, Malta, Mauritius and San Marino are rolling over. In eerily uniform official letters to the Secretary-General of the OECD, the kind that read like coerced confessions, the respective representatives all promise to implement the OECD's recommendations and follow, if necessary, with legislation of their own to end privacy and facilitate "exchange of information in tax matters."

The OECD's statist overreach must be seen in the context of an increasingly centralized Europe. Europeans are being herded by stealth into a supranational European State. With a vision predicated on rigid central planning, homogenization of laws throughout the continent, and heavy taxation and inflation of the money supply, the EU's putsch can't but evoke unfavorable comparisons.

From its equally suspect quarters, the UN is pushing for an international tax collection organization, for global taxes, and for an emigrant tax. This master plan will see individuals cornered by governments and paying a ransom if and when they wish to exit a particular jurisdiction. The UN plans for governments the world over to be able to tax income earned outside their borders (something the United States already does), the outcome of which will be a well-coordinated confiscation of private property.

The OECD no more reflects the "will of the people" than does the EU or the UN, although, like them, it hides behind the same democratic dross. The EU does not speak for Europe's diverse 374 million people. And apart from its bureaucrats, nobody knows for whom the UN speaks. Still less does the OECD represent any more than a cartel of enforcers for high-tax governments. Ironically, any corporation that acted like that would be prosecuted under antitrust law.

23. MUTANT MARXISTS IN 'THE HEART OF DARKNESS'

August 28, 2002

There's a Joseph Conrad kind of symbolism in the location of the United Nations-sponsored World Summit on Sustainable Development. A collection of central planners has convened in Johannesburg, South Africa, to further centralize control over private property and streamline the distribution of wealth from freer, more prosperous nations to despotic, underdeveloped ones.

The intellectual and ethical impetus for this renewed assault on freedom and prosperity is the repugnant Marxist theory of environmentalism. Conservation is the central planners' Trojan Horse for a globally coordinated assault on individual rights.

These "watermelons"—green on the outside, red on the inside— adroitly combine elements of socialism with fascism: They want to see an expansion of the "public commons," their euphemism for nationalization of resources. But they are not impervious to the methods of the Fascist State: Impose on private property owners a globally harmonized regulatory and taxation regime.

The degradation-to-the-environment hypotheticals popularized at the Summit are mutations of Marxism. The theory used to be that capitalism was going to cause the impoverishment of the worker. The exact opposite transpired. Greater economic freedom, especially in developed nations, has enabled those who, in previous centuries would have lived brutishly short and nasty lives, to afford the accoutrements of modernity. The theory now is that capitalism has taken a slight detour—the worker's demise will indeed follow as soon as the capitalist is through despoiling the environment.

On the ideological interface between socialism and environmentalism, economist George Reisman says this: "The Reds claimed that the individual could not be left free because the result would be such things as 'exploitation,' 'monopoly' and depressions. The Greens claim that the individual cannot be left free because the result will be such things as destruction of the ozone layer, acid rain and global warming."

Reds, and now Greens, agree that wise bureaucrats alone have the wherewithal to make decisions for billions of people.

The 20th century was a monument to these decision-makers. A handful of communist commissars replaced with their own commands, and at the point of a gun, the voluntary decisions, valuations and exchanges made by millions of people. To achieve this, governments—not capitalists—murdered roughly 80 million people. The devastation the Reds wrought was not incidental but inherent to the ideology of collectivism and statism.

The Greens harbor similar designs. They are quite prepared for "a major portion of all mankind" to suffer and die "for the alleged sake of the lower animals and inanimate nature."

Eco-idiots, however, need to be disabused of their romantic view of nature. As Reisman points out, most "resources" in nature are useless lumps of nothing. If not for man, iron, aluminum, coal and oil would lie purposeless and pristine in the wildernesses.

Man discovered that these elements could be used to assuage human needs. Once he identified and ingeniously matched the human need with the material thing, he went on to devise ways to harness the resource. Most "resources" provided by nature become goods of value only when man connects the dots. If not for man, the matter and energy abundant on earth would come to naught.

The ability to discover and transform natural resources into usable goods, as well as to develop "resource-enhancing and sustaining technologies" is the unique province of man.

The environmentalist may sway with Mother Earth's rhythms but he hasn't the mental stamina to grasp the pulse of the very thing that feeds him. About the voluntary cooperation between men, about the division of labor, and about the way the price system conserves resources he is ignorant.

No surprise then that for every enlightened suggestion made at the "Heart of Darkness" Summit (such as eliminating protectionism and tariffs), there were lots of foolish condemnations of the supposedly disastrous production and consumption patterns in industrial societies.

The alleged impending shortages forecasted, however, are a feature of "public ownership," the Sacred Grounds of the Summit's voodooists. Depredation, overuse and wastage are attributes of government-managed resources. The tragedy of the commons occurs when everyone and no one owns the resource.

As we speak, government-managed forests are going up in flames. Lives and property have been lost. This is to be expected. Be it in fishery or forest, communist custodianship removes all the attributes of private property, namely, the incentive to conserve. Lack of ownership is the death knell for the resource. Only when it is owned, and not just leased for periodical plunder, will a forest continue to be a viable and renewable source of riches, monetary and other. The solution clearly lies not in better regulation of a resource but in its privatization.

"The horror, the horror" are Kurtz's last words in Conrad's *Heart of Darkness*. They capture the counter-civilization, savage-lauding spirit of the South African Summit. The totalitarian, myth-worshipping environmentalists are hostile not only to The Good Life but to life itself.

24. INSIDER TRADING, OR INFORMATION SOCIALISM?

June 19, 2002

Mainstream media seldom fail to shed darkness on whatever topic they tackle. Since the arrest of former ImClone CEO Dr. Samuel Waksal for prematurely ridding himself of his soon-to-tumble ImClone stock, the media have not deviated from this mandate. Pointmen like Howard Kurtz of the *Washington Post*, the wild-eyed James Cramer, and Chris Matthews have been whooping it up uncritically for the actions of the Securities and Exchange Commission (SEC).

When the SEC implicated Waksal's pal Martha Stewart for possible insider trading, obstruction of justice, and conspiracy, the jeering in the press reached a climax. The doily doyenne sold her ImClone shares around the time she and Waksal were supposed to pretend they were not apprised of—or entitled to act on—any special knowledge. Stewart has now resigned from the board of the New York Stock Exchange. To the delight of the jackals, she may soon be forced to step down as chief executive of Martha Stewart Living Omnimedia and even face a prison term.

Information Socialism

While it's easy to come up snake eyes when trying to understand the vague and ill-defined laws Martha Stewart and Sam Waksal are accused of violating, the premise of the law is not hard to divine: Competition in capital markets must proceed from a level playing field. All investors are entitled to the same information advantage irrespective of effort and abilities. In a word, socialism!

There is no end, seemingly, to the ingenious methods legislators will devise in order to forcibly, and at the behest of the voter, suppress natural advantage. The law unethically distributes tangible property at the point of a gun. Distributing advantages like IQ, beauty or knowledge is somewhat more complicated, a fact that has forced lawmakers to be extra-enterprising. And so we have non-discrimination laws to ensconce ugly flight attendants on airlines and obese fitness instructors in gyms. SATs are routinely—and ingeniously—standardized to reward congenital stupidity.

To the same tradition belong insider-trading regulations, according to which an individual must not be able to profit from non-public information, gleaned because of his position within the firm. Essentially, lawmakers have come up with a winning formula to punish those who are poised to benefit from the risks and rewards of their occupation.

Non-Public Information

The test of a true and sound principle is in its universal applicability. If insider trading is good law, why criminalize the use of non-public information only in capital markets? By parity of reasoning, and in the aim of "fairness," why not broaden the proscription?

Aren't professionals who get jobs through "networking" acting on non-public information? Are they not the recipients of an ostensibly unfair advantage? For acting on inside information, Attorney General John Ashcroft should certainly be forced to do the perp walk, says Bill Anderson of the Mises Institute. Like the rest of government prior to September 11, Ashcroft had non-public information that terrorists might hijack U.S. airliners. While We The People were sitting ducks, the AG acted on his knowledge: Just before the dreaded date, he began to fly exclusively on private aircraft.

The Benefits of Insider Trading

Insider trading may even benefit the market in general. It facilitates the circulation of information about the status of the company and prevents misallocation of funds. It's hard to imagine that the share price of Enron or WorldCom would have reflected so poorly on the real value of the stock if insider trading had been permitted. Those with inside information would have dumped their stocks as soon as they got wind of irregularities, and others would have followed, saving many people a great deal of money and sorrow.

As a matter of property rights, it's up to the rightful owners of the company—the shareholders—to regulate information about the company and to decide what their employees do with information gleaned about it. Because they stand to profit from the knowledge, insider trading encourages employees to learn about the firm. With this in mind, shareholders might even want to allow such trading. If they decide to forbid trading on inside information, shareholders can so stipulate in an employee's contract.

If a stock is destined to tank, everybody is going to lose money. For a variety of reasons, some people are in a position to lose less than others. What could possibly be the objection to this other than envy? It's both fit and proper that when he sells, the insider will make more of a profit than the late seller who doesn't have his hard-won advantage. Ultimately, when he sells his shares, signaling to other shareholders to follow suit, the insider is performing a service in the market. If investors are too stupid to grasp the information conveyed by a sale, they should not be investing in the market.

Supporting Innovators

Another ruinous link in the Sam Waksal saga is the Food and Drug Administration (FDA). Aided by a renowned cancer scientist by the name of John Mendelsohn, Waksal was working on the development of the new cancer drug, Erbitux. On average, it takes the FDA 12 years to approve a substance. The agency allows approximately five out of every 5,000 substances to be tested in clinical trials. Of these, only one is approved for patient use.

During the month of December 2001, ImClone's promising drug moved from the FDA's vacillation stage to its chopping block. It was after the FDA's snub that Waksal attempted, but failed, to sell his ImClone stock. It's a testament to the tenacity of the entrepreneur that, despite the FDA, the Waksals of the world continue to drive pharmaceutical innovation. In the interest of both fairness and the support for further innovation, one ought to have no misgivings when the person who took all the risks recovers some of his investment.

Does it Violate Rights?

Part and parcel of an ill-defined and unconstitutional law is that it, in the words of legal scholar James Ostrowski, "Legalizes naturally criminal behavior by the state and its agents while criminalizing naturally lawful behavior by citizens."

All the more reason why it's incumbent on the fair-minded to consider this: By selling their property on the basis of an information advantage, have Sam Waksal and his alleged tippee Martha Stewart violated the rights of other ImClone shareholders or potential buyers? The answer has to be a ringing no! Neither the rights of ImClone shareholders nor the rights of other potential buyers have been violated, because there is no such right as a right to a guaranteed profit or a right to avoid losses.

In their discussion on whether insider trading constitutes fraud, economists Walter Block and Robert McGee invoke the example of the merchant who is first to sell his grain "where wheat fetches a high price." He knows that other merchants will follow, and the price of grain will fall. It would be virtuous of him if, then and there, he lowered his prices, but he isn't morally—much less legally—obliged to do so.

Is our trader then obliged to tell buyers that share prices may soon drastically fall? By seeking to be rid of the stock, Waksal conveyed all the information to which a potential buyer is entitled. Why would he be attempting to sell the stock if he did not expect share prices to soon fall? Equally, when insiders buy stock, what reason other than the expectation of a profit could there be for such a purchase? It's one thing to concede that it would be decent of the insider to go public with the information. It's quite another thing to jail someone for not spilling the beans.

While Martha was not bound by contract to ImClone shareholders, Sam Waksal was. If he violated his contractual obligation to his shareholders by selling his shares, pursuant to the FDA's criminal rejection of Erbitux, then Sam Waksal ought to incur a civil—not criminal—liability. Waksal's investing partners, Merck KGaA and Bristol-Myers Squibb, to whom he indeed had a fiduciary duty, were fully in the loop. Waksal, it seems, didn't mislead them about the FDA's shenanigans, and is hence not in violation of his contractual obligation.

Conclusion

"Socialism in its contemporary watered down form," writes Martin Pot of the Paris-based *Institut Héraclite*, "is little more than envy disguised as principle." If we can credit the purveyors of information and opinion in our society with anything, it's with demonstrating that both the legal and the personal attacks on Martha Stewart spring from this "grand" tradition.

While the yipping in the press easily leads to the impression that business is becoming increasingly corrupt, it's the accelerated activity of bureaucrats that lurks behind the glut of SEC-driven prosecutions. As Cornell's Jonathan R. Macey averred, the SEC is teetering perilously on hounding any trader who trades on "the basis of an information advantage." A trend that if not halted will see the agency bring ruin to capital markets.

Absent a moral obligation to divulge information, criminal charges are a grotesque overreach, a position reiterated in the Supreme Court's older interpretations of securities laws. The Court rejected the notion that all trading parties have to have parity of information, maintaining that "there is no duty to disclose nonpublic information." These more constitutional—less casuist—rulings conceded that it is up to company shareholders and their employees to regulate insider trading through contracts.

Either way, it's a lemming's lunacy to turn people like Waksal and Stewart by legislative fiat into common criminals. A society that destroys its most productive and gifted members because they accrue more information than others and act on it has little to recommend it.

25. MARTHA'S AS GOOD AS GOLD

October 16, 2002

Writer Maralyn Lois Polak first caught my attention with her smarmy "Saint Martha, and the Whores in the Temple" column. Like many a media liberal, Ms. Polak proves incapable of advancing a substantive argument against Martha Stewart. Instead, she offers up a string of personal assaults, based on the peculiar symbolism Stewart has acquired in Ms. Polak's mind. That she projects almost paranoid ideation on a woman she doesn't know says everything about Polak but very little about the victim of such riffs of outrage.

On the prowl for Martha, the liberal—and this includes neoconservatives, who howl for her head just as loudly—likes to set the scene by denouncing mammon. Ms. Polak self-righteously disavows money as "… more of an affliction, like genital herpes, something you worried would return uncontrollably, passed on to others through sweaty but dubious transactions you usually regretted later." The problem is that Polak doesn't understand the *meaning* and *morality* of money.

Money is first and foremost a medium of exchange. It arose naturally to replace a primitive barter economy. Once upon a time, Ms. Polak would have been forced to directly exchange her articles or books for anti-herpes medication. Finding someone who possessed herpes-calming meds, but at the same time wanted a dose of epistolary clap, may have proven tough.

As people went about making a living by exchanging things—for that is all the maligned free market is—they came to realize that if they didn't facilitate indirect exchanges, many would starve. Money simply replaces a direct-barter economy with an ability to make indirect exchanges. That Martha has more money than Ms. Polak, or me, means that many more people are willing to trade their cash for a Martha than for a Polak or a Mercer.

Like Hank Rearden in Ayn Rand's *Atlas Shrugged,* Martha can say this: "I am rich and I am proud of every penny I own. I have made my money by my own efforts, in free exchange and through the voluntary consent of every man I dealt with—the voluntary consent of those who work for me now, the voluntary consent of those who buy my product."

The morality of her abundance I don't doubt, although I'm not entirely sure what Martha manufactures. Whatever it is, leave it to Ms. Polak to discover the inherently corrupting power of the product. Consumer sovereignty? Free will? "No such thing," the grim socialist will bay. People aren't rational beings who make decisions based on preferences. Rather, they are marionettes in the hands of Monster Marthas. Writes Polak: "Martha Stewart helps keep millions and millions of women down by giving them more and more meaningless, trivial busywork to preoccupy them from achieving real major changes in their already over-scheduled lives, let alone lasting accomplishments like … composing sonatas."

An aside on sirens and sonatas is in order. Feminists have, admittedly, done an impressive job of jamming cyberspace with online catalogues of obscure women composers. I hate to break it to the faithful: Real history as opposed to "Herstory"—to use the feminist sobriquet—tells of a stark lack of aptitude for composition

among women, which, incidentally, way preceded the appearance of
The Martha.

No one cares how many ancient Greek poems Sister Sappho set to
music. Good music always was—and remains—male. My daughter,
far more forgiving than her mother is on matters musical, would
take Bach or Bon Jovi anytime over what she calls the "Tuna Tour":
The simpering Sarah McLachlan or the Jewel-type bimbo with a
bedroom whimper for a voice. (Relatively skilled women like Stevie
Nicks or Alana Myles are a rarity.)

I got distracted (hmmm ... Bon Jovi). Back to the lacunae in
Polak's thinking.

To Ms. Polak, Martha's knack for giving people a touch of the
patrician for prices the peasantry can afford is an oppressing plot, for
which almost all women have fallen, except for, drum roll, please:
Ms. Polak. But if the Marxist notion of Martha's power to subjugate
is valid, why is it, then, that Polak and her confreres have managed
to see through and avoid the mesmerizing tug? Polak's answer is in
the mold of her previous reasoning: She is smart. Evidently, Ms.
Polak has always possessed the smarts to see that Martha is a
"manipulative business woman," who preys on women's need to be
perfect. Other women are just not that astute.

At the root of this meandering is the profound contempt the
liberal has for the masses and their right to buy a tea cozy without
being declared *non compos mentis*.

26. BUBBLEHEAD SEARCHES FOR BULLIES OF
BRANDING

August 18, 2000

In happier times, Toronto's garment district was abuzz with
Trotskyite debate and the wrangling of trade union leaders, laments
Naomi Klein in her book, *No Logo: Taking Aim at the Brand Bullies*.

Now, she says, the district's warehouses have only one "remaining capitalist function," and that is to showcase advertising billboards.

From here on in, the book is devoted to the machinations of a capitalist cabal, intent on colonizing the minds of consumers by peddling larger-than-life brands over and above products; the kind of brands that expand to rob people of their "public and personal spaces," their culture, their jobs, even their freedoms. The lineup of culprits is long: Microsoft, Nike and the various "sneaker pimps," Intel, The Gap, Tommy Hilfiger, Calvin Klein, Apple, The Body Shop, Starbucks, and so on.

A self-confessed "mall rat"—which would explain her obsession with the gimmicks of marketing to the exclusion of an understanding of market forces—Ms. Klein is a leader of the anti-globalization movement, and has been described by the *Times of London* as "probably the most influential person under the age of 35 in the world." All the more surprising considering that this soundbite-rich, deeply silly monograph is more conjecture than fact; Ms. Klein draws causal relationships where none exist, and finds culpability in the absence of any proof.

It sounds flaky, she explains, but the corporate takeover really gained momentum after a 1993 event known in marketing circles as "Marlboro Friday." It was then, ironically, that the branding of products seemed poised for its demise: On that apparently fateful day, Phillip Morris slashed its prices in response to competition from "bargain brands." According to Ms. Klein's subjective interpretation of market competition, if a brand like Marlboro was "stooping to compete on the basis of real value," the public must have called the corporate bluff and rejected the cachet of the name brand.

Alas, the brands recovered. In their truest and most advanced incarnation, they have become "about corporate transcendence." Products that will flourish in the future are increasingly presented as concepts rather than as commodities. For the next 446 pages, the same savvy American consumer who forced Phillip Morris to fight harder for its market share on "Marlboro Friday" suddenly turns into a helpless pawn of the marketing moguls.

Like a solemn commissar, Ms. Klein bolsters her theme with
scores of exuberant, non-incriminating interviews with ad executives
and CEOs, which she portrays as sinister confessions. The endless
accounts of advertising gimmicks are meant to expose the malignant
franchises that devour local shops, public spaces and "host cultures."
The fluffy jargon does nothing to conceal that in reality, this is an
unremarkable selection from the trillions of capitalist acts between
consenting adults.

Advertising has become this sophisticated and, as a result of the
dizzying array of choice in the market, has shifted to selling lifestyles,
attitudes and atmospheres. Long gone are the days when advertisers
merely educated and informed the few who could afford their
products. The plenty generated by mass production means
producers must labor to capture consumers' attentions.
Corporations can no more be demonized for their promotional
methods than lovers for preparing candle-lit dinners as preludes to
seduction.

Further, in her discrete demarcation between big and small, local
and transnational business, Ms. Klein ignores the fact that consumer
patronage grows a small business into a large one. To her,
consumers are dim. They buy products they neither need nor want,
and even when their purchases are unsatisfactory, they keep at it. If
they are so incompetent, why allow them to vote?

Ms. Klein describes the horrors of the branded neighborhoods,
schools and towns—"public" areas that fall prey to the logos and
brands of corporations. This happened because of tax-base erosion,
for which Ms. Klein blames the Reagan, Thatcher and Mulroney
trinity. With big, good government in retreat, big, bad business is
forced to pick up the slack. The fact that Ms. Klein's monopoly
public schooling is producing ignoramuses becomes the fault of
corporate cash infusions that have allowed big business to infiltrate
campuses.

Ms. Klein extends this seamless corporate conspiracy to the co-
opting of the pharmaceutical industry, the censorship of news, the
upstaging of sports events and the overthrowing of local retailers by

branded superstores. She descends into obscurantism when describing the apocalyptic branding of life: "Cross-promotional brand-based experiences that combine buying with elements of media entertainment and professional sports to create an integrated branded loop … using ever-expanding networks of brand extensions to spin a self-sustaining lifestyle web." What in bloody blue blazes does this mean?

Evidently in no small part, corporations are also responsible for censorship. Klein claims that somehow private enterprise can threaten free speech, and issues an indictment against Wal-Mart for pulling sexually explicit magazines in accordance with customers' wishes. This champion of local activism cries "censorship" when the moms and pops in a community peacefully exercise the power of the boycott! What escapes Klein is that only the state has the legal power to infringe speech rights—when government bans publications, they vanish or go underground. When a private outlet decides to heed the wishes of its buyers by not carrying a publication, the item can be purchased elsewhere. Alas, the distinction is lost on Ms. Klein.

Ms. Klein rounds up by anointing those who vandalize billboards as the leaders of the new anti-corporate resistance movement. Somehow Ms. Klein, who despises the falseness of consumerism, has failed to detect the poseur in these self-styled "culture jammers and anti-corporate campaigners."

27. CONGRESSIONAL CHURLS TROLL FOR VOTES

February 20, 2002

"Fascism," wrote the Tannehills in *The Market for Liberty*, "is a system in which the government leaves nominal ownership of the means of production in the hands of private individuals but exercises control by means of regulatory legislation and reaps most of the profit by means of heavy taxation."

Friends of fascism—privileged members of the media and political punditry—have been cackling over the downfall of the upper echelons at Enron and cheering the Regulator.

Front and center is the Larry Kudlow and James Cramer combo, hosts of CNBC's America Now, who pepper their shrill jeers with a blood-curdling call for disproportionate, symbolic sentences. Kudlow, who fancies himself a free-market guy, shamelessly champions the accretion of the Securities and Exchange Commission (SEC), when he ought to be calling for its elimination and for the freeing of accountants from their status as stooges for the state. Cramer's Tourette's-inflected screeching is only slightly less terrifying than his central planner's zeal.

But to the representatives-cum-inquisitors at the abominable congressional hearings goes the cake, or rather, the carrion.

Contrary to the claim of Rep. Peter Deutsch, D-Fla., the market system didn't fail. Enron came up with an innovative way to trade energy. Soon, other companies got a whiff of the initial exorbitant profits, entered the same market, and, as *Wall Street Journal* analyst Susan Lee commented, "competed away" the Enron advantage, putting the squeeze on the company's margins.

The market punctured the dot-com hype, and it did the same to Enron when Enron emerged as no more than hedge funds and hot air. As we speak, the same self-regulating market has companies wooing the wary investor with open accounting practices, offering transparent, cash-flow-based financial statements, as well as vouching that their auditors do not double up as consultants, *à la* Arthur Andersen. So why call on the Regulator?

Any serious student of economics knows that regulation hinders wealth creation, often forcing the entrepreneur to replace viable, voluntary trades and transactions with bureaucratic, politicized decision making. Rather than concentrate on satisfying consumers, proprietors must divert resources from innovation and production into getting around the bureaucrat's tax and regulatory laws.

When Bill Gates neglected to schmooze Washington, Joe Klein, the Justice Department's top dog, picked up the scent and gave chase. The lesson being that if he wants to survive, the entrepreneur must also pay protection money to his political masters.

If, as Rep. Billy Tauzin, R-La., concluded, the Enron mess is a "simple story of old fashioned theft," why were the accused being subjected to a tribal (congressional) exorcism? Doesn't criminal law adequately adjudicate fraud or whatever the Enron crowd's putative crime is? Apparently not when there are votes to troll for.

This was apparent at the backslapping session of the "Subcommittee of the House Energy and Commerce Committee on the findings of Enron." The cringe factor peaked, as representatives attempted to outdo one another with expressions of outrage, veiled threats, libel and presumption of guilt for the accused.

Rep. Deutsch compares Enron top guns to the Mafia and, in particular, to *The Godfather*. A bilious-making Rep. Bilirakis, R-Fla., accused Enron executives of perpetrating something "almost as bad" as the terrorists perpetrated. Evidently, "destroying the faith of the American people in the system" approximates mass murder.

The foulest delivery, however, was that of Rep. Bobby Rush, D-Ill., Cleaving to the mass-murderer analogy, Rush ventured that, unlike the Enron type, a terrorist still possesses "ideals of justice and righteousness," if twisted and perverted. The "economic terrorist at Enron" can claim only "selfishness and greed" as his credo. To shore up his thug credentials, Rep. Rush dragged in "one of the world's most outstanding citizens," and demanded he be saluted. The specimen was none other than Monsignor "Shakedown," the Reverend Jesse L. Jackson! And these scavengers are deemed fit to "regulate" decent Americans, as they go about making a living?

The accused, of course, all came under scrutiny for resorting to their Fifth Amendment rights. Rights, apparently, are reserved only for the Guantanamo gangsters.

Sadly, even Dick Cheney's admission that regulation costs the average American household $8,000 per annum is unlikely to turn Americans against these ghouls. Some discouraging revelations about human nature emerged from an experiment designed by economists at the Universities of Warwick and Oxford. Subjects overwhelmingly chose to destroy the wealth of another, even if this, without fail, meant burning away a good portion of their own. So long as they continue to destroy and distribute property, regulators will be mirroring the minds of the majority.

28. BONO AND HIS BAND OF BANDITS

April 3, 2002

What an obscenity democracy is! The latest victory our democratic institutions can boast, the latest lien we've apparently authorized against our paychecks, is a commitment to more foreign aid.

American voters have allegedly delegated to the president and Congress the right to allow bureaucrats abroad to take a shot at their wallets. The democratic license extends to faceless administrators at the United Nations, the IMF, the World Bank; you name it, they all can take a stab at your pay stub.

Since the beneficiaries of foreign aid reside in Washington, Geneva, Brussels, and assorted mansions dotting Third World landscapes, it takes a great deal of cash to maintain them in style. Which is why, worldwide, the UN is seeking approximately $166 billion annually in foreign aid.

It doesn't take much skill to loot the voter. Cued by our democratically elected representatives, Bono, a chap who fronts a three-chord band of unimpressive droners, has now joined this mob in clamoring for your cash.

Like our elected representatives, U2's Bono doesn't care that forced transfer of money is always theft. To the wealthy Bono, the fact that more than half the American voters support the reigning thieves who orchestrate the theft is enough to render the robbery permissible.

Economist Walter Block offers a characteristically animated illustration of the democratic principle at work. Here it is, moderately adapted for my purposes:

"Suppose two hoodlums break into my apartment and are in the process of walking off with my television. When I object that they are stealing, they agree to hold a referendum on the issue." Bono, the philosophical bandit, says, "How many object to taking Ilana's television?" I raise my hand. Bono then asks, "How many favor this action?" Bono and his accomplice, World Bank President Jim Wolfenson, outvote me.

Bono, who is oblivious to the immorality of democratically approved distribution, thinks you won't even feel the pinch. So what if the average American family now pays government more than it spends on housing, food, and medical care. So what if you work for government until roughly May 18 of every year. Big deal: What's another hour or so of bondage?

If "for the children" used to be your cue to head for the hills, now, clutch that purse when politicians pronounce that a new spending scheme is part of a terrorism-fighting strategy. Having capitulated to the yammer about poverty being a cause of terrorism, President Bush is aiming to make foreign aid part of an official anti-terrorism strategy. This fatuity promises to end for good the debate on the corrupting effects of foreign welfare, because anything that ostensibly fights terrorism is sacrosanct.

Bush may imagine that with your kindness and your moolah he will call off the Islamist mullahs! Foreign aid, however, will occasion no such epiphany in murderous hearts because at the heart of Islamist terrorism is a violent and brutal belief system. What the president will achieve is to re-victimize the victims of Islamic aggression.

The ethical arguments against foreign aid notwithstanding, foreign aid, like any welfare entitlement, cripples the recipient by putting in place incentives that reinforce sloth and corruption. Third World nations are poor because they have failed to adopt the institutions of capitalism. Their governments are growing by the day, many industries remain nationalized, taxes are prohibitive, regulations are rampant, and price control's a cause of endemic shortages.

Private property rights, the cornerstone of prosperity and justice, are, at best, precarious in Third World countries. It took economist Hernando de Soto and his team roughly 289 days, "as well as $1,231 in payment fees, to legally open a small garment shop in Peru, an objective that took a single morning in the U.S." Similar conditions exist in other Third World countries into whose corrupt coffers Bono, Bush et al. will plow your funds.

Foreign aid infrastructure, moreover, is directly responsible for growing the political class in these countries at the expense of the productive private sector. As the size of government increases, the growth of real GDP decreases. Indeed, to the World Bank is owed the dubious distinction of propping up despotic governments and undermining free market reforms in the Third World.

Bush has gone from preaching "trade not aid," and being charmingly unaware of celebrity, to instituting trade tariffs, and pledging to Bono a 50 percent increase in U.S. foreign aid over three years. This is the essence of democratically sanctioned theft. It is also why an unknown sage once said, "If voting changed anything, they'd make it illegal."

29. FOREIGN AIDS

December 4, 2002

If I didn't know better, I'd say that William Jefferson Clinton was well qualified to be a poster boy for the dangers of AIDS, and that the 42nd president of the United States' op-ed in the *New York Times*, marking World AIDS Day, was in line with his new duties. Alas, as a former AIDS counselor in South Africa, I know something about Mr. Clinton's chances of infection: The former president's risks are quite low, his sexual philandering notwithstanding.

If he wasn't writing in his capacity as an advocate against risky sexual behavior, what's Mr. Clinton's angle? Now that educational efforts are proving ineffective in halting infection rates in the Third World, The Village Idiots are shifting the goalposts. Whereas our "moral duty" was once discharged by supplying Third Worlders with condoms and educational prophylaxis, it must now extend to making treatment available to every sufferer—or so Clinton says. Like his wife, Clinton galvanizes the royal "We" revealingly to support his theories of collective ownership and culpability (and hence more foreign aid).

The foremost authority on foreign aid, the late Lord P.T. Bauer, pointed out that a responsible demand for aid mustn't avoid examining those "… popular attitudes and behaviours in the poor societies" which cause and perpetuate the misery.

Professional confiscators and colossi of ignorance like Clinton and U2 lead singer Bono would rather justify their activities with the false claim that human misfortune is a result of external contingencies that can be fixed by social planners like themselves. They hammer home the wicked lie that the wealthy—individuals and nations—thrive at the expense of the poor and essentially deserve to be relieved of their possessions.

Never mind that rich nations were streaks ahead of sub-Saharan Africa and Southeast Asia well before colonization. Countries like Australia and Switzerland were rich absent any meaningful ties to the undeveloped world. As Bauer proves, this was the result of the West's human resources, not its exploitation of the backward world.

Bono certainly doesn't come clean. While he points an accusing finger at the West, the self-righteous activist praises Africans for being a "rare and spirited people," concealing that if the spirit didn't move them in some pretty wild ways, rates of infection in Southern Africa would not have reached 20 to 33.7 percent of the adult population.

Africans are having unprotected sex irrespective of the mortal dangers of AIDS, a phenomenon economists might explain with reference to time preference rates. This is the degree to which different people—and peoples—will discount the future in favor of immediate gratification. The number of people infected especially in Southern Africa bespeaks a high time preference: the consistent risking of the future for momentary benefits.

Nowhere do Bono and Clinton mention the endemic sexual violence in Africa—it too plays a considerable role in spreading AIDS. In South Africa, a woman is raped every few minutes. My African female clients told me that if they wanted to avoid being brutalized, they didn't dare ask an African man to wear a condom. But I clean forgot: Violence in Africa, once attributed by liberals to the legacy of colonial meddling, is now conveniently put down to a lack of Western intervention.

Indeed, Bono never thinks to hang his empty head in shame as he proceeds to both slander and stiff Westerners by using his political pull. Goes without saying that in the process, Bono also fails to mention what Bauer so cogently referred to as the conduct of the recipient governments. This too is the proper object of scrutiny in the question of aid.

"Expulsion and slaughter of productive minorities" is certainly a factor in the increasing economic deterioration in South Africa and more so in Zimbabwe. Life for the productive white minority is perilous. Once wealth creators leave or are targeted by crime and oppressive economic policies, not least nationalization of their land, economic conditions worsen for all, especially the poor. I've a feeling, though, that Bono would have no sympathy for the Jews of Germany during World War II or the Chinese of Malaysia— somehow, it's hard to imagine he or Clinton mustering compassion for groups that are, or were, persecuted by governments because of their self-sufficiency.

All in all, such boneheadedness stands to benefit from a lesson in ethics. And Bauer, who disputed the notion that "foreign aid is ... the discharge of a moral duty to help the poor," delivered it:

> Foreign aid is taxpayer's money compulsorily collected;
> it is outside the area of volition and choice. Indeed,

contributors not only have no choice but quite generally do not even know they are contributing. It is sometimes urged that in a democracy taxpayers do have a choice, which restores the moral element to foreign aid. This objection is superficial. The taxpayer has to contribute to foreign aid whether he likes it or not and whether he has voted in its favor or against it.

30. MEDIA CONCENTRATION? TRY GOVERNMENT CONCENTRATION!

June 25, 2001

I have no reason to celebrate the transfer of more than 100 Canadian newspapers including half-ownership of the *National Post* from Conrad Black's Hollinger Inc. to Izzy Asper's CanWest Global Communications Corp. Shortly after the CanWest media acquisition flurry, I was fired by the new owner of the Vancouver-based *North Shore News*, after writing a successful weekly column there for two years. On the heels of the same press purge, I was booted from a perch I'd held at the *Calgary Herald* for a year.

My American readers will recognize Conrad Black as the Chairman and CEO of one of the world's largest newspaper groups. Among its more than 200 publications, Hollinger International counts *The Daily Telegraph* in the United Kingdom, *The Jerusalem Post* in Israel, and the *Chicago Sun-Times*. Conrad Black is a conservative and a relatively hands-off proprietor. When he pens the occasional op-ed piece, it is always a wonderfully wrought *tour de force*. The new media boss' lesser facility with ideas and words has not prevented him and his progeny from tirelessly agitating in editorials for the governing Liberal party. Mr. Asper[*] is becoming known for his editorial activism, an accusation that revived the Canadian apoplexy over "media concentration" or "cross ownership"—always a familiar bugaboo in the minds of bureaucrats and other befuddled statists.

Still, my firing had little to do with "media concentration" *per se* and its alleged effects on freedom and diversity of expression. Free speech rights are not suppressed when certain opinions are expunged from privately owned media. Government alone has the power to violate speech rights by using the force of the law. When government bans a publication or an opinion, it disappears or goes underground. You procure the publication or voice the opinion at your peril! A private outlet has no such power. Unless we presume we have a right to his property, Izzy Asper's misguided editorial edicts were entirely his affair.

The only true monopolies are government monopolies. A company is a monopoly only when it can forcibly prohibit competitors from entering the market, a feat only ever made possible by state edict. In the free market, competition makes monopoly impossible. If Canadians don't like Izzy Enterprises, they ought to vote with their cash and stop buying the *Vancouver Sun* and the *National Post* and stop watching BCTV. "Galaxy 500" doesn't lack for television channels. Radio, magazines and, above all, the Internet, render moot concerns over media concentration and freedom of speech.

A large market share is not a monopoly. If a Hollinger or CanWest expands without regulations, subsidies, licenses, or franchises, then they've done so fair and square. They've supplied at good prices products and services consumers want. Indeed, the notion that business concentration has anything to do with monopoly power is based on discredited theories. Free-market competition is a dynamic process, and market share is in constant flux. One day it's Conrad; the next it's Izzy—unfortunately.

It is also an unfortunate reality, however, that Canada is home to incontinent legislators. And they have been out marking their territory. To the extent that it is the beneficiary of a regulated broadcasting monopoly, CanWest benefits from government largesse. But, in Canada, government has also partially nationalized the newspapers. What else would you call legislation that prohibits an owner from selling more than 25 percent of any newspaper to a foreign owner? To that extent, CanWest suffers the malign effects of the Regulator. Izzy's empire would certainly not be as large if non-citizens could buy Canadian newspapers. If Canadians enjoyed freedom of contract and full property rights, no one would complain of too much concentration and too little diversity.

Besides being a morally bankrupt assault on property, antitrust laws that break up "concentrated" industries penalize entrepreneurs for their exceptional productivity. The resulting loss of efficiencies—such as the economies of scale and superior management that are instrumental in the successful concentration—does consumers no good.

To understand why there is a demand for the flaccid fare that Canadian and American media purvey—why there is such an eerie uniformity of opinion across our nations, the kind Izzy Asper's conglomerate only reflects—we must look to the effects of the government-regulated, taxpayer-funded public school monopoly. Why are Canadians and Americans so partial to collectivism? Why have we no concept of freedom other than sexual? Why do we fear private enterprise and love Big Brother? Largely because the public school system monopolizes the dissemination of ideas. John Dewey and his progressive acolytes founded modern public education with the express intention of forcibly reconstructing society. Monopoly schools remain instruments of coercion designed to strengthen "correct" social-democratic welfarism at the expense of traditional communities. Unlike libertarians, conservatives, unfortunately, have seldom objected to this monopoly, so long as their values prevail within it.

Public Broadcasting is another cultural foot-and-mouth that ought to be the proper focus for those who cavil about monopoly. The Canadian Broadcasting Corporation (CBC) is an undisputed enemy of self-government. Its multimedia tendrils, nourished with taxpayer dollars, choke the national psyche and propagate the Nanny State. Canadians practically live and die with this icon. CBC dominance, moreover, is nurtured by the protectionism of the Canadian Radio-television and Telecommunications Commission. Any group seeking broadcasting rights must convince CRTC bureaucrats of the "public interest" inherent in their endeavor. Not only can it restrict access to the electromagnetic spectrum, but the CRTC also enforces and censors content.

The Canadian counterparts to Ralph Nader, the meddlesome Maude Barlow of the Council of Canadians, and Robert Hackett of NewsWatch Canada, perennially excoriate the Regulator to step in to ensure chain-owned newspapers don't abuse "the public agenda." These busybodies forever invoke the force of the law in the service of a tyranny they term the "public good." It is when they enlist "our children," or declare, "It takes a village," that my own instinct is to grab the kids and run for the hills. Pravda Inc. is far more sinister than Izzy Inc.

* Mr. Asper passed away unexpectedly in October 2003.

31. COMMIE CARS

May 1, 2002

If there was any doubt that environmental dogma has won the day, the debate over exploration in the Arctic National Wildlife Refuge has resolved it. Coated with a patina of science, this dogma continues to insist that there is inherent discord between our system of production and the environment. Essentially, not much has changed since the environmental movement's forefathers advocated forcefully halting development and ending consumer freedom through government regulation. With one exception: This scourge now informs official public policy.

It so happens that the low prices at the pump signal (at the time of writing) that oil supply, so far, is stable. But not even the on-and-off threats of an oil embargo by the Arab world have dampened the powerful environmental lobby's opposition to oil exploration.

In addition to the domestic moratorium, thousands of regulations and restrictions have been foisted on the industry over the years in a bungling attempt at conservation. One scheme to limit fossil-fuel consumption is legislation—in California, Massachusetts, New York, Vermont and other jurisdictions—compelling automakers to manufacture electric vehicles.

It's one thing for automakers to voluntarily invest in these technologies. It's quite another for central planners to coerce the automaker into manufacturing lumps of metal for which there are no buyers. This is tantamount to the confiscation of property. Intimidated by regulators, General Motors and Toyota Corp. sank roughly half a billion dollars into manufacturing pure electrical cars, only to abandon the endeavor for lack of a market, losses which are, invariably, transferred to the consumer in the form of more expensive cars across the board. Steep car prices mean that people hang onto their cars for longer. Older cars are more polluting than newer ones. You get the picture: Regulation here indirectly causes more pollution.

Right now, even I wouldn't trade my 1986 Toyota MR2 ("Mr. Two," as he is fondly known), for a new, battery-powered car that manages only between 41 and 71 miles of driving before it needs refueling. Re-charging the thing is akin to kidney dialysis for cars— find a socket and stay hooked up for several hours, that is if you can locate a re-charging station.

The electric car is a marvelous metaphor for the legislator's attempt to shackle the "wayward" consumer. Purchase one, and you had better avoid straying too far from the socket in your garage. Or, alternatively, be sure to equip yourself with a very long extension cord, lest your vehicle turn into something not nearly as useful as a pumpkin.

With such pox-like features, you'd expect the thing—of which 4,450 to 15,450 are required by law in California—to be as cheap as the lowly Russian Lada. (The Lada was the mobile scrap metal

manufactured by decree of the former USSR's Ministries Council.)
No such luck.

The manufacturing cost of our own "People's Car" is roughly
twice that of a comparable conventional vehicle. The benefits to the
consumer are non-existent, much less to the environment, unless a
steady discharge of lead, cadmium, and nickel—the byproducts of
batteries—is a blessing in disguise.

Ordinary Americans are not fooled. Faced with a choice between
a roomy SUV, or forcing the kids to share the backseat with a giant
battery or an enormous tank of hydrogen—all "features" of the new-
technology chariots—consumers have not exhibited a great deal of
option anxiety.

As for the hybrid gas-and-electric vehicles, other than "limousine
liberals," with backup fleets, like Cameron Diaz, this perilously
sluggish accelerator has few bidders. The price of gas would have to
climb to $3.55 per gallon to make it worthwhile for the buyer to
purchase this $20,000 plus toy—an event which government is
more than capable of orchestrating if it decides to levy European-
style gas and emission taxes. Currently, any demand for these lame
ducks will be a demand artificially manufactured by government
policy, not driven by market forces.

Perhaps the biggest obfuscation in the gimmick-car racket—
which President Bush has fallen for, if to judge from his energy
plan—has to do with the source of the energy. Whether a vehicle is
propelled by hydrogen-powered fuel cells or electricity, both
electricity and hydrogen don't magically materialize in the vehicle.
They must first be generated. Be it coal, natural gas, nuclear or a
hydroelectric dam, these cars are only as clean as the original source
of energy that generated the vim that powers them.

Other than to increase the consumption of gas, because people
drive more in them, mandating so-called fuel-efficient cars is a grand
exercise in the compulsory misallocation and waste of capital. It
proves that the development of technologies is best left to the
market, not to busybody bureaucracies.

32. PURGING PAUL O'NEILL

December 11, 2002

Dismissed Treasury Secretary Paul O'Neill presented some strange contradictions, not least of which was his opposition to a tax cut. Tax cuts, especially for those from whom the most money is filched, are morally imperative and economically efficient. At the same time, O'Neill supported tax reform, denouncing the U.S. income tax code as "9,500 pages of gibberish."

His favoring of a flatter and lower tax while simultaneously shunning tax cuts made sense once O'Neill's concerns about the deficit became known. Less explicable was the cavorting with Bono. U2's front man was another of O'Neill's bad habits, although, in his defense, it was the only bit of global outreach O'Neill seemed to endorse. His affinity for Bono and his opposition to tax cuts got O'Neill praise from a lot of dullards. He must, however, be appreciated for more often than not infuriating the very same people.

The American public O'Neill enraged. The masses wanted a meddler and the Republicans wanted to use the politically appealing pleas the people made as the *quid pro quo* for more government intervention in the economy. O'Neill refused, quite admirably, to show the required leadership—with his optimistic *laissez faire*, he often thwarted the political agenda.

Cultivating the kind of bedside manner ordinary Americans demanded was not for him. O'Neill was especially tough during the days the pampered employees of Enron held marathons on "Donahue," demanding that you and I—who have never and probably will never see the kind of funds these so-called victims were once in possession of—bail them out. "Companies come and go," was O'Neill's quip, "it's part of the genius of capitalism."

On personal responsibility, O'Neill was unwavering: "People get to make good decisions or bad decisions, and they get to pay the consequences or to enjoy the fruits of their decisions." No American should be made to compensate people who knowingly signed a contract and who chose to sink all their savings into the once-great company. O'Neill's refusal to be an "inspirational leadership" (read: nanny) was, if anything, rather inspiring.

With the truths that kept tumbling out of his mouth, the refreshingly impolitic and plainspoken O'Neill certainly infuriated the right people. He dared, for one, to speculate on the costs of waging war on Iraq. And so he should've. War is as good for the economy as is burning down a neighborhood to create jobs for construction workers.

Blunt about the banditos of Latin America, O'Neill expressed hope that policies be implemented to ensure that foreign aid destined for Brazil, in this instance, does some good over and above padding a Swiss bank account. On the heels of his statement, the Brazilian Mickey Mouse money lost more than five percent of its value. Washington blamed O'Neill, although it's the very least we should be able to expect an official to say about money mulcted from us, the taxpayers. If a currency plummets when the truth is spoken, too bad. If it takes lies to keep a currency buoyed, then the sooner truth intervenes with a correction, the better.

Or as O'Neill put it: "There is a real doubt about the effectiveness of interventions or words about intervention. It is not possible any more to actually fool the markets for very long." Something Greenspan and his congressional backers should take to heart. They can drop interest rates to zero and make borrowing hazardously cheap, but they cannot sustain the bluff behind this credit expansion. Increasing the quantity of easy money has only decreased its purchasing power, a reality no amount of talking or tinkering can change.

To expect O'Neill or any politician to be honest about what's going on with the legal—but illegitimate—tender would be naive. Tiny consolation that it is, O'Neill did dare to speak favorably about the safety of nuclear power plants. In light of the energy crises exacerbated by a moratorium on building such plants—courtesy of the environmental nuts—O'Neill's veracity was overdue. Thanks to mass hysteria and Jane Fonda, people still believe that Three Mile Island was a disaster. But as the truism goes, "More people died in the back seat of Ted Kennedy's car at Chappaquiddick than died as a result of that accident." (One person—Mary Jo Kopechne—died as a result of Kennedy's criminal negligence.)

Easily the most powerful factor in the O'Neill sacking is the election in 2004. The president is in campaign mode. With an unemployment rate of six percent, and climbing, Bush can't tolerate a cabinet member who ventured that many welfare programs are bonanzas for bureaucrats. Not if he wants to peddle welfare largess for votes.

Granted, O'Neill was recalcitrant on the administration's stimulus package. But so is Stephen Friedman, who will replace the sacked Larry Lindsey on the president's National Economic Council. Since the newly hired Friedman also opposes tax cuts, it is not unreasonable to conclude that O'Neill's objection to tax cuts was not the main reason he was required to fall on his sword.

33. SIMIANS* IN SEATTLE

December 7, 2000

The WTO protestors in Seattle enact an annual ritual that sees their troops descend on the city to commemorate—and re-enact— the destruction wrought in previous years. Like lower primates, the anti-traders hoot, throw rocks and bottles of gasoline, and generally do a good job of demolishing private property. In one riot, the louts even managed to relieve a police officer of an eye. The vandals who aren't dragged off invariably beat a retreat, knuckles trailing the pavement and the debate not much more elevated.

The WTO must, of course, be opposed with vigor, but not for the reasons the protesters trot out. As an organ of the United Nations, the WTO should strike terror in the heart of any true free trader. The organization is the concoction of international statists;

it's a powerful bureaucracy concerned with managing, not freeing, trade; a central planner whose goal it is to harmonize labor, health, and environmental laws throughout the world.

Llewellyn H. Rockwell, President of the Ludwig von Mises Institute, surmises that had the WTO not incorporated the legal mechanisms for regulating the world economy rather than freeing its markets, the Clinton administration would never have supported its creation. Before the charter was ratified, Rockwell predicted that "the WTO would convert peaceful trade into policy imperialism. It would allow economic exchange with some countries under approved conditions, and impose a variety of sanctions on others. The conditions will include all the legislation beloved to the U.S. left-liberals..." In short, a mercantilist takeover that bears little resemblance to free trade.

The prophecy is not far off. WTO-directed practices consist in each country pushing for the next nation to abandon "trade distorting domestic support programs," while insisting on its right to keep subsidies and tariffs alive in its own. It's not free trade, but it bears a remarkable—if ironic—resemblance to the protesters' version of a planned economy. The two solitudes—the WTO suits and the protesting simians—may be ideologically closer than the latter would like!

There are plenty of good reasons to reject the WTO, but those escape our ersatz humanitarians. Instead, the well-fed dilettantes who flock to Seattle target the very processes that sustain life on earth—commerce, and the division of labor that gives rise to voluntary exchange between all people.

No matter how self-sufficient a person strives to become, his particular aptitude coupled with scarcity of time and resources make peaceful exchange with others necessary. The top-notch lawyer may be perfectly capable of repairing his car; he may, in fact, be better at it than the mechanic. Since his time is scarce, it is more productive for the lawyer to spend it in counsel; it pays him to hire a mechanic. Differences between individuals impel people—rich and poor—to cooperate and trade to mutual advantage.

The notion that this process must stop at the political border is nonsensical. Similar considerations direct nations—developed and undeveloped—to specialize in producing what they are best at and exchanging these products and services for the things they cannot produce or are less efficient at producing.

Immutable differences resulting from climate and geography account for why, instead of erecting hothouses and paying exorbitant electricity bills, Norwegians are better off trading with Caribbeans if they want bananas. In economic parlance, such trade confers an absolute advantage.

International trade has the added benefit of allowing nations to develop economies of scale. As economist Thomas Sowell explains in *Basic Economics*, some industries require the kind of capital outlay that is uncompetitive and unviable unless produced and marketed in especially large quantities. For small countries that lack a local demand, foreign markets are essential.

Free trade between nations also indirectly promotes peace, since economic interdependence is a powerful deterrent to war. How ironic, then, were the parallels drawn by some commentators between the mission of the WTO protest and the causes peace activists championed in the 1960s. It's unclear how smashing Starbucks for creating jobs in underdeveloped countries compares, as an act of moral suasion, to picketing Dow Corning for manufacturing napalm. What's crystal clear is that by protesting free trade, the agitators are opposing both commerce and comity.

Another myth has it that free trade suppresses local wages. Not so. Where inefficient industries are faced with competition—local or foreign—workers will migrate to more efficient industries. Free trade simply forces a more efficient allocation of scarce resources.

Vital to expose are the violation of real rights and freedoms buried in protester cant. To secure votes, government seeks to regulate trade for the benefit of domestic industries and special interests. To avert prosecution under our protectionist laws, a foreign trader must raise his prices. The local consumer is then forced to either patronize more expensive, less competitive local industries or pay the foreign trader's new price. Tariffs, quotas, anti-dumping rules or any other trade barrier mean that the consumer is forced to subsidize less efficient local industries, making him the poorer for it. Should hundreds of industries shrink or go under in order to keep politically efficient industries in the lap of luxury? This is not in the interest of the consumer and it violates his freedom of contract and association.

Another arrow in the protesters' anti-trade quiver is to vilify the likes of Kathy Lee Gifford and Nike for investing in poor countries and creating jobs in places where none likely existed. Let us deconstruct: Nike or Starbucks is either offering higher, the same or lower wages than the wages workers were earning before the company's arrival. A franchise would find it hard to attract workers if it was offering less, or the same as other companies. It must be then that these so-called villains are benefactors who offer the kind of remuneration unavailable prior to their arrival.

If forced to pay Third World workers in excess of their productivity, the entrepreneur will go bankrupt, disinvest, and leave the locals to starve. When Clinton called for sanctions on developing countries that don't adhere to "labor standards," he let posturing against corporations and pandering to armchair anarchists take the place of guarding people's freedom to gain advantage through the use of the only resource they have, their labor.

Economies in which child labor is a sad fact are more appropriately compared to medieval England or Europe. Child labor is not the problem in Chad or Bhutan, poverty is. Child labor is merely a solution to this problem. Had a government in England of the 1500s outlawed child labor, the death of even more children would have followed. If the protesters have their way, many children will perish.

Alas, these realities are not for our street-fighting effete to entertain. Not one among these environmentalists, union groups, and anarchists spoke for "the poorest of the poor." While loitering about the streets, our cherubs chomped on their dirt-cheap tofu and Big Mac burgers. The cheap transportation that got them there and the technology that disseminates their sub-intelligent message were once luxuries reserved for few. Thanks to economic freedom and mass production these are now staples for the masses. Our humanitarians suffer no shortages, yet they want to prevent Third World nations from aspiring to the same plenty.

What whooshed past protesters was not beyond the grasp of Kofi Annan. Writing in *The Wall Street Journal*, the Secretary General of the UN condemned rich nations for imposing tariffs on goods imported from developing countries, and for using quotas and antidumping penalties to stop poor nations from selling their products bellow market prices. Even a central planner like Annan understands that protectionist policies are detrimental to the Third World.

With some luck Annan may also come to realize that unfettered trade and not the debilitating welfarism of foreign aid is what will inch backward societies forward. No such an epiphany can be expected from the protesters; they are, after all, paternalistic westerners who need to preserve their Hollywood image of the authentic—if starving—foreigner.

*A simian is an ape or a monkey.

34. PHILISTINE PHILOSOPHER

July 6, 2000

A pointed put-down from ancient Greece came to mind as I gagged through Canadian pop-philosopher Mark Kingwell's *National Post* column:

> Demosthenes: "The Athenians will kill you some day when they are in a rage."
>
> Phocion: "And you, when they are in their senses."

The editorial was a trendy mumbo-jumbo that ought to deface the more frivolous sections of a newspaper. Following a barrage of incoherent verbiage about "cross-over," "synergy," and "total brand experience," Kingwell offered up a hackneyed assault on Bill Gates and his profits.

A primer for this leftist sophistry is Naomi Klein's book *No Logo: Taking Aim at the Brand Bullies*. Kingwell is credited with acting as Klein's mentor while she assembled her miscellany. A sound-bite bellwether in her own right, Klein uses terms such as "brand bullies," "brand bombing," and "brand convergence"—echoed in Kingwell's prolix—to underscore that the masses buy into a vision of the world an evil capitalist cabal sells for its own gain. In both instances, the reader should avoid confusing an orgy of alliteration with conscious thought.

Yes, Microsoft makes good software, allows the professor. For a company that stole its ideas, or so Kingwell claims, Gates' billion-dollar enterprise even markets itself with "moderate success." But the billionaire's attempts to "justify his own outrageous wealth" simply infuriate Kingwell.

Why is the wealth of Gates so outrageous? It is so only if your departing point is that Gates forced all those who bought the bundled Windows Operating System and Internet Explorer to do so at the point of a gun.

Here's the rub: There is no bullying in a supply-and-demand free market. When a sovereign consumer decides to part with the $128 or so in lieu of Gates' Windows and Explorer deal, it is because he values the product more than the cash. Are people too simple to execute this basic cost-benefit evaluation? Had the consumer valued the Netscape, LINUX, or SOLARIS products—none of which offered a combined Internet browser and Operating System at a rock-bottom price—more than the cash these companies were demanding for their cumbersome alternatives, buyers would have purchased those instead of giving Gates the larger market share.

Bill Gates' market share is derived from the consumer's vote of confidence. When Joe Average invested in the bundled products, he voted for the product that would give him the best bang for his buck. Indeed, democratic capitalism is a fail-safe mechanism that ensures the capitalist is roped into serving the masses. If he fails to serve, absent government intervention, the entrepreneur doesn't profit.

Much as I would like the rarified music of Bela Bartok to sell millions, the numerous have spoken. Through their dollar votes, they decide what should be produced, by whom and in what quantities, and it is Brand Britney (Spears) the masses want most.

Concealed in Kingwell's sneering is the deep contempt the Left holds for the no-longer-noble proletariat. So stupid are ordinary people, such pawns of package are they, that they lap up products they neither need nor want. Kingwell's apoplexy is really an unintentional paean to capitalism. For it is thanks to mass production, namely capitalism, that the average incomes in North America are so high. And it is capitalism that explains why goods that were once luxuries reserved for few—such as good food and clothing, vehicles, homes, computers, art, entertainment, and foreign travel—are now mass-market commodities. The average man can, very plainly, afford to buy *fluff* over real *stuff*.

Why a man so hard at work on his own brand would strike such a pose against marketing is unclear. Kingwell's disdain for wealth is less baffling. Unlikely as it is to be based in scriptures, and very definitely not on the "Jewish legal tradition according to which wealth honestly acquired is a blessing," his disdain for wealth is borne of a *dirigistic* impulse to replace "the social order in which the most ingenious citizens are impelled to serve the masses," in the words of economist Ludwig von Mises, with a system "in which they no longer will be the customers who give the orders, but wards of an omnipotent authority." Boring...

35. WHO STOLE MICROSOFT?

May 11, 2000

Not content with divvying up Bill Gates' company, the indecorous Judge Thomas Penfield Jackson took to making insulting public pronouncements about Mr. Gates' personality and the intelligence of the Microsoft lawyers. A quick précis of the case, however, leaves little doubt as to which was the cerebrally impaired, malevolent party.

What distinguishes the U.S. postal system from Staples, Toys "R" Us, Rockefeller's Standard Oil, Sara Lee, Eastman Kodak and Microsoft? The former company is a monopoly; the latter are not, but have been so accused in accordance with antitrust legislation. The U.S. Post Office is a monopoly because its market dominance is derived not from what it offers consumers, but from an exclusive grant of government privilege. As monopolies, the postal service and the local gas and electric companies do not compete or engage in a voluntary exchange with consumers. Rather, they control the market by forcibly prohibiting others from entering it.

Extend this premise, and you arrive at the natural conclusion that in a free market, where voluntary exchange between consenting adults is the guiding principle in trade, there can be no monopoly other than that created by government. How is it, then, that Microsoft was hounded for being a monopoly? This is made possible through legislation that frames as predatory the process whereby an innovator captures a large market share. This, despite the fact that the only way to capture a large portion of the market is by dint of government legislation, as the post office does, or through offering good service for a very low price, as Microsoft does.

Recall that as a competitive strategy, Microsoft had bundled the Internet Explorer with the Windows operating system. It did so for free, and with the aim of outdoing the competition. Microsoft then licensed its operating system to PC manufacturers with the proviso that they take free of charge its Internet Explorer.

Were users prohibited from loading Netscape's Navigator or any other Intel-compatible operating system onto their PCs? Of course not. Could Microsoft have prevented PC makers from installing competitive products? Hardly. That Netscape lost revenue is evidence of nothing more than Microsoft's competitive edge and Netscape's failure to offer the consumer a similar deal. Netscape then ran to Überbureaucrat Joe of the U.S. Justice Department for a remedy.

Clearly Microsoft has arrived at its considerable market share by offering the consumer more total product for the least cost. Let's imagine, however, that a company could eliminate competition in a free market. Such an evil empire could restrict its sales with the intent of raising prices and doing some serious profiteering.

But had Microsoft charged a high price for the browser it tied *gratis* to its Windows operating system, its rivals would have been thrilled, and well positioned to take such a market by storm. (Incidentally, flexible antitrust law would have nabbed the company for predation under this contingency as well.) Microsoft did the opposite: It gave away the browser, causing Judge Jackson, in a decision more voodoo than veracious, to declare Microsoft a monopoly.

The other mischief Microsoft might have attempted so as to drive and keep out competition would have been to drop its total product price even lower. But to be truly "predatory," Microsoft would have to have kept it there over time, eventually going bust. For the duration that it managed such a Kamikaze feat, the company's rock-bottom prices would have benefited consumers. This goes to show that, government monopolies excepted, there is no such thing as a predatory price.

Despite a 1998 court decision that magnanimously upheld Microsoft's right to tie the two products, coupling the browser to Windows, according to Judge Jackson's Conclusions of Law, was not only incontrovertible proof of a monopoly and harmful to consumers, but part of Microsoft's "larger campaign to quash innovation that threatened its monopoly position."

What of the objection, then, that by bundling its Internet Explorer with its Windows operating system, Microsoft failed to offer the consumer a choice? What of the contention that it attempted to freeze out other suppliers, as well as prohibit consumers from coupling one of these Microsoft products with that of one of this company's competitors? One problem with this line of reasoning is that it attempts to discern the motives of businessmen. This is always a risky procedure, too uncertain to support a judicial finding of wrongdoing.

Another more grave difficulty with this charge is that it is open to a *reductio ad absurdum*: were this act to be made the basis of unlawful behavior, we would have jails overflowing with white-collar victimless criminals. For example, it is impossible to purchase a McDonald's burger coupled with a Wendy's bun; neither fast food establishment will make such a concoction available. The consumer who wishes this particular combination of goods will just have to visit each store, buy a burger from each, toss out the McDonalds bun and the Wendy's burger, and eat whatever remains.

Similarly, it is impossible to purchase a Ford chassis and a BMW motor. Those who wish to drive in such an admixture will be forced to buy one of each of these automobiles, and fashion this amalgamation for themselves. However, if we are going to penalize Microsoft legally on this ground, we must also include in the indictment all fast-food purveyors, all automobile companies, all TV manufacturers (some consumers may wish the SONY innards had the RCA tube or vice versa), all publishers (some readers may want the cover of the bible and the inner pages of *Lolita* or *Playboy*, or, who knows, vice versa), etc. In short, the indictment would have to catch any entrepreneur who has irked someone with the way he has configured a product.

Antitrust legislation considers a large market share or a concentration in the market to signify both monopoly and predatory practices on the part of a company. As such, the antitrust chimera is based on discredited theories about competition. Relying as it does on a model of ideal or perfect rather than rivalrous competition, the legislation aims at a market neatly carved among competitors.

Judge Jackson's circular reasoning culminated in his asserting that the fact that Explorer is not "the best breed of Web browser" is further evidence of Microsoft's predatory behavior. If the proliferation of bad products on the market is an indication of a lack of fair competition, we ought to sue rapper P. Diddy on behalf of Johann Sebastian Bach or Jennifer Lopez on behalf of Franz Liszt.

*A section of this column is a product of my collaboration with William Anderson, Walter Block, Thomas DiLorenzo, Leon Snyman and Christopher Westley on the paper, "The Microsoft Corporation in Collision with Antitrust Law." The paper appeared in the *Journal of Social, Political, and Economic Studies*, Vol. 26, No. 1, Winter, 2001.

36. PHONY PRIVATIZATION

February 2, 2001

Debate over the deregulation of power markets always begins with a reference to that *bête noire* of deregulation, the State of California. This is all the more reason to dispel the notion that the California energy market was in any way decontrolled. On the contrary, there was only a hint of deregulation in the state-managed electricity wholesale market California implemented in 1998.

Not only had the State forced the electricity companies to sell their power plants to independent investors, but the new owners were compelled to sell electricity to the state-controlled power exchange, which, in turn, set the daily power prices. In this false free market, utilities were prohibited from entering long-term contracts with electricity producers and had to buy power on a daily basis.

Californians and their politicians have a fetish with natural gas plants, which are expensive and relatively unprofitable. Because these were the only plants permitted, natural gas prices soon soared. The growth in population and economic development in California during the 1990s further contributed to a dramatic increase in demand for power. Retail prices, however, remained capped. With voters-cum-ratepayers being strategically shielded from the real scarcity that prices ought to reflect, shortages were inevitable. Clearly, a hybrid market, not a free market, caused the implosion in the Golden State.

With the Federal Energy Regulatory Commission (FERC) pushing forward in an effort to ostensibly deregulate energy markets, there is a renewed concern that it may be *déjà vu* all over again, especially if market principles continue to be applied to what is still, root and branch, a government operation.

The FERC fully intends to restructure U.S. electricity transmission networks. The first sally in this scheme is to dispossess the utilities of operational control over their power lines and make them answer to independent regional transmission organizations. Local politicians, especially in the South and West, have voiced concerns that this measure will allow their utilities' relatively cheaper power to be sent outside the region, forcing their electricity rates up.

California's crisis justifies their concerns. While Californians have a perfect right to return to the Dark Ages, they are not entitled to expect residents of enlightened states to pay for their energy-averse policies. Which is what happened: Californian environmental fundamentalism led to policies that rejected diversification in energy supply. Other states were then forced by central planners to subsidize this folly.

In addition to casting doubt on whether the FERC is really moving to free up markets, this "deregulation" impetus raises the issue of states' rights. The powerful federal regulator's alleged quest to create a competitive wholesale market involves "equal access," namely the distribution of energy from the have to the have-not states, a process that not only rewards states whose regulations prevent diversification in energy supply, but also overrides state authority.

While power outages coincide like clockwork with regulated power markets, there are unfortunately no shortages in visceral, anti-intellectual arguments. Government messes up in California, and the foot soldiers for the Total State cite the mess as proof for the need for yet more government intervention—a disaster that is a culmination of decades of regulation is blamed on markets that were never allowed to work.

To further dim debate, out of the woodwork has emerged a new, more sinister breed of regulator. He portrays himself as a market enthusiast, with a difference; his is a middle of the road, genteel "free" market, better suited to what is referred to in administrative circles as the consumer's special relationship with electricity.

But this is a *non sequitur* if ever there was one, since the claim supports just as well the exact opposite argument—so crucial is our need for it, how can electricity possibly be left to bureaucrats whose bungling is rewarded with increased budgets; who fob bankruptcy onto taxpayers; whose incentives for making profits and avoiding losses are weak at best, and who regularly override the consumers' vote with political expedients?

Such middle of the road interventionism leads directly to socialism, warned economist Ludwig von Mises. Interventionism, and in particular price control, eventually causes a failure to bring supply and demand into balance through the price system. When politicians make a commodity cheaper, when they fix prices below market level, the result is increased demand and shortages. The irony of price controls typical of the regulated market is that they stifle incentives to produce, causing higher prices in the long run. What's more, if demand continues to rise, chronic shortages ensue, and the legislator is then forced to step in and begin fixing prices of labor and materials, and so on eventually at every stage of production.

Our state-mediated utilities may be able to buy and sell on the free market. But, unlike private firms, they need not respond to profit and loss signals. So long as they have taxpayer funds to make good their errors, these hydra-headed creatures have the option to produce at a loss. Thus, in a market in which the state has a hand, prices will never fully convey the information they relay in an unhampered market, and will invariably fail in guiding producers to meet consumer demand.

Electricity is best entrusted to fully free markets. Only private enterprise raises initial capital voluntarily and applies careful entrepreneurial forethought to all endeavors. Left to their devices, entrepreneurs will, in the long run and in response to price signals, build more capacity—electricity-generating plants—and prices will inevitably fall. Only entrepreneurs in competition with one another have the incentive to satisfy the customer, on whom they depend for their very survival.

California's Governor Gray Davis wanted to fully nationalize the grid. He threatened to sue power companies—even jail their managers—for not selling their juice below market value. He sought to ban power producers from exporting electricity to other states. Theft of private property was also on Gray's agenda, as he threatened to use "eminent domain" to seize power plants. Ludwig von Mises was right. The road to socializing the means of production is paved with interventionism.

37. MEPHISTO'S MEDICARE: A PARABLE

Canadian identity is founded on the national welfare programs. What is left but to laugh along with the architect of one such socialized program?

October 26, 2000

While doing his rounds on earth, Mephistopheles, Mephisto for short, paused to take stock. He had been successful. His was a benevolent tyranny painlessly relieving people of their liberties.

Mephisto liked to think of the pact with his flock, which he fondly called The Tribelings, as a voluntary exchange. As is always the case, what you give up you value less than what you get. And The Tribelings value the goods they think he provides more than their freedoms. The Agency over which Mephisto presides has an inexhaustible list of therapeutic wants, sardonically referred to in-house as human rights. The Agency's charges, The Tribelings, expect no less from the Agency; this is a precondition for power.

Somewhat bored, Mephisto longs for the days when achieving compliance was a rough-and-tumble affair. But, and here he flashes a gleam of dentition, his facility with the art of propaganda is no less magnificent. The literature about a free society he has not banned but simply reclassified. The men who once spoke of individual freedom in ideas, in trade, in the enjoyment of one's property—of human agency, responsibility and self-government—were now The Rubes. The Agency's agitprop, however, is cast as progressive.

Modeled on the latest health-care trends in North Korea and Cuba, The Firm is Mephisto's crowning glory. Like all Agency Corporations, The Firm is not subject to the land's bankruptcy laws. Mephisto busts a gut, because, while The Firm is insolvent, The Tribelings bankroll it indefinitely with their tax dollars. Compounding this, prices of services in The Firm are pegged at zero. This drives The Tribelings to use the service voraciously, with the result that endemic shortages ensue.

The Firm a.k.a. Mephisto's Medicare has just received a large infusion of funds, and The Tribelings are scurrying about arbitrarily trying to figure out where it is needed most. Should it go to technology, staff, maybe towards new databases to keep tabs on The Tribelings, or how about equipment? Mephisto knows that under freedom, prices are like a compass: pegged to supply and demand, they ensure the correct allocation of resources. In The Firm no such knowledge is available. No one knows the prices of services The Firm provides. But for all Mephisto cares, let The Tribelings use derrière doctors (proctologists) if misallocation of capital causes shortages of surgeons.

By design, Mephisto's Monopoly produces a different kind of worker. More mediocrity, less malcontents is his motto. To that end, Mephisto's seminal paper entitled "The Equilibrating Effects of Industrial Action among Doctors" has helped stem privatization rumblings, and with them unease over the subversive power of freedom. In the paper, Mephisto explains how, when wages are tied to a negotiated deal with labor rather than to the individual physician's performance, the position of the bad practitioner is reinforced. And all hail to that.

In Mephisto's country, rated Number One according to the World Health Hegemony, the professionals can only but work for The Firm, that is if they want to use their skills. If their instinct for freedom is strong, they must flee Canada's jurisdiction. While many of them have been expunged, Mephisto must labor to suppress the thinkers in The Firm. This he has done by entrenching a perverse incentive scheme. The hard rule in The Firm is that competency is rewarded with increased workload, but no extra pay, pervasive sluggishness guaranteed.

Mephisto's Medicare, in fact, is a pit of perverse incentives. Can you get kinkier than to make failure tantamount to success? If a hospital consistently underperforms, the administration celebrates. Why? Because this means more Agency funds to ostensibly fix the problem. Absent competition, The Tribelings are trapped. As the Eagles song goes, "You can check out anytime you like, but you can never leave." The Underperformers, or The Winners, as they are known in Agency speak, shoulder no responsibility. There is no out-of-pocket payment for the odd slip of the scalpel. The Tribelings pony up in blood and treasure for such pooling of risks or insurance. A perfect system of unaccountability, Mephisto calls this.

A particularly enjoyable stint is pressing peon practitioners into occasional slavery. Mephisto makes it an offense for doctors to refuse to treat defaulting Tribelings, thus ensuring that The Agency gets their free labor. No matter that on occasion some doctors, angered over not receiving payment for performing medical services, rise up and sue The Agency's assorted front organizations. Guess who always pays? The Tribelings do.

III. Criminal Injustices and Patent Wrongs

38. TRUTH OBSCURED IN JOHNNY JIHAD'S PLEA BARGAIN

October 9, 2002

There's a reason the American Constitution emphasizes "the right of trial by jury." The justice system's mandate is to unveil the truth. This can only be done in a court of law, and in accordance with due process. The plea bargain is nothing more than a negotiated deal which subverts the very goal of the justice system: In the process of hammering out an agreement that pacifies both prosecution and defense, truth usually falls by the way. As the predominant method of adjudication in the United States, the plea bargain taints the system.

The outcome of the wheeling and dealing in the case of John Walker Lindh, aka Suleyman al-Faris, aka Abdul Hamid, was that the American Taliban agreed to plead guilty only to supplying services to the Taliban, as well as to carrying an explosive during the commission of a felony, both in violation of the United States Code. The plea is peanuts compared to the original indictment.

There's no doubt that closing such a high-profile case without having to present a jury or judge with evidence and witnesses, and, in turn, without allowing the defendant to present his case, is a sweet victory for any politically ambitious prosecutor. No surprise then that U.S. Attorney Paul McNulty counted the deal as a triumph against terrorism. For his part, Lindh's defense attorney bizarrely claimed for himself the feat of having his client certified as a "court approved, non-terrorist." Both advocates are capitalizing on the perks of the plea bargain. Defense attorney and prosecutor alike can pencil in a victory on their scorecards. This, in the absence of the arduous search for truth and without any regard for the original indictments.

The overwhelming power of the state compared to the limited resources and power of the accused means that ordinarily the accused is the compromised party in a plea. This truism is hard to sustain in the Lindh case, if one endeavors to come to grips with the facts of the case.

Suffice it to say that Johnny Walker Lindh's Islamic conversion was nowhere near as harmonious as that of Yusuf Islam. The lyricist formerly known as Cat Stevens confines himself to composing "A's For Allah" devotional sing-alongs.

Understandably, the family of CIA agent Johnny Michael Spann is piqued. According to the Criminal Complaint, Spann conducted the interviews at the Qala-i Janghi compound near Mazar-e Sharif, in Afghanistan. Lindh was among the Taliban and al-Qaida men captured and brought there by Northern Alliance forces. "Some of the brothers were very tense," Lindh related to journalist Robert Young Pelton. "We're going to die either way," they reasoned. According to Lindh, "the brothers" decided to aim for the virgin-strewn heavens.

To Lindh and "the brothers" at Mazar-e Sharif dying in the course of an uprising meant *martyrdom*. For Mike Spann it meant *murder*. The CIA officer was consequently beaten and shot.

Lindh belonged to the Arab section of Ansar, which was a sort of foreign legion affiliated to the Taliban army. It was also part of Osama bin Laden's al-Qaida group. Lindh confessed to having trained at the al-Qaida-run al Farooq base, where, aside from having a brief audience with OBL, he also practiced terrorism warfare. When rumors about bin Laden's sending "50 people to carry out 20 suicide operations" against the U.S and Israel reached a crescendo in the camp, Lindh cowered. He failed to warn anyone back home.

By his own earlier account, Lindh appeared to be in on the Mazar-e Sharif uprising plot. As one of the prisoners interviewed by Spann,

Lindh refused to answer any of Mr. Spann's questions, much less did he offer him a "Hey man, watch out, and may Allah be with you."

Is Lindh guilty of conspiring to murder Mike Spann? Lindh certainly failed to warn the victim. Because of the Bush administration's criminal negligence of the intelligence, a message from Lindh warning about the impending September 11 terrorist attacks would have been to no avail. Had he, however, done that meager thing and warned Mike Spann, Lindh would have discharged his moral duty. As it stands now, this pattern of moral rot has been rendered legally legless.

The questions, nonetheless, linger. In his Statement to the Court, Lindh correctly points out that the U.S. hadn't always proscribed fighting alongside what were once the Mujahideen. On the contrary, the U.S. supported the Taliban's predecessors in their fight to repel the Soviets. Yet another effect of this plea bargain is to further hush the irreconcilable implications of U.S. meddlesome foreign policy.

Still, the facts indicate that, in the process of negotiating into being a crime that was palatable to all parties, Lindh was let off lightly.

39. PATRICIDE AND PROSECUTORIAL MISCONDUCT

September 11, 2002

When he discovered that he had unwittingly killed his father and married his mother, Oedipus Rex gouged out his eyes—not an unusual response from a hero of Greek mythology, who took his taboos very seriously.

Mitigating circumstances aside (Oedipus Rex didn't know these were his parents), patricide in contemporary America has decidedly different moral implications. Let's just say that, unlike the perpetrator of such an abomination in Greek mythology, the American throwback offers no spellbinding images of an internal struggle.

Fourteen-year-old Derek and 13-year-old Alex King murdered their father Terry King with a guilty and evil mind, and few inhibitions. Patricide was not the only taboo violated in the case. Prosecutor David Rimmer turned the case into two trials. In each, Rimmer presented to the jury an opposing theory, thus subverting the very foundations of the legal system.

Pretty boys Derek and Alex King killed *pater* because he was an obstacle: The boys wanted to live happily ever after with their neighborhood pedophile, 40-year-old Rick Chavis. Aside the perks of endless TV and video games, no chores, no school, and no church, Chavis had inducted Alex into the ways of Greek Love.

There were other proclivities Chavis uncorked in little Damien. Like so many American "cherubs," Alex was prone to believing in his uniqueness. And for brazenly daring to "stare the princely King kids down," daddy King was going to get it. "Staring down," and rule setting, according to Chavis' tutoring—not that different from the message kids get from most progressives—amounted to emotional abuse.

Well, there's one poor Cat who will not be staring at a King again … Providing a remarkably vivid and consistent confession, the boys told of how they bludgeoned their father to death with an aluminum baseball bat, as he slumbered in a recliner.

The boys soon recanted their confessions, and fingered Chavis, after their defense team claimed Chavis had killed the boys' father because he was obsessed with angel-faced Alex.

Matters were rendered unclean when, in trial B, the defense's case became the prosecution's case. The same prosecutor, who had the boys wielding the bat in one trial, argued to a different jury that Ricky Chavis wielded the very same bat.

Tough-on-crime conservatives show little care for the Rights of Englishmen. They care not that "… the foremost task of a justice system is to find justice and serve the truth." I can hear them say, "Throw the book at the contemptible pedophile, just so long as something sticks."

Prosecutorial power to bring charges against a person is an awesome power, stress Paul Craig Roberts and Lawrence M. Stratton in *The Tyranny of Good Intentions*. Backing him, the prosecutor has the might of the state, and thus must never "override the rights of the defendant in order to gain a conviction."

Prosecutorial duties are dual. While acting as the plaintiff, the prosecutor must also take pains to protect the defendant's rights.

More of a Benthamite bureaucrat than a truth seeker, Rimmer attempted, with insufficient evidence, to accuse Ricky Chavis of helping plan the murder. When Judge Frank Bell rejected this ploy, Rimmer came back with another.

Chavis was at home at the time of the crime. He received a call from the boys, collected them, washed their clothes and, the following day, delivered them to the local sheriff's office. Whereas it's the duty of a prosecutor never to bring the full force of government against an individual in an attempt to make indictments stick, Rimmer did just that: He charged Chavis with the murder.

Can anyone honestly claim that this prosecutor discharged his obligation under the law—that he presented both the grand jury and the trial juries with a single, coherent case in which he believed? Can anyone sincerely claim Rimmer provided evidence of guilt beyond a reasonable doubt before laying charges against Chavis?

Unlike the defense attorney, whose job it is to defend the accused, regardless of guilt, the prosecutor's job is to jail only those who are actually guilty. It is not unethical for a defense attorney to get a guilty client off—if the prosecutor can't meet his burden of proof, it's not the defense's fault. But it is unethical for the prosecutor to prosecute someone he does not firmly believe is guilty.

Not only were David Rimmer's dual trials under mutually exclusive theories inconsistent with his prosecutorial duties, they were tantamount to prosecutorial misconduct and violation of due process.

The jury convicted the boys of second-degree murder without a weapon. Analysts postulated that this incongruent sentence amounted to a jury's pardon. After all, the boys were so young and beautiful. Turns out, the jury that tried the boys viewed them as mere accomplices, and accepted Chavis' guilt. Miraculously, the jury that tried Chavis did not.

40. BUSH'S AFFIRMATIVE ACTION AMBUSH

January 22, 2003

In what is surely an unusual move, given that the Bush administration had no legal involvement in the case, the president announced his intention to file a brief challenging racial preferences in student admissions at the University of Michigan.

Following Mr. Bush's deft deployment of the Trent Lott affair to curry electoral favor with minorities, it appeared that, by taking a stand ostensibly against affirmative action, the president had done an about face. Or had he?

Anyone who suggests the Michigan undergraduate and law school programs are not racist cannot be serious, and if he is serious, should not be taken seriously. At the undergraduate level, African-American, non-white Hispanic and Native-American students receive 20 points out of 150 solely because of their race. A perfect SAT score nets a student only 12 points. It takes 100 points to gain admission, making the hue of one's skin good for a fifth of the admission points. The law school completes the project with a relatively straightforward quota.

Michigan is not unusual. Many undergraduate institutions, and most law schools and medical schools in the U.S., practice affirmative action. Like the Constitution, "the Civil Rights Act of 1964 gave the government no license to set quotas for hiring personnel by private enterprise or admitting students to institutions of higher learning, yet the federal bureaucracy acts as if it had," affirms Harvard scholar Richard Pipes.

The problems of affirmative action, as libertarians will point out, are the peculiar province of state-controlled schools. In a free market for education, schools would be able to establish any admission criteria they like. If a school wants to give preference to African-American albinos, that's the prerogative of private property. Predictably—although ironically—the ideology promoted in state-controlled schools is also responsible for producing a mentally monolithic population. This is to be expected when the state has the power to define and enforce politically correct diversity.

Politicking aside, a closer look at the Bush brief should quell denunciations from Democrats and minorities. Bush agrees that the American "Constitution makes it clear that people of all races must be treated equally under the law." "Yet we know that our society has not fully achieved that ideal," he equivocates. "Racial prejudice is a reality in America."

The prevalence of deep-seated racism the president infers from the fact that African-Americans lag behind whites in academic and socio-economic achievements. This, of course, is a *post hoc* error, one that most Americans thoroughly reject.

Upheld by Mr. Bush, this error is the central tenet of affirmative action. According to the president's diversity doxology, justice is achieved when racial and ethnic groups are reflected in academia and in the professions in proportion to their presence in the larger population, an impossibility considering individual and age-long inter-group differences. Absent such representation, Mr. Bush concludes that racism reigns.

This *non sequitur* is even harder to sustain when considering the Asian minority, a minority that has had its own historical hardships. In professions and academic pursuits where mathematical precocity is a factor, Asians are overrepresented and consistently outperform whites. If underrepresentation signals oppression, then overrepresentation equally must reflect an unfair advantage. Surely justice demands that overrepresentation of any group, not only of white males, be similarly corrected by the state? (How about making the NBA reflect America?)

Malaysian governments certainly adopted this logic toward their Chinese population, whose starting status as indentured laborers didn't stop them from rising to dominate business, professions, and universities. To achieve "racial balance," pro-Malaysian affirmative action laws were mandated in all government-controlled institutions.

Did not Hitler awaken to the same logic? In proportion to their numbers, Jews were also overrepresented in the economic and cultural life of Germany. In Malaysia, state ideology created a climate that was conducive to pogroms against the Chinese population; these were not looked upon unfavorably. Despite an antipathy toward the Jew—antipathy far in excess of the alleged racism African-Americans complain of nowadays—Jews remained active in German society until the state stepped in and stripped them of their rights. Hitler used the state apparatus to find a "Final Solution" to the Jewish advantage—the "Final Solution" was a *reductio ad inferno* of state-approved affirmative action.

The U.S. federal government has gone the Malaysian route for its black minority. As syndicated columnist Paul Craig Roberts reports, "In all 22 independent federal agencies and in 16 of 17 executive departments, blacks are massively overrepresented" in proportion to their presence in the population. Understandably, the plaintiffs in the Michigan case want the state to relinquish its compelling interest in promoting whatever it construes as diversity.

Bush refuses to second this; his brief shies away from addressing "the outer bounds of the Constitution," but only the case in its narrowest sense. Since he accepts racial discrimination as a cause for African-Americans' lag in achievement, the president intends to reject only the methods associated with this faulty formulation. Diversity directives are to go full throttle ahead so long as they are "racially-neutral."

Mr. Bush's "road map" includes encouraging schools to come up with racial cue cards such as "a statement people can make about whether they've overcome hardship." Berkeley and Texas, for instance, already make unusual hardships and life experience a crucial consideration in admissions. "The kind of hardships" that'll be given extra credit are "largely peculiar to preferred minorities such as having been shot," notes commentator Steve Sailer, wryly. In short, the quest for diversity is unlikely to encompass the Midwestern experience.

The Condi, (Andy) Card and Karl (Rove) Crack Team has achieved a triumph of triangulation. The Bush base, of which 92 percent is white, will swallow the bait, believing, as it did after the landmark 1978 case of Bakke, that quotas had been outlawed. Despite Bakke, universities continued to take race into account. Same in this case: With presidential approval, the Michigan point system will be palliated somewhat, but business as usual will see public funds diverted to other, less conspicuous, race-friendly recruiting methods, much to the glee of the "civil rights" industry. Mr. Bush's appeasement of both sides, while further entrenching the politically correct and favored side, is a prime example of slimy Clintonian tactics.

41. MEDEA OR MADONNA?

July 16, 2001

When her lover ditched her in favor of a match with bluer blood, Medea, a character in Greek Mythology, takes her revenge by killing their sons. A rapacious murderer and schemer to rival any villain of the opposite sex, Medea has, however, been rehabilitated in recent decades. Even at their most ferocious, our society now insists that women are no more than passive victims, capable of few free choices. Medea has found a place in the annals of women's studies courses as a symbol of a woman in revolt against the patriarchy.

Assisted along by this view is Medea's latter-day sister, Andrea Pia Yates. Yates, whom the media persist in calling "a Houston mom," methodically drowned her children aged six months to seven years.

One reporter wondered why the police had offered no explanation for how Yates drowned five children without any escaping. Let's see: How difficult is it to corral your unsuspecting, completely trusting and likely adoring charges for bath time? A promise of ice cream after ear scrubbing used to do wonders with my once-tiny tot.

The reporter's assumption about the woman's daintiness forms part of the "vocabulary of motive" that was deployed by the experts and the media. Accordingly, a woman will engage in violence only when provoked, or brought to the brink of desperation. Premeditated brutality is simply not part of her biology. If a woman is driven to kill, it is for good reason. Conversely, when men kill or abuse, it is because they are hardwired to do so. If she kills her newborn, and, in the case of Yates, throws in the rest of the brood for good measure, the woman is said to have likely suffered from Postpartum Depression. Deployed as a legal defense, PPD may see her exonerated.

Canadian killer and sex offender Karla Homolka combined with feral gusto an active social life with the dedicated activity of abduction, murder and rape. She availed herself of the Battered Woman defense. Homolka is immortalized on video partaking in the rape and killing of three women, including her sister. Because of her gender, the experts—the same people who pontificate about Yates—don't consider Homolka a sadist or sexual deviant. The consensus in psychological circles is that sexual deviance in women is practically non-existent and hence recidivism unlikely.

Consequently, Homolka did not receive the mandated treatment our state-run prisons administer to sex offenders. What she got was a jailhouse protocol called "Improving Your Inner Self." This New Age fatuity has helped her, in her words, to "get rid of mistrust, self-doubt, and misplaced guilt." While this monster was growing her dangerously gargantuan ego on the taxpayer's dime, research had already begun to unveil sexual deviance in women, indicating that it was far more prevalent than previously presumed. The public, however, continues to be shielded from the realities of women's crimes.

The rhetoric intended to exculpate Yates was relentless. "Yates," we were told, "had spent her adult life catering to the deepest needs and visions of others." When she did commit acts of aggression, these were only ever turned on herself in the form of a failed suicide, leading one mental health maven to characterize the murders as a form of suicide by proxy. Yates, he says, lost touch with reality to such a degree that she thought of killing her children as killing herself. He doesn't explain why, with all the confusion about her psychic boundaries, Yates herself emerged unscathed, which is more than we can say about the children.

No less repugnant are the collectivist explanations for this crime. "There's blood on everybody's hands," fluted one infanticide expert. The premise here being that children belong to "Rotten Rodham's" Village, and that somehow, because raising kids ought to be a tribal affair, the responsibility for killing them must also repair to members of the clan.

Anyone who has been at the receiving end of abuse from a mother, a wife, or a female lover, knows that these explanations simplify and infantilize women. We persist in draining the crimes women commit of moral or rational content, writes Patricia Pearson in her 1997 book entitled *When She Was Bad*. Pearson combines "chilling real life examples with scholarly research" to show that violence committed by women is every bit as vicious, albeit different, as violence perpetrated by men.

Stripped of the clinical vernacular that attenuates their deeds, women hold their own in the country's crime statistics. "Women," writes Pearson, "commit the majority of child homicides in the United States, a greater share of physical child abuse, an equal rate of sibling violence and assaults on the elderly, about a quarter of child sexual abuse, an overwhelming share of the killing of newborn, and a fair preponderance of spousal assaults." The African-American man living in Chicago, for instance, is at the greatest risk of being killed by an intimate partner. Eighteen percent of black men killed in

Chicago between 1966 and 1996 died at the hands of their mates; 65 percent of these men had no record of violence, abuse or other. "Ten to 20 percent of the six to eight thousand Sudden Infant Deaths reported each year in the U.S. conceal accidental or deliberate suffocation," usually by mothers. How many deadly assaults by mothers are finessed as the "condition" termed Munchausen syndrome by proxy is hard to assess.

Indeed nowhere are the myths about female pacifism more robust than in spousal violence orthodoxy. Hundreds of well-controlled sociological surveys reveal one of the most astonishing episodes of dishonest science in our times. Women assault their partners as often as, or more often than, men do. Gender symmetry in violence between couples is as well documented as it is well concealed by government number crunchers.

In the acclaimed *Moral Panic: Biopolitics Rising*, Professor John Fekete documents the dozens of two-sex surveys conducted in Canada and in the U.S. over the past 30 years, all of which "show that women in relationships with men commit comparatively as many or more acts of physical violence as men do, at every level of severity." It is a slap for a slap, beating for beating, knifing and shooting for knifing and shooting, on the evidence of women's own self-reports. The fact that women are more likely to be injured in domestic altercations points to differences in physical strength between men and women, not in culpability. Physical weakness is not to be equated with moral innocence.

Women's aggression is different to that of men, which is why it's so easy to misconstrue. From an early age, women opt for underhanded and manipulative strategies such as "bullying, name calling, excommunicating and gossiping," to achieve their ends. Consider honor killings, undoubtedly the grisliest of crimes against women. In the Palestinian Authority alone, fathers and brothers murder 20 to 40 women every year in order to defend family honor. But when studying female aggression in the territory, anthropologist Ilsa Glaser observed that women's gossip plays a causal role in the events leading up to the butchering. By spreading rumors about the targeted woman, and by putting pressure on the men to act, women were instrumental in instigating the murders. Although preparing the grounds for murder is not tantamount to taking a life, the fact remains that women are in on the act.

Anthropological insight strongly advances our case. In her book *Mother Nature: A history of mothers, infants and natural selection*, Sarah Blaffer Hrdy shows that the maternal instinct, which supposedly elevates women above men, is not as natural as mother's milk. In primate species, mothers are known to reward males who kill their young by soliciting copulation with them. And there are many conditions in the wild "under which mothers abandon and cannibalize the young." If, like me, you are not fond of extrapolating from monkeys to men, then Hrdy supplies human parallels of "sex-selective infanticide in several of the world's cultures." Here, as in the Palestinian Authority, women are active participants.

All of this suggests that the old stereotypes must be replaced with a nuanced understanding, one which recognizes that if women can match men in almost every way that is good and fine, they can also harbor the potential to be as sinister as men.

42. VICES ARE NOT CRIMES

May 8, 2002

Darryl Strawberry is perhaps not the most savory character, but a criminal he is not. He has been classed—and hounded—as a criminal by a law that brutally punishes adults for the substances they ought to be able to *ingest*, *inhale* or *inject* at their own peril.

The former major-league star was recently sentenced to 18 months in prison for violating probation, following a 1999 conviction on drug and solicitation of prostitution charges.

So Strawberry is a cokehead with an appetite for unwholesome sex. Will someone tell me why this is the business of anyone other than he and his unfortunate wife?

There is no shortage of meddling third parties that find certain consensual, capitalistic acts between adults to be offensive. Some people want to stop the trade in pornography. Others would like to make it prohibitive for adults to purchase cigarettes or junk food.

For one thing, "Consumer sovereignty," as libertarian economist Pierre Lemieux notes, "reflects the assumption that each individual knows better than anybody else what is good for him. This idea runs counter to state paternalism, whether in smoking, pension plans, drugs or whatever."

For another, any transaction that was at the time of occurrence voluntary, and hence beneficial to the participants, can, retrospectively, be denounced as harmful and regrettable. A litigious culture facilitates this trend. Government and other busybodies, however, would do well to consider that if an exchange is voluntary, then both parties expect to benefit from it.

Where no force or violence is involved, a voluntary exchange is, by definition, always mutually beneficial, inasmuch as, at the time of the exchange, the buyer of the drugs valued the purchase more than the money he paid for it, and the seller valued the money more than the goods he sold.

Third parties have no place in transactions between consenting adults, unless these transactions infringe directly—not foreseeably—on their property or person. Strawberry and his suppliers have appetites and values I don't share. But I fail to see how their decadent deals infringe on my rights.

Having arbitrarily decided that certain patterns of consumption are potentially worse for individual and society than others, the policy pinheads have proceeded to preemptively trample the constitutional rights of people like Strawberry, before the foreseeable harm to society occurs.

If we accept state aggression based on prior restraint arguments, then aggress we must *ad absurdum*. Why not prevent all teenagers from driving, or, even better, all socialist parents from procreating, lest they sire proponents of state theft?

"Vices are those acts by which a man harms himself or his property. Crimes are those acts by which a man harms the person or property of another," wrote Lysander Spooner, the great 19th-century theorist of liberty. And government has no business treating vices as crimes.

Drug use is a private choice. Incarcerating people for their consumption choices has the logical consistency of arresting a survivor of suicide for attempted murder. If for harming himself a man forfeits his liberty, then it can't be said that he has dominion over his body. It implies that someone else—government—owns him. People ought to be arrested only for crimes they perpetrate against another's person or property.

Be mindful, though, that the coercive, therapeutic state is a poor substitute for the avenging state. Justice Florence Foster, who presided over Strawberry's case, had repeatedly opted for compulsory treatment for the eight-time all-star.

Law-enforced medical treatment, however, must be as volubly opposed as prison. Over and above the immorality of coerced wealth distribution, treatment schemes paid by the taxpayer ensure that those of us who choose to refrain from drug taking subsidize the lifestyle of the addict. Less addiction will come about, not by distributing resources from the risk averse to the reckless, stealing from responsible adults, and rewarding the rash and imprudent—but by making the addict responsible for the risks he takes.

This is not an easy task given that some self-destructive behavior has acquired disability status and is legally protected. When insurers cannot transfer to the addict the full costs of the risk he poses, they must make those of us who choose to watch our diets, exercise, and refrain from smoking or drug taking the repository for these costs. Insurance must be permitted to exercise its mandate to discriminate between risk groups. With such discrimination comes the incentive on the part of the insured to avoid lifestyles or behaviors that incur costs.

Reducing addiction lies, then, in withdrawing the perverse incentives that reinforce the maladaptive behavior. To use 12-step locution, state-mandated treatment programs are "enablers." The dismal failure of state programs launched by the addiction industry, the high rates of recidivism they yield, and the pesky fact that most quitters among smokers do so solo—goes to show that addicts quit when they decide to. And they are more likely to be nudged in that direction when made to shoulder the consequences of their lifestyle.

Once the state retreats from punishing vices, it will fall, once again, to custom and religion to reinvigorate those informal checks on behavior the therapeutic state has undermined. Shame, loss of face, being denied membership, excommunication, counseling and support are some of the ways moral communities have, in previous eras, kept their members in check.

Drug addiction, of course, is a chosen habit or lifestyle—not a disease. A society that cleaves to a worldview that parlays misdeeds into diseases does so at its own peril. Darryl Strawberry, sadly, happens to have a serious and genuine disease. Strawberry's metastatic cancer is yet another good reason to set him free and cut him loose.

43. PINKO PLUMPS PENAL ABOLITION

May 18, 2000

Avi Lewis, the onetime host of the Canadian Broadcasting Corporation's *Counterspin*, portrays himself as one who challenges ideas "fundamental to our culture." This is his facetious spin. Avi is Old Left establishment. He is the son of former Canadian UN envoy Stephen Lewis and raging feminist Michelle Landsberg, grandson of one-time national NDP leader David Lewis, connubial comrade to Naomi Klein of the banal anti-free market sloganeering, brother-in-law to Seth Klein of the far left Canadian Center for Policy Alternatives. Avi is a pedigreed pinko and not terribly original at that.

Having failed to stray from the ideology of his kin, Avi is not that far removed from the powers that be. He champions a little more regulation and thought control than the reigning Canadian Liberals, more of a command economy and more welfare dependence. His fetish is the culture of the commons—but, like the Liberals, divisive identity politics is his modus. No one beats Avi for substituting soundbites for substance and smart aleck for intellectual acuity. Given the profile, is it any wonder Avi was in his postmodern element in a segment on penal abolition?

The movement for restorative justice holds that problems plaguing the criminal justice system are reason enough to abolish it. Its position is purely result oriented: Incarceration doesn't reduce rates of re-offense and doesn't bring back the dead, ergo abolish it and heal the criminal in the community. Justice, the activists say, must be sought in a redistribution of wealth and resources. As one activist claimed, punishment only stigmatizes difference.

I was unaware that criminality was an expression of cherished human diversity, and thus even more surprised when the activist claimed that "redemption" for psychopaths would be better achieved through therapeutic than punitive means. Lewis, who failed to get the goods on the efficacy of unconditional love with psychopaths, confined himself to a rant about the "hyperbole of the crackdown crowd."

A hallmark of an Avi Lewis argument is that you can invariably drive a four-by-four through it. True, crime rates in Canada have been going down. Public demand, however, for tighter parole and tougher young-offender laws, for example, need have nothing to do with falling crime rates. Why should aggregate crime trends impact individual sentencing? Do we reduce the sentence for murder in the first degree because there were fewer such murders that year?

Penal abolitionists see crime solely as a consequence of inoptimal social conditions. Thus they conclude that the disproportionate percentage of blacks and natives in jails is proof of systemic racism. Doubtless there are racist elements in the criminal justice system, and some false convictions, but people go to jail, first and foremost, because they break the law. The fact that most incarcerations are drug related calls not for the abolition of the criminal justice system, but rather for the repeal of all laws against the production, use, and trade in drugs.

Next, a smirking African activist proceeded in tortured phrases to compare the cruelty of our penitentiaries to those of Africa. Ms. Agomoh recommended that we look at traditional tribal methods for meting justice. It might not be easy in this day and age to get away with impaling perpetrators as Shaka Zulu did. Adopting Winnie Mandela's more humane and contemporary necklacing method—placing a diesel-doused tire around the putative criminal's neck and igniting—may also make some victim's rights groups hot under the collar. Clearly, Agomoh has spent too long in the West, which would account for her romanticized delusions about African tribal justice.

Still less can Ms. Agomoh claim for her ideas an African pedigree. It's quite marvelous how self-appointed African advocates embrace and use the distinctly Western tradition of human rights: the dignity of the individual and the respect for diversity—all outgrowths of the Enlightenment—but then proceed to slam the West, a trend that pleases leftists almost as much as does skewering the white man for all ills.

Criminologist Don Andrews was the most unabashed utilitarian to make an appearance on the show. Andrews vituperated "this retribution accountability stuff," and claimed that we punish not because we get public protection from it but because it makes us feel better. Punishment to him is to be adjudged only in as much as it measurably retards recidivism. If punishment doesn't accomplish this, regardless of what is right or wrong, it must be abolished in favor of quick expedients.

Whether punishment makes people feel good, whether it reforms the criminal or safeguards the public is immaterial, although I would argue that a society with a moral code is safer in the long run than one without. Punishment is a public declaration of moral values. It is an extension of natural law. Descend into the Don Andrews and Avi

Lewis amoral abyss, and you abolish the very fabric of our ethical
tradition.

44. RIGHTS IN IDEAS INFRINGE RIGHTS IN REAL
PROPERTY

January 26, 2001

Prior to the U.S. Court of Appeal's decision in the Napster case,
all indications were that the parties to the litigation were adjusting to
a reality in which copyright might become a thing of the past.

TVT Records, one of the largest U.S. independent record labels,
had become the first label to drop its copyright infringement lawsuit
against Napster. TVT upstaged Bertelsmann AG, which strategically
remained party to litigation against the song-swapping outfit while
promising to forgo action once Napster transformed itself into a fee-
based membership service.

Edel Music, too, had hopped on board. The players seemed to
have sensed that they could no longer stem the tide: Could the new
technology have blown the lid off the anti-free-market protectionism
that is copyright and patent law? In explaining TVT's change of
heart, president and founder Steve Gottlieb said: "I am afraid that
copyright owners' resistance to finding workable solutions with
Internet music providers may result in consumers, artists, and the
industry itself ultimately being harmed. . . .It is high time that the
industry embraces a service that the public has so emphatically said
they want."

Once the dust settled, the expectation was that TVT and Napster
would offer Napster's 45 million-plus users the opportunity to
exchange copyrighted music files online under a business model that
compensates recording artists and record companies.

In the decision that followed these developments, the U.S. Court
of Appeals for the Ninth Circuit found Napster liable for
contributory and vicarious copyright infringement. Users were said

to be engaging in direct infringement of the plaintiffs' distribution and reproduction rights. The court conceded that Napster is capable of and has the potential to provide other non-infringing uses. While this would have acted as a legal defense against contributory infringement, it was outweighed by the fact that Napster possessed actual, specific knowledge of direct infringement.

The judge found that Napster was able to locate the infringing material and hence capable of properly policing its system. This, combined with a direct financial stake in the infringing activities, caused the court to find Napster liable as a vicarious offender as well.

One hope was that the Audio Home Recording Act of 1992 (AHRA) would grant Napster users protection on the grounds of "fair use," since it allows audio music swapping for noncommercial use. This too failed. Because they got for nothing something they would ordinarily have paid for, Napster users were deemed to be engaging in commercial use. The judge further ruled that since a Napster user copies an entire work, he is harming the market by (1) reducing CD sales among college students, and (2) making it harder for the record companies to enter the arena of digital downloading.

This standard underscores that copyright aims at maintaining a market for certain interests through the force of the law, a good point from which to segue into the crux of the Napster saga: Are the legal rights that politicians gave to originators of ideas—as embodied in music, software programs, books, or practical inventions— justified? And what property rights should the law protect?

The answer depends on the definition of property and what makes it ownable. Tangible goods, we all agree, are properly the objects of property rights. This is because they are economically scarce. But why should this not be the case for intangibles such as the ideas intellectual property (IP) laws protect? Here we arrive at the heart of the issue. "He who receives an idea from me," wrote Thomas Jefferson, himself an inventor, "receives instruction himself without lessening mine; as he who lights his taper at mine, receives light without darkening me." Jefferson was very definitely not articulating the fatuous "information-wants-to-be-free" argument made by the

Left regarding IP. He was, however, enunciating what is the essence of ownable property.

Indeed, the notion that the mere act of creation confers ownership is problematic. Drawing on Lockean principles of homesteading, property theorists like attorney N. Stephan Kinsella reject it in favor of economic scarcity as "the hallmark of ownable property." Scholars like Sir Arnold Plant and Tom G. Palmer, along with virtually all property theorists of the Austrian school, recognize that scarcity precedes property.

Economic scarcity results when my use of an item conflicts with your use of it. While an abundance of computers can be had on the market, my use of this particular PC excludes your use of it. We might come to blows were we both to insist on occupying the thing. If I could conjure computers with a magic wand, they would be abundant, not scarce, and it would be immaterial if this one were removed. In the case of scarce resources, property rights are essential to prevent conflict.

Intangible Goods

Not so for intangible things such as the ideas copyright and patents protect. However valuable, ideas are not economically scarce: My listening to a piece of music doesn't conflict with or exclude your doing the same. The same applies to a book: A copy made of the thing doesn't remove from its author the configuration of ideas that is the book.

Granted, copyright law protects only the physical instantiation of an idea. Humming a song won't secure copyright in it. The idea must be written down to become fixed in a tangible medium. Here is the nub: Copyright is vested in a physical object that can be owned quite legitimately by someone other than the author of the book, the singer on a CD or the code writer of a software program. It is in the rightfully owned property of others that the copyright owner acquires a stake.

Say I write a novel and you decide to film a movie based on my novel's plot, using your own filming equipment. Were I only to proclaim I owned the ideas in my novel, I would merely be exercising my free speech. But when I want to prohibit you from using your equipment as you please, and can use the force of law to do so, I am violating your property right. Under the law as it now stands, my act of creation is all it takes for me to be able to exercise control over you.

Put another way, imagine you could reproduce at almost no cost copies of a scarce, tangible item like a desk I designed. Would I be justified in prohibiting you from using your copy of my desk simply because I possess the original item? Would it be right to demand that you pay me a stipend for every copy of my desk you made using your own desk copier, so that I might secure for myself a tidy source of revenue? If you dare resist my attempts at extortion, I will galvanize the law. After all, you are cutting into an income I imagine I am owed.

Copyright redistributes wealth, as the workings of the AHRA makes evident. Here, manufacturers like Yamaha or Philips that market digital audiotape recorders and CD-R burners must pay a statutory royalty as a penalty for making devices that could foreseeably be used to infringe copyright. Such manufacturers must pony up for the potential undermining of the *value* of copyrighted material. Notwithstanding the incoherence of assigning rights in some imagined value the copyrighted material may have, wealth here is distributed from manufacturer to music industry. Similarly, consumers who purchase blank recording media must pay special excise taxes to the music industry.

No less egregious is the patent monopoly. Consider the Prozac patent, recently—and surprisingly—struck down by an American court. Ordinarily, the patent monopoly held by Eli Lilly & Co. would have prohibited competitors from using their own property to make generic copies of the drug. This is all a patent is; it grants to the holder no more than the right to prohibit someone else from implementing an invention he may have arrived at quite independently.

Some conservative organizations, abandoning free-market principles, defend patent monopolies. The Fraser Institute, for example, has fiddled with econometrics in an attempt to show that denying Eli Lilly & Co. the Prozac patent monopoly causes a net loss to the economy, reducing wealth and the incentive to invent. Such staple utilitarian arguments are not only unjust and unprincipled, but also incoherent.

The Fraser Institute compared the three billion savings to consumers from the introduction of competition from generic drugs with the $66 billion loss to pharmaceutical company shareholders after the removal of Eli Lilly's patent protection. It then concluded that patent monopoly benefits the economy.

But as economist Ludwig von Mises wrote, "Just as there is no measurement of sexual love, of friendship and sympathy, and of esthetic enjoyment, so there is no measurement of the value of commodities." Neither is there a "method available to construct a unit of value." Values are subjective. While consumers gained from the removal of the Prozac patent monopoly, others—notably investors—lost. By what shift of logic does an expert decide that the loss to one party is more important than the gain to the other? Clearly, to sanction state-granted, exclusive monopoly privileges on the central-planning grounds that this redistribution of wealth promotes prosperity in society is not an enduring basis for principled legislation.

Legally Binding Promises

Rather than resort to discredited central planning and its attendant specious measurements to justify imposing patent monopolies, conservative organizations should rediscover the advantages of the free market. It offers other, much simpler, and much more elegant options—contracts are among them—to ensure that the originator of an idea receives a share of the profit. Under certain conditions and with certain provisos, promises made between parties become legally binding. Employees in high-tech companies, for instance, are bound by contract when they agree to keep quiet about trade secrets. A variety of contracts are available to allow parties to protect their assets and profits. Confidentiality, nondisclosure, royalty, and non-compete agreements can be expected to proliferate in copyright-free commerce. These arrangements differ from the current copyright regime in that they bind only parties to the agreement. Intellectual property rights bind everyone.

Given that protectionism distorts the market, its removal needn't be dreaded, except by those who turn to government to capture wealth. Imitation *haute couture* and knock-off fragrances, paperbacks, and drive-in movies have not decimated the original articles or industries they emulated, although they may have scaled them back somewhat. How many tears would you shed if Bill Gates were worth only several—not dozens of—billions? Since Microsoft owes a good portion of its wealth to the copyright monopoly, this would be the upshot of its removal. If the company relied only on profits from initial sales and from support services, would that be so bad? In the case of music, no protection may indeed mean fewer of the three-chord warbles that currently pervade the industry. Why is that such a bad thing? And who says someone has a right to make others provide him with a market? Certainly no true free-market proponent.

Intellectual Property rights are invariably enforced in the tangible world of scarce resources. Recognizing property rights in nonscarce intangible resources diminishes rights in tangible scarce resources. Laws that elevate rights in ideas to the extent they override rights in tangible property must give pause—more so given government's penchant for imbuing things with economic value (such as occupational licenses and cable franchises) so as to grant monopoly to one interest or another.

The copyright system ought to be abolished because there can be no justification for the use of force against legitimate property owners. And force is, very plainly, what flows from the enforcement of the law. Since ideas should not be treated as property, laws that target those who have not violated person or property are wrong.

45. BATTY PATENTS

June 12, 2002

It's distressing when an ardent capitalist like Doug Bandow of the Cato Institute plumps for government grants of privilege. The columnist's support for patents does, however, contain a welcome admission that a patent is a government grant of monopoly.

In practice, a patent allows the inventor to use the force of the law to prohibit someone else from practicing the invention. Government grants the patent holder the right to forcibly restrict entry into the market. Restricted entry causes restricted supply. The patent holder thus creates a scarcity of the product, allowing him to inflate prices. This is not how market-based profits are generated, but it is quintessential central planning.

Mr. Bandow justifies this monopoly on the grounds that companies must be allowed to "enjoy the fruit of their labor," a misleading way of couching the fact that with patent privileges, government guarantees to the pharmaceutical kingpins a return on their investment. Surely Mr. Bandow doesn't believe companies have a right to a secured investment.

What many patent advocates share with leftist, non-libertarian, patent abolitionists is that both defend or repudiate patents on utilitarian—not principled—grounds. Many proponents of patents sanction them on the basis that patents contribute somehow to the "greatest wealth or happiness for the greatest number of people." Leftist abolitionists, for their part, grouse about the need for a "Creative Commons," for the good of "society."

Any attempt to pronounce conclusively on the benefits to society of patents is something of an economic impossibility. "Society" is a collection of individuals with disparate needs, which is why there can be no objective value to a commodity. The removal of Bristol-Myers' patent over the diabetes-fighting drug Glucophage will permit competition from generics, which will, in turn, save diabetics money. Bandow or other central planners would likely counter by claiming that, because the loss to pharmaceutical-company shareholders is likely to be many times the savings to diabetics, the economy on the whole is poorer.

Nonsense on stilts!

The value of a commodity is subjective. No "expert" can decree the loss to one party more important than the gain to another. What is amply clear is that profits from the patent monopoly are illegitimate and come at the expense of all but the special interests they are designed to favor.

More compellingly, no wealth-creation calculus can justify the overturning of property rights, which is what patents achieve. To clarify what is properly the object of property rights, let's hark back to some imagined, primordial time we'll call BG (Before Government):

The homesteading of previously unoccupied, tangible property is the way property is justly acquired. Duly, Tribe A moves into an unoccupied cave and makes it its own. The cave, in a word, is now spoken for.

Next, Cavewoman A invents a bat-catching widget. The tribe not only has a home, but it now has a steady supply of bat stew. Shortly thereafter, an irate Batlady discovers that the neighboring Tribe B is using the same device. For "stealing" her idea, Batlady demands that the elders unleash the tribal warriors to punish the neighbors.

The elders are wise and peaceful. They huddle to debate the alleged theft by Tribe B of Batlady's idea. The timeline supports her claim: The neighbors began using the device well after it was invented and produced by Tribe A. No evidence, however, of trespass could be found on Tribe A's property. None of its widgets were missing. Tribe B clearly fashioned the copycat batcatchers using their legitimately owned wherewithal.

The elders, who astutely entertained the obvious possibility of concurrent invention, concluded that, Batlady's pride notwithstanding, Tribe B stole nothing from them. The state of affairs was as Thomas Jefferson would one day describe it: "He who receives an idea from me, receives instruction himself without lessening mine; as he who lights his taper at mine, receives light without darkening me."

Since all this happened BBG (Blissfully Before Government), Tribe A directly approached Copycat Tribe with a contract, inked in ochre and blood. Accordingly, Batlady would divulge her next muse to Copycat Tribe in exchange for a couple of lavish mink coats for Tribe A's womenfolk.

Having applied the natural law, never did it occur to the elders to demand that The Copycats pay royalties in lieu of each and every one of their widgets, for decades to come. It seemed clear to our elders that they had no legitimate stake in the Copycat Tribe's widget property. They did, however, initiate a voluntary contract to protect their prized advantage. Absent coercive Big Brother, batty patents would not exist.

46. CIPRO SHORTAGE: A PATENTED SCARCITY

October 25, 2001

During the anthrax attacks, Bayer AG, the German pharmaceutical giant and manufacturer of the anthrax-fighting drug Cipro, experienced a windfall. The sudden demand for Cipro could not have come at a better time for a company that had been in a slump and was hemorrhaging due to a considerable operating-profit shortfall. The financial press's accounts of how Bayer was scouting for bailout partners soon gave way to details of Bayer's moves to triple its Cipro production. With Cipro, Bayer was vying for some of the $643 million the Bush administration had planned to put toward increasing stockpiles of antibiotics.

Scrambling to fill every order placed by government, the company ran its facilities 24 hours a day, seven days a week; placed its Connecticut plant on an accelerated production schedule; and even reopened a defunct German plant. In the event that the unspeakable occurs, however, Bayer's likelihood of single-handedly meeting consumer demand for Cipro will be slim, if not anorexic. Tripled production and all, Bayer's promise to crank out 200 million tablets over a short period may do little to satisfy a spike in demand driven by almost as many Americans.

At the height of the anthrax crisis, government asked Americans not to stockpile the medication but to rely on the government's math: If the crunch came, the government promised to be able to treat 12 million people for 60 days of incubation. It is unclear why the government is justified in facilitating access to the medication for only a fraction of the population. If every single paying American wishes to secure a course of Cipro, if only as a psychological antidote, why not? Only in a command economy does government dictate when the demand for a good has been—or ought to be—sated. In a free market, consumers direct supply and demand. And in a free market, increased demand leads to increased supply, as producers compete with one another to meet the demand. When the demand for Cipro has approximated the supply of Cipro, buyers—not the government—will have indicated their needs have been satisfied.

With more people bidding for Cipro, the drug was fast becoming scarce at its current price. When shortages of a good persist in the face of steady demand, it's safe to say that government incursion into the economy is at fault. Energetic price-fixing and stockpiling by bureaucrats are a symptom of—and an *ad hoc* response to—deficiencies brought about by ongoing policies of intervention in the economy, not of "market failure."

In the Cipro addle, the likely culprits are Food and Drug Administration regulations and the patent system. FDA regulations go some distance toward explaining why our choices are limited so as to make Cipro the only drug that has been approved for the treatment of the inhaled—and the most lethal—form of anthrax. Getting a new drug approved today costs about $500 million and takes approximately ten years. The sclerotic FDA does not, however, explain why, once a shortage has occurred in an already approved drug, the self-regulating market mechanisms cannot kick in to remedy the problem. Patents explain this.

The acute scarcity of Cipro is indeed a side effect of the law. As bad as FDA regulation is, patent law constitutes even more of a barrier to entry into the pharmaceutical market. In terms of the length of the patent granted, the patent system hasn't changed significantly. The anthrax crisis, preceded by the events of September 11, has served to simply amplify the manner in which patents subvert the market and invite—even require—further central-planner tinkering.

Any coherent explanation for the shortages or elevated prices of certain drugs must proceed from the understanding that patents allow the manufacturer to create a scarcity of the product by restricting its supply in order to raise the price.

How then would consumer demand have been heeded in a market unhampered by patent? The same events that have hitherto occurred would have unfolded; the sudden urgent demand for the drug would have been followed by a shortfall of supply. Large demand and short supply would initially send the price of Cipro rocketing. At this stage, demonstrators would take to the streets, riding the same old ass and hollering, "Profits equal plunder." The bellicose collectivists never understand that our very lives depend on the ability of the manufacturer to read and act on vital market signals. Profits in an unhampered pharmaceutical market would signal to the many drugmakers that it's time to enter into Cipro production.

These processes have all transpired, save one: Drug makers are not permitted to respond to one of the street signs of the free market, to profits. The law prohibits pharmaceutical companies from competing for Cipro market share, supplying the demand, and, in the process of creating competition, dealing a blow to the Bayer monopoly price tag. Because of specific patents Bayer has obtained, other companies cannot bring supply and demand into equilibrium, and satisfy buyers.

Whether one thinks that granting an inventor a near 20-year monopoly on the manufacture, use, or sale of a product is the right thing to do is quite apart from acceding that a patent places a barrier on entry into the market. This barrier is the essence of monopoly. Capturing a large market share by pleasing consumers does not a monopolist make. But appealing to government for a grant of privilege that gives the rent-seeker the legal power to restrict access into the market, so that he is undeterred by competition, qualifies. Ensuring that there is only one price and that a competitive price—a function of the presence of other sellers in the market—cannot arise is also the practice of a monopolist.

While making her something of an untouchable to the international pharmaceutical kingpins, certain provisions in India's patent law account for a thriving generics industry. Compare the monopoly price of $350 U.S. for a course of Cipro to the roughly $20 per course of treatment set by profitable Indian generic companies.

The patent has survived challenges, which would explain why, in turn, the monopoly price remains unchallenged. In the absence of competition, the product's high price does not markedly reduce sales or force a market adjustment on the seller. Irrespective of price or less-than-robust sales, the Cipro patent has pretty much guaranteed that Bayer reaps a considerable profit.

The moral claim of concurrent inventors notwithstanding, the fact that Bayer's Cipro patent does not expire until December 2003, and the fact that Bayer is the only company that is allowed to produce ciprofloxacin until then, leaves us with the possibility of shortages. There is no telling whether Bayer might relent and license the drug to other drug makers, thus enabling generics to fill the demand generated in the aftermath of September 11. The anthrax threat has, however, drastically altered the consumer's tolerance.

Understandably apprehensive, Sen. Charles Schumer (D-N.Y.) inadvertently expressed unease about the hampered drug market.

"I'd still feel a lot better with several competitors," ventured the senator, adding that "it goes without saying that if we increase the number of manufacturers producing ciprofloxacin, we are more likely to have enough on hand, should we need it."

The Centers for Disease Control and Prevention have, in the interim, expanded the range of anthrax prophylactics to include doxycycline and others, with the result that the pressure has since been somewhat lifted off Cipro as the first-line agent of choice in treating anthrax. It would, however, be a mistake to consider the case of Cipro a mere fluke; it's a harbinger of things to come. So long as companies receive from government a protracted monopoly on the manufacture, use or sale of a product, the "public's health" is not safe.

The fact that Health and Human Services Secretary Tommy Thompson went ahead and asked Congress to suspend the patent on Cipro in the event that Bayer AG does not lower the price for its most powerful customer is neither here nor there. It tells us nothing substantive about the patent system, but it speaks volumes about the nature of government. It tells us that government can as easily revoke monopoly privileges as it can revoke genuine liberties. It tells us that when you make the law—just or unjust—you can also break it.

47. INTERMINAL MONOPOLY TURNS TERMINAL

March 29, 2001

What precisely do the activists mean when they contend that the intellectual property regime overseen by the WTO is disadvantaging underdeveloped nations? Do they mean that the arbitrarily determined 20-year exclusive patent monopoly granted to pharmaceutical companies is just dandy when implemented in rich countries, but that it suddenly sours when applied to the Third World? Is a change of geography and demographics enough to turn ostensibly legitimate property rights—for that is what patents are—into coercive tools? This seems unlikely, unless, of course, the rights in question are not legitimate rights.

Consider South Africa, the scene of the last patent imbroglio. Why is it that if a pharmaceutical company purchases a share in a condo in South Africa, its title in the land does not imperil the locals, not unless it incinerates toxic waste into the air, or causes some doyen of wealth distribution a fit of envy. Yet with a property title in a brand-name AIDS drug the company effectively acquires a lien on the rightful property of others, in this case, South Africans. The company can prohibit South African manufacturers from using their legitimately owned laboratories and equipment to make a replica of the drug.

Which is what has transpired: The government of South Africa enacted legislation to help deal with the AIDS crisis. The amendment, which was to allow parallel importing of and domestic production of generic AIDS drugs, was greeted with fury by the pharmaceutical kingpins. A court interdict initiated by the Pharmaceutical Manufacturers Association, which represents largely North American and West European pharmaceutical multinationals, soon stumped the legislation. South Africa was thrust into in legal battle with 39 drug companies.

South African firms, presumably, have not stolen their equipment. Neither have they trespassed or broken an entry to obtain the molecular combinations for AZT, 3TC or ddI. These are in the public domain (and most probably available on the Internet, where Prime Minister Thabo Mbeki apparently gets his conspiracy theories about AIDS). So why should South Africans be prohibited from making these drugs?

My friends at the Fraser Institute, a Canadian free market think tank, have adopted all manner of tautology in proclaiming that patents unequivocally deserve a property title. Such a title, which gives the owner "the exclusive right to control an invention or a productive process," also allows the patent holder to prohibit someone else from practicing the patent, even if he arrived at the invention independently, an exceedingly common occurrence among inventors.

According to the Institute, patents share with tangible property "the mutual quality of exclusivity in the eyes of the law." (See *Competitive Strategies for the Protection of IP*, 1999). Whether the institute's scholars appeal to convention or to the "evolutionary nature of rights," the argument amounts invariably to legal positivism: If the state evolved these rights, then they must be property rights. Or as Dr. Owen Lippert puts it, if they make all the right duck sounds, then patents—like tangible property—are property.

It is equally questionable to make appeals to the common law tradition in justifying patent rights. Patent is a creature of statute. Having derived its authority from the will of the legislature rather than judicial precedent, exclusive patent rights are not grounded in the common law. Rather, patent law is an excrescence of it, a lingering privilege given to Friends of the Crown, so to speak.

The *Washington Post* came closer to the truth when it surmised in an editorial that rich nations can simply afford to grant pharmaceutical companies near 20-year patents, even if lengthy patent rights mean high prices, because their citizens are able to afford the drugs they need.

Not so South Africa, where 20 percent of adults are infected with HIV, and where most live in poverty. For them, the patent protection conferred on the AIDS antiretroviral drugs, and produced by the likes of Merck and GlaxoSmithKline, Bristol-Myers Squibb, Boehringer-Ingelheim, and F. Hoffmann-La Roche, has grave repercussions.

Naturally, the lawyers for the drug companies deny that the case has anything to do with access to AIDS treatments. It centers, they claim, on bringing South Africa into compliance with international law and treaties regarding intellectual property rights. A tack to which the Fraser Institute is partial. In a recent issue of the *Fraser Forum*, Lee Gillespie-White sets out to demonstrate that less patent protection will not make AIDS drugs more available to Africans. Her information tells her that in other sub-Saharan countries where patent protection is absent, drug availability has not increased.

She has a point: removing patent protection may not always be a sufficient condition to alleviate the shortage of drugs in Africa. The blight of poverty, lack of infrastructure, despotic governments, and activist pressure hamper overall investment in the continent. The well-studied case of Brazil does, however, indicate that, while a lesser reverence for patents may not be a *sufficient* condition for the increased availability of antiretrovirals, it is probably a very *necessary* condition.

A 1996 bill that gave Brazilian generic manufacturers the go-ahead saw them marketing a combination of AZT and 3TC that sells for only $1.50 a day, compared to $18 a day in the U.S. A study by *Médecins Sans Frontières* found that the introduction of generic AIDS drugs in Brazil has meant that it now costs the same to treat 1000 patients there as it does to treat 552 in Thailand, where generic drugs are less available. Since 1996 mortality from AIDS in Brazil has dropped by 50 percent.

The generic jolt orchestrated by two leading Indian generic manufacturers in Africa (India does not recognize international patent laws) is certainly not part of the plan set out by central planners such as Gillespie-White, who prefer more western aid to Africa. First Cipla Ltd. of Bombay offered to sell to Africa a combination of three AIDS drugs for about 40 percent below the discounted price offered by the brand-name drug companies. Another Indian generic company, Hetero Drugs Ltd., jumped in, beating Cipla's discount with an unheard of $347 a year per patient. Aspen Pharmaceuticals, a local South African company, moved in, ready to begin distributing Hetero's drugs once the legalities were dispensed off.

The real free market cat was loose among the pigeons.

Merck responded hastily by committing to supply AIDS drugs to the developing world at cost; its new price on Crixivan, one of its powerful brand name protease-inhibitors, undercuts Hetero's considerably. So too has Bristol-Myers disavowed profits in Africa.

Brand-name companies are strategically choosing the battles they lose. They know that what governments give they can take away, and the pharmaceuticals would sooner sell at cost in Africa than risk their long-term patent privileges. If this strategy wins out over the right of the generic manufacturer, the market will have been shackled rather than freed; welfare will have displaced agency.

Following the slashing of drug prices in Africa by Merck and now Bristol-Myers, predictions of doom concerning a global price war among drug companies abounded in the financial press. Fearing, no doubt, that the loss of a captive market for patented drugs might deflate the stock value of brand-name companies, this press argued that a dangerous precedent was being set for the drug industry. Soon developing countries with only a small AIDS problem will demand the same prices, then other worthy afflictions will be added to the entitlement inventory, to be followed by the demand for equal treatment—and cheap drugs—for the well-off. The fear being that by capitulating to pressure, the price-slashing pharmaceutical companies will be writing off the entire developing world as a profitable market for AIDS and other research.

Slashing prices in Africa, however, is a response by the pharmaceutical industry not so much to market forces, but to the vilification of the industry by activists and the fear that governments (and the WTO) will lessen their commitment to enforcing patents. Remember that global government is also beholden to—and infiltrated by—powerful activists and NGOs. These interests mistakenly conflate the regime of patents with an unfettered pharmaceutical market. They blame the lack of access to AIDS medications in poor countries on market failure when nothing could be further from the truth: patents, of course, are inimical to the free market.

The meddling in the market by global governments like the United Nations (UN) and the European Union (EU) and their malignant offshoots, the WTO included, certainly does nothing to ease the situation. Not content with striving to "harmonize" labor, health and environmental laws the world over, the WTO, together with the World Intellectual Property Organization, has set its sights on homogenizing intellectual property regimes. Developing countries have been gulled into signing on and can face trade sanctions if they violate these agreements.

By enforcing the exclusivity of patents in international treaties under the guise of upholding a free market order, these centrist establishments are sustaining distorted, inflated drug prices. Patent policies seem especially incoherent in light of the fact that governments, in their drug benefit plans, are strong supporters of the cheaper generics, yet it is they who drive drug prices up by conferring patent monopolies in the first place.

In Article 31, the WTO's "Agreement on Trade-Related Aspects of Intellectual Property Rights" does devolve some power to signatory states by allowing the use of compulsory licenses of patents. Accordingly, the state may allow the use of patented material "without the authorization of the right holder." Compulsory licenses can help economically underdeveloped countries ward off the perils of patents, although they still require that the party practicing the patented method or product pay reasonable royalties. Bear in mind though that compulsory licenses are granted by governments as a contra-indication to their own meddling in the market, and are not a principled long-term solution to patent monopoly or to the proliferation of mercantilist World Planners.

How long before compulsory licenses are attenuated is anyone's guess. The Pharmaceutical Research and Manufacturers Association and the International Federation of Pharmaceutical Manufacturers Associations have been actively lobbying the United States and the EU trade officials to ban or restrict the use of compulsory licensing for medicines. An enthusiastic user of compulsory licensing domestically through eminent domain and anti-trust assaults, the U.S. government has been using considerable pressure to stop poorer countries—of late South Africa, Brazil and Thailand—from deploying this tool for pharmaceuticals.

Local initiatives like parallel imports, unless thwarted by our hegemonies, remain good free market tools. A free market, after all, means that entrepreneurs can shop around internationally for the best-priced drugs without checking with the patent holder first or capitulating to the WTO. If the U.S. gets its way, however, South Africa will be forced to repeal legislation allowing parallel imports, leaving her at the mercy of prices dictated by patent exclusivity rights.

Removing government-granted patent rights ought to go a long way toward defusing competing interests. At the very least, pharmaceutical companies may have to stop bedding down with governments—local and global—and, instead, seek their fortunes on the free market.

Utopia aside, there is life after patent. Eli Lilly has emerged from a stock depression, and is doing well after being stripped of three years worth of patent protection for Prozac. As is usually the case when patents are hard to protect, the company intensified its R&D efforts. The confidence it is generating is mirrored in a climbing share price.

Absent patent protection, companies can feasibly protect their investment and potential profits for a good number of years through trade secret and licensing arrangements. Profits generated by initial sales and other support services may still be very lucrative. Economist Fritz Machlup (in Moore, 1997) pointed out that "patent protection is unnecessary as an incentive for corporations in a competitive market to invest in the development of products and processes. The short-term advantage a company derives from developing a new product and being the first to put it on the market may be incentive enough."

48. TOKERS ARE TERRORISTS NOW

December 24, 2001

This is the age of bureaucratic free-association. The president stretches on a couch and his minions say "terrorism," prompting him to conjure from the recesses of his mind various loose connections to regions of the economy and to life in general, while suggesting a legislative "remedy."

To one Dr. Freud's invitation to free associate in response to the magic "terrorism" word, Mr. Bush blurts out "bailouts and handouts to business." "Come on," warns another excavator, "If you don't do better I'll get out the Rorschach test." "You know how you hate the scary inkblots." "Okay, okay," cowers the president, "How about we go after low-tax jurisdictions? Or, I know, I'll unleash DEA agents on infirm medicinal marijuana users." "I've got it, yes, yes," shouts the president, "anyone, but anyone who takes drugs is complicit in supporting terrorism."

When he sobers up, the president should come clean and tell Americans how, with drug prohibition, government subsidizes organized crime—including terrorism—the world over. The truth is that terrorists owe a debt of gratitude to governments for the solid financial base they enjoy.

The drug trade is indeed firmly linked to terrorism—the avails from the trade finance roughly 25 percent of the world's terrorist activity. But it is prohibition of drugs, which is the doing of governments, that is directly responsible for the excessive profits the drug trade yields. Had governments not outlawed these substances, profits would not be excessive and terrorists and organized crime would be forced to look elsewhere for a quick fix. The avails from drugs, moreover, would be much less likely to be funneled to unsavory causes if the trade were in the hands of legitimate, law-abiding businesses.

Ask any poverty-stricken Afghan farmer, and he will tell you that the production costs of common drugs are low. A poppy is not an orchid. Neither is cannabis a particularly fragile plant. These chemicals are derived from hardy plants. As with other illegal commodities, the price is pushed up by the high costs of circumventing government law, as well as by the reduced supply brought on by prohibition. The price of pure heroin for medicinal purposes is a fraction of its street price. The difference amounts to a state-subsidy for organized crime, al-Qaida included.

Allah's will notwithstanding, the Mad Mullahs had refrained from tampering with the flower that fed them, issuing no more than token bans on poppy cultivation. They even allowed narcotics refining to continue unabated. The Taliban's hands-off approach flowed from the importance of the drug trade to the financing of their exploits. In their precincts, the Northern Alliance also took no strident action against cultivation and trafficking.

In fact, the areas devoted to poppy cultivation in Afghanistan have more than quadrupled since 1990, which goes to show that someone is buying, and that curbing demand, the much-touted strategy in the prohibitionist's arsenal, is ineffective.

The urge to experiment with psychoactive drugs has and will always be with us, with the predictable result that demand-reducing initiatives in the West have met with a dismal failure. This enduring demand, coupled with exorbitant profits brought about due to outlawry, have caused poppy to displace wheat production in Afghanistan.

Afghanistan is the narcotics artery of the world—it cultivates 72 percent of the opium now circulating the illegal market and a good share of cannabis. Any attempts here to drastically reduce supply will reverberate the world over, resulting in rising opium prices. Not only will supply reduction be a boon for traffickers sitting on large stockpiles, but it will ensure that the potential profits induced by reduced supply bring a renewed influx of dealers into the trade.

American prohibition piety is incorporated into practically every U.S. international treaty. Since the jurisdiction of the U.S. now comfortably extends into Afghanistan—we can expect the crops of pretty Afghan poppies to be savaged by drug warriors. That intractable 1988 UN Drug Convention will be invoked and, like transcontinental locusts, the drug warlords from the International Narcotics Control Board will descend on Afghanistan.

The poppy fields might have been wrested from Taliban control, but the new Afghan government, prodded by U.S. and UN prohibition policies, will alight on the long-suffering people of Afghanistan and punish them if they ingest, inhale, inject or trade these substances. An Americanization of the drug dilemma in the region will mean that an already brutalized people will endure more suffering.

Legalization, however, will see prices plummet, inclining fewer pushers to enter the trade. Farmers will be more likely to turn to other crops, thus ameliorating the severe food shortages. In a country with a poor infrastructure, the "relatively stable value of opium and its nonperishability means that it can also serve as an important source of savings and investment among traders and cultivators," in the words of a U.S. State Department report.

Contrary to the report, it is not strictly true that drug production in—and trafficking from—Afghanistan is responsible for "increased levels of terrorism and drug-related violence in neighboring countries," or for corrupting local authorities—prohibition is.

Here's the correct sequence: First comes government, which declares arbitrarily that heroin use is potentially worse for individual and society than compulsive eating, bungee jumping, gambling, alcohol consumption, fatty foods or tobacco. It then proceeds to terrorize peaceable people, leaving it up to gangsters, whose market share is captured with guns, to satisfy demand.

Freedom and choice—not prohibition, incarcerations and coerced treatment—are the best salve for a people that has been infantilized for too long. Bring the rule of law to Afghanistan, but let the people grow poppies.

49. THEY'RE COMING FOR YOUR KIDS!

April 25, 2008

Imagine: One day you're frolicking in the open air on a large compound, doing your daily chores, and feasting on hearty homegrown fare; the next you're gagging on a diet of T&A courtesy

of MTV, and fast-food compliments of your fat foster mom. As the
makeshift mom hollers at you to swallow your zombifying meds—
the Texas foster care system is notorious for pumping its charges full
of psychotropic drugs—her flaccid live-in lover eyes you lustily.

As I write, many of the kids kidnapped by Texas rangers from the
Yearning for Zion ranch are being scattered across the state to far-
flung group homes and shelters. In the land of the free and home of
the brave hundreds of children can be rounded up and removed from
their families based on a hunch or a hoax. No hue and cry will
ensue—not from professional civil libertarians, nor from members
of the unwatchful dogs in the media, or from presidential candidates
vying to uphold—or is it just to hold—the Constitution.

How about it Hillary, Barack? Have you a message of hope for the
children seized from the sect known as the Fundamentalist Church of
Jesus Christ of Latter-Day Saints (FLDS)? Of course you don't.
During an election season it would take a village idiot to defend the
quaint idea of the autonomous family. To do that would involve an
implicit retreat from the position that children are first and foremost
wards of the state, and their parents nothing but low-level civil
servants who must obey the state's child-rearing directives, or else.

The-state-as-parent is a leftist legal doctrine that has been eagerly
embraced by the rigor-mortis riddled Right.

Whether they are "plural" or single, Wicca or just weird,
bohemian or bourgeoisie—parents should take the kids and
skedaddle when they hear that phrase "in the best interests of the
child." It is simply a license for the state to substitute its own
judgment for that of the parents. Today it's polygamist parents—
Kool-Aid drinkers is Bill O'Reilly's favored sobriquet. Tomorrow
it'll be the offspring of home-schoolers or global warming deniers.

The "Texas Department of Child Abduction," which writer
William N. Grigg "sometimes wittily refers to as the Department of
Protective and Family Services," acted on an anonymous call from a
shady character named Rozita Swinton. Rozita was released by the
Texas ruffians after being briefly detained. The innocent victims of

her mischief-making are being held indefinitely, separated from their mothers.

So how about it? Am I free to call the police anon, sic them on someone I dislike and then sit back and watch the show? Apparently so. At least in the kangaroo court of Judge Barbara L. Walther, for whom a tip from a complainant who never materialized constitutes probable cause.

The rules of evidence have been revised in post-constitutional America. If you thought that wrenching babes from their moms ought to be predicated on the testimony of a competent, credible witness, you were wrong. And you were utterly insane if you imagined the defendants ought to get to confront the witness against them in a trial before being punished.

That Sixth Amendment stuff is so yesterday.

In post-constitutional America the right to be free of unreasonable searches and seizures certainly no longer applies uniformly. Ditto due process. Creepy people, for whom the goons in government have been gunning, are as good as convicted criminals. In the case of the FLDS cult's kids, the burden of proof has been shifted from the state to its victims.

Rest assured, if these children have not yet been forced into premature sex, they most certainly will be once they hit the foster-care circuit. The nation's foster parents, bless them, are not known for being upstanding professionals who collect strays out of kindness. Fagin on welfare is more like it. The famed character from Charles Dickens' *Oliver Twist* also offered his young charges a "free meal" and "lodgings for nothing."

Nancy Grace (who pimped out her infant twins on TV) and O'Reilly have fulfilled their providential purpose in this case. Both self-styled child champions have been evangelizing for state overreach. I've given up on looking for clarity of thought among TV's tomfools. But whatever happened to compassion?

Children in foster care are more likely to be sexually and physically abused, even killed. I will say though, just to be "fair and

balanced," that only four children died in the care of the state of
Texas in 2006.

Whatever are your voyeuristic fantasies about the sex romps on a
polygamist commune, of this you can be certain: Relative to the
loose, licentious, libertine and precarious foster-care environment,
the children seized in the raid on the FLDS property have led a
sheltered, chaste life. The gravest abuse still awaits them.

Misplaced compassion is common in sentimental, sensation-
driven America. The country cried with Ellen DeGeneres as the
comedian slobbered on camera, and begged the "Mutts and Moms"
canine adoption agency to return to friends a terrier the agency had
removed.

Will no member of the American Idiocracy shed a tear for tots
torn from their loving mothers? I realize the FLDS females are
quaint, demure (not to mention slim and unslutty!), and don't
occupy pages on myspace.com. Still, have a heart, won't you?

50. DON'T TASE ME, BIG BRO

August 15, 2008

Baron "Scooter" Pikes had been confined, cuffed, and was non-
confrontational. There was no need to kill him. Nevertheless, Scott
Nugent, a Louisiana police officer, stunned Pikes repeatedly with a
Taser. The man was dead "before the last two 50,000-volt shocks
were delivered," surmised CNN. An autopsy revealed no evidence
of drug use in Pikes' system—he had been detained for possession.
Nugent was indicted this month on a charge of manslaughter.

The Taser X26, "once playfully dubbed the 'Thomas A. Swift
electric rifle' (after the exploits of the fictional Tom Swift, a teenage
inventor made famous in a series of juvenile adventure novels
published from 1910 to 1941)," has become a fixture in the
increasingly fractious interactions between the police and the people.
Tasers are now "fired more than 620 times a day and have been used

a total of more than 680,000 times worldwide." This, according to an exposé in the Institute of Electrical and Electronics Engineers' *Spectrum* magazine.

"Research by the Police Executive Research Forum has raised the concern that multiple activations of Tasers may increase the risk of death," cautions Sandra Upson in the *IEEE Spectrum*. Unlike medical devices, "Tasers don't have to undergo testing … at least not in the United States. Even if Tasers are proven to be entirely safe," Upson worries that "there's the bigger question of whether the stun guns encourage police brutality. A Taser shock leaves almost no visible scarring or bruising, as a clubbing or a beating typically would. Could the absence of physical scars lift a psychological restraint on officer behavior?"

Put it this way: When, as Matt Garfield of *The Herald* wrote, "a 75-year-old woman who refused to leave a nursing home where she had gone to visit an ailing friend" is stun gunned; or when a university student is shocked for aggressively quizzing his Highness Sen. John Kerry; or, when a 14-year-old harmless skateboarder is thrown to the ground and threatened by a pig of a policeman—abuse is afoot. When another three, even bigger, pigs hand over an 18-year-old high-school boy, arrested for speeding, to a group of feral felons, who then rape him to shreds—it is then that you know each one of us is in danger of becoming "the State's bitch."

Who can forget how "The Homeland Security State" came together in all its brutality to extinguish the life of the fragile Carol Anne Gotbaum? Gotbaum met her demise not in a Pakistani or Saudi airport, but in Phoenix's Sky Harbor. The petite 45-year-old, who weighed 105 pounds, became distraught—not dangerous—when she was detained at the airport and not permitted to proceed to her destination: an alcohol rehabilitation clinic in Tucson. Unhinged, Gotbaum took off down the concourse hollering. Was this unstable woman soothed by savvy PR professionals? Not on your life. Gotbaum was scrummed by meaty policemen, tackled to the ground, and a knee jabbed into her skinny spine. She was then thrown in a holding cell, where she was shackled and chained to a bench. Minutes later Carol Anne Gotbaum was dead. Her bruised body was autopsied and the police exonerated, naturally. Famous forensic pathologist Dr. Michael Baden said: "If she asphyxiated, someone else did it ... the most likely cause of death has to do with asphyxia and could be a result of too much pressure on her chest when they were putting on the handcuffs and the shackles."

In mitigation, it has been suggested that rampant displays of excessive force might be indicative of poor training. Somehow the sight of a burly brute standing over a helpless, slip of a woman screams sadism more than sloppy training.

"In the United States, about 670 people die each year under police restraint, according to the U.S. Department of Justice's Bureau of Justice Statistics," confirms the IEEE's Institute of Electrical and Electronics Engineers-United States of America Mark W. Kroll." These incidents include arrests and attempts to control an uncooperative person who needs medical assistance, as well as suicides after arrest. ... One study found that 100 percent of in-custody deaths involved the use of handcuffs."

Something has gotten into the country's lymphatic system—and the infection becomes most apparent in these street-level scuffles between the State and its subjects. We are, it would seem, witnessing a tipping point—an inversion in the existential preconditions for liberty, described by Thomas Jefferson thus: "When the people fear their government, there is tyranny; when the government fears the people, there is liberty."

51. 'MAD DOG' SNEDDON VS. MICHAEL JACKSON

July 5, 2005

Dan Abrams, MSNBC's top lawyer, assured the Jackson jurors that they had returned the right verdict. On the law, they were beyond reproach. He then proceeded to ream them out: "what do you think Michael Jackson was doing in bed with these kids? What would you do if a man in your neighborhood did the same (which is?)? Wouldn't you call the cops? Confess to being star-struck!

The jurors had dared to apply the law to the facts of the case; they refused to convict Jackson based on assumptions and inferences. And that enraged the chattering class—from jurists to journalists, from politicians to pundits. Even more preposterous—so preposterous it elicited unflattering comparisons to OJ's enablers—"the jurors failed to 'get past' the testimony of the accuser's mother and ... convict Jackson." In other words, the jury had the temerity to toss the testimony of a professional grifter and a liar. In so doing, they admirably fulfilled what remains of the institution's mandate: jurors are not supposed to "get past" the testimony of a swindler—or a family of them, for that matter.

In the majestic tradition of Anglo-Saxon law, juries were once trusted to forestall government tyranny. Thomas Jefferson considered "trial by jury as the only anchor ever yet imagined by man, by which a government can be held to the principles of its constitution." Lamentably, the Founders' Blackstonian view of the jury as a bulwark against government abuses has been supplanted by the notion of the law as an implement of government, to be utilized by all-knowing rulers for the "greater good."

Such Benthamism has allowed zealous prosecutors (and their graceless handmaidens) to discard a defendant's rights. Thomas Sneddon's nickname says a lot about the Santa Barbara DA's métier and mood. And "Mad Dog" definitely breached his prosecutorial obligations. Of his "Rights Of Englishmen" (due process, habeas corpus, the right to counsel; no crime without intent, no self incrimination, no retroactive law), Jackson was most egregiously deprived of a prosecutor who pursues truth and justice; tries the defendant in the courtroom, not in the media (as Sneddon did), makes sure there is strong evidence against the defendant before indicting him (Sneddon didn't); refrains from bringing the full power of government against an individual citizen, and avoids piling on charges as a means of gaining a conviction (ditto).

The DA kicked off the proceedings by depriving Jackson of a preliminary hearing. A preliminary hearing compels the prosecution to lay out the evidence—the basis of its case, if you will—to the satisfaction of a judge. "In California, prosecutors may initiate a criminal action either by filing a complaint, or by obtaining a grand jury indictment," explains FindLaw's Jonna M. Spilbor. "The overwhelming majority of felony cases in California are done by complaint." But once a grand jury indictment is filed, the defendant loses his right to a preliminary hearing, and, with it, the opportunity to prepare for trial.

Glaring discrepancies exist between the initial felony complaint and the indictment, chief of which is that the conspiracy count is conspicuously absent from the complaint. Was the count that carried the stiffest sentence conjured in the process of throwing at Jackson everything but the kitchen sink? Was conspiracy a "clever" prosecutorial afterthought? Or did the "complaining witnesses" suddenly "recall" they had been abducted and imprisoned at Neverland?

All of the above, it would seem. The accuser's mother, the key witness in the state's case, "remembered" late in the game that the family had been imprisoned in Neverland. Pesky things that they are, the facts, however, indicate that her kidnapping and "coerced confinement" included a trip to a beauty parlor, where she was depilated of bodily bristles; dental appointments, shopping sprees, and dinners out—all on Jackson's dime. By admitting this woman's testimony, Sneddon, then, suborned perjury. As to sonny's incarceration: the accuser testified he didn't want to leave, "Because I was having lots of fun."

Furthermore, the nature of the conspiracy must, by law, be described in the indictment (it isn't) and the co-conspirators named (they aren't). "Defendants need to know who they supposedly conspired with, and what they supposedly conspired to do—and to know it when the indictment is issued, not later," noted Spilbor.

Last I looked, *ex post facto* law was unconstitutional. But with Superior Court Judge Rodney Melville's blessing, a law was passed to allow Sneddon to parade Jackson's prior accusers into court. By admitting into evidence prior alleged acts committed by Jackson— acts never proven in a court of law—Sneddon hoped to demonstrate "Jackson's pattern of behavior." But, as FindLaw's Julie Hilden warned, "Evidence of prior criminal behavior that does not result in a conviction is a classic example of prejudicial evidence." Indeed, that Jackson paid off an accuser is no proof of his guilt, yet it was treated as such. Absent convictions, these charges ought to have been ruled inadmissible. In any event, who's to say that the housemaids (sons in tow) who mulcted Jackson of millions were not flaunting their preferred "pattern of behavior," extortion?

When it comes to popular and popularizing crusades like child sexual abuse, contemporary America has sustained the spirit of 1692 Salem. Merely accusing someone of sexually abusing a child is enough to strip him of his rights. And convictions can be obtained with no proof or evidence of guilt other than the word of the accuser. Thus it mattered not that the evidence in Jackson's case consisted solely of the say-so of a family of transients and tramps: the accuser's mother—and coach—is a felon in her own right. From welfare fraud she graduated to extortion, chiseling JCPenney of $150,000 for alleged... sex abuse (they paid. Does that mean they're guilty?). If a history of criminality was not sufficient to render Mrs. Arvizo unfit to testify in a court of law, the odd ideation she exhibited ought to have done the trick: Arvizo testified Jackson was going to eliminate her family by dispatching them in a hot air balloon!

Described as really smart and cunning, Arvizo's five-foot-seven, hirsute "child" (the accuser) was every bit as acquisitive (a shoplifter) and imaginative (a liar) as mom. He and his brother had helped buttress their mother's assorted bilking schemes. Or as a wise juror put it, the lad lied habitually because that's all he knew. That Jackson plied him with "Jesus Juice," and licked his forehead is something only the shakedown clan witnessed. The alleged molestation occurred, if to go by tiny's timeline, after Martin Bashir's devastating exposé ("Living with Michael Jackson") aired, and while the Los Angeles Department of Children and Family Services was searching Neverland, sicced on Jackson by busybody, Gloria Allred. A subsequent raid (carried out by 75 lawmen!) on Jackson's home produced some legal porn, proving only that, as weird as he is, Jackson's carnality, at least, is shared by millions of Americans.

Expecting a prosecutorial touchdown, *Countdown With Keith Olbermann* aired a rather cruel segment called "Prepping for the Pokey," in which the TV Talker pondered how Jackson would fit his prosthetic proboscis in jail. The only man (Jon Stewart disappointed) to have distinguished himself from the pack was Geraldo Rivera. The Fox News reporter conceded Jackson's conduct was creepy and said as much. But he understood that creepy is not necessarily criminal. Hooray for Geraldo.

And hooray for the twelve wise men and women who stood between Michael Jackson and a parlous prosecutor.

IV. Private Life on the Public Stage

52. ON SEXUAL BOMBAST AND BLISS

May 25, 2000

A surefire way to be labeled a desiccated dogmatist is to express some reservations about the way matters sexual are discussed in public forums. I never cease to recoil at the explicitness in the daily discourse diet, although one would sooner admit to being a member of the Hollow Earth Society than confess to being something of a prude. From *Friends* to *Fraser* to *Sex and the City*, it is *de rigueur* for these true-to-life characters to dilate on their sexual proclivities and practices with the same ease once reserved for discussing a lesser carnal refreshment like afternoon tea.

Turn to the printed media and you have the award-winning Christie Blatchford of the *National Post* briefing readers at every opportunity on how priapically deprived she is. Evidently as desperate, Ann Kingston, Blatchford's colleague, does not finesse her words either. Ms. Kingston went into raptures over the advent of a kind of mechanical female Viagra. "The Eros System," she promised, was sure to get women in the mood "to mambo." Ms. Kingston's excitement was tempered only by indignation over the fact that the device did not make front-page news (Hallelujah), for which, predictably, she blamed men. Although it is unclear why the always full-cocked male species would want to thwart her sexual pleasure.

Even more repelling than the prurience was Ms. Kingston's inability to interpret for her readers the statistical insignificance of the data behind the marketing gush: The glowing results that promised, according to this columnist, to make the device the unrequited woman's contraption of choice, were derived from a sample six woman strong!

The Vagina Monologues is a stage performance that has, for some time now, been the rage in the United States. Eve Ensler is the playwright responsible for these soliloquies from down under. Having been summarily dismissed by cultural critic Camille Paglia as possessing of "a dreary, pedestrian, unliterary mind," Ensler has yet to be laughed off the cultural stage. *Au contraire*: Ensler's claim that the survival of women as females hangs on her dialogue with "this much mumbled-about body part" is taken quite seriously.

The said enclave, of course, is not a "much mumbled-about body part"; it is much revered. Men, it has been observed, struggle to emerge therefrom and spend the rest of their days trying to resubmerge therein, a reality, admittedly, more filled with bathos than pathos. Granted that the mesmerizing power women have over men is lost on females like playwright Ensler, but does she of the asinine genital-speak not realize that some things are best left veiled and mysterious? Women of her ilk are first to holler about the objectification of their sex, yet are complicit in ensuring that the act itself suffers the very same fate: sex is being reified; made an object, a fashionable accessory, a part of a healthy life-style, or the bulwark of some imaginary emancipation.

In an orifice, I suggest, women like Ms. Ensler have found a suitable interlocutor. The rest of us gain nothing from such uncouth conversation. If anything, this sort of self-aggrandizing obsession is bound to increase the prevalence of sexual dysfunction.

From Viktor E. Frankl, the leader of the Third Viennese School of Psychotherapy, comes real insight into achieving sexual bliss. The concept of "hyper-intention" originated by Frankl explains why those who buy into the sexual bombast, the public posturing and the exhibitionism, may be left high and dry. Try as they may, individuals who make achieving sexual gratification "the object of intention and attention" are doomed to fail. In the achingly beautiful book *Man's Search for Meaning*, Frankl explains that "pleasure is, and must remain, a side effect or by-product" of a relationship. It will evade those who make it a goal in itself. "Sex is justified, even sanctified, as soon as, but only as long as, it is a vehicle of love," writes Frankl.

All these sexual loudmouths front and center, including our withered, national, sex tele-educators—Sue Johansen of the *Sunday Night Sex Show* springs to mind—deflect from the partnership that should come with sexual satisfaction, and diminish, denude, and reduce the act to no more than friction.

53. THE IMPORTANCE OF BOUNDARIES

August 14, 2002

The Public Diary

Not all bloggers (keepers of a web log) are self-aggrandizing. Some do offer a thoughtful, well-written and ego-unencumbered web diary. The blogging process does, however, seem emblematic of the blurring of boundaries in the culture, certainly those between what is private and what is public. In years of yore, a daily diary was considered private, and not only because it was intended for secrets. Keeping a diary implied that there was a demarcation between what a person shared with the world and what he kept to himself. For the cultural conservative, such distinctions have meaning.

A state of flux between the private and public is not part of a cultural conservative worldview, but is in keeping with a liberal libertine outlook. Whereas some utterances were kept for the diary because they were sexually or emotionally charged, others remained clandestine because they were manifestly trivial. Either way, good taste combined with humility to make the diary a closeted thing. The closet, sadly, has come to signify oppression, not discretion. The upshot of populism in punditry, at least, is that bad commentary is promiscuously outed—few and far between are the commentators and conversationalists who have honed their craft.

Libertarian writer Virginia Postrel appears to confer the web-diary with a mystic, cosmic rhythm, calling it "one of the most interesting new spontaneous orders in the world of the Web." In as much as it fails to speak of the individual person as the source and initiator of this woolly wonderment, "spontaneous order," despite its Hayekian pedigree, is a collectivist metaphor. It has little of the Misesian or Randian emphasis on the purposeful, conscious, and rational nature of individual human action. This is reflected in the blogger phenomenon. The fact that millions of people are moved to mouth daily on the web is no more significant to freedom than the fact that billions of humans have a bowel movement every day.

Chances are that if you are of the up and coming blognoscenti, a part of you believes that your impromptu daily thoughts ought to be public. Chances are you are not terribly concerned that, of the cyberspace ejaculate you emit, stuff will come back to haunt you like a nasty paternity suit.

Public Indecency

Hardly a dog of a commentator missed the opportunity to lift his leg in protest against Anna Nicole Smith and her reality show. Smith is indeed a wall of trashy flesh. Even her dog is lewd and repulsive, but she is so obviously vulgar that hyperbolic attacks on her are not worth a straw. More disturbing is the specter of girls who, in quick succession, grant an MSNBC-TV interview, after being abducted and raped. More unsettling than Smith is the mother of a slain and raped tiny girl, out and about on *Larry King Live*, a week after her child's dreadful demise. There is nothing these people will not say and express in public. They have no private selves.

More warped than the blatantly freaky Smith is the spectacle of mass contagion, where members of the public turn into professional mourners, flocking to funeral happenings for victims they never knew. Like "spontaneous order" or achievement, neither is grief a tribal affair. Communities don't grieve; individuals who incur loss do. These phony displays among regular folks are at the root of our festering cultural commons. Professional pornographers like Smith are just a sideshow.

Crossover Kids

Permissive liberals and people who need Braille to understand a well-aimed barb will fume at the words of author Florence King: "...children have no business expressing opinions on anything except, 'Do you have enough room in the toes?'" But true-blue cultural conservatism puts a premium on the proper boundaries between children and adults. Such boundaries are essential to the moral hygiene of a society. It is from the progressive, libertine parent that we would expect a child of such narcissism and precocity that he or she thinks of adults as his peers, and takes to preaching to his elders.

But no, some of the most hubris-stricken kids are emerging as commentators from so-called conservative quarters. The real cultural conservative knows that even in the unlikely case that the child is the new H.L. Mencken, and is smarter than all the adults around him, respect necessitates that he bide his time. Even the intellectually gifted take years to synthesize intellectual material and make it their own. This process is a culmination of insight, life experience, humility, and authentic intelligence.

The cultural conservative adult who lets a kid be a pal and peer is a liberal. He cannot claim to be a cultural conservative. He must, moreover, own up to being mired in self-contradiction. Writing on the topic of Western Civilization, historian Alan Charles Kors reminds us that avoiding self-contradiction is the touchstone of truth—being mired in self-contradiction, the touchstone of error. To the Greek philosophers, to be mired in self-contradiction was to be "less than human, less than coherent, less than sane."

54. TOO BAD, MRS. TOOGOOD, WE'RE TAKING YOUR KIDS

October 2, 2002

Had I been caught on camera administering an admittedly vigorous hiding to my daughter, my first instinct would be to flee much like Madelyne Gorman Toogood did. Toogood's unflattering film debut was broadcast repeatedly nationwide. To flush her out, trumped-up charges were brought against her sister, who was taken into custody and held for three days.

Toogood relates how she was afraid to surrender because she feared, justifiably, that the law would remove the children. "I left with my other two children and flew to my mother," she explained. Anchorwoman Paula Zahn donned an inquisitor's cap on her severe, helmet-shaped hairdo: "You obviously changed your hair color," she interrogated Toogood. "Were you trying to avoid being caught?" Well, duh.

The power that allows the state with impunity to usurp the parents as the primary agent in the lives of children is the judicial doctrine of the state as *parens patriae*. Knowing that the state has the right to kidnap my child and replace me as a parent, without much ado, might also have me scampering for dear life, my daughter in tow.

Toogood is a member of the migrant community of Irish Travelers. That, and her lack of penchant for self-pity and psychobabble, did not bode well with the media. (I wonder how they would spin it if she were a Mexican migrant.) When she emerged from hiding, Toogood was so obviously overcome with sorrow—for her child, not for herself: "My baby is with people she doesn't know...my little girl is probably terrified now, please give her to someone she knows," Toogood pleaded, relating how little Martha, whom doctors have pronounced unblemished and in perfect health, is accustomed to snuggling in mom's bed nightly. Just the kind of idiosyncrasies I'd be agonizing over. (The thought of possible sexual abuse, the incidence of which is increased in state care, would have been enough to drive me to distraction.)

The assorted execrable commentators, however, nonchalantly spoke about the need to *place* Martha with a loving family. In most situations and despite human fallibility, children love and need their parents more than anything, and vice versa. Does the state or its intellectual bootlickers in the media and therapeutic community believe that a child can be jettisoned into a new family and habituate to it like a hamster or a dog? Who loves a child more than a parent?

The same anchors and experts, whose vigorous defense of child killer Andrea Yates began while Yates was still rounding up the kids for their deadly dip, and who tirelessly promoted Yates' imaginary disease—the same people who daintily avoided describing the gruesome Medea-like savagery Yates inflicted on her children— were merciless about Toogood: "What kind of a monster would do what Toogood did?" And "have we stumbled on a career criminal," they gobbled.

Pinko liberals almost always plump for the state, but get-tough-on-crime so-called conservatives are not much better. First, they fail to understand that the law must protect people from—not subjugate them to—the formidable power of the state. Mock conservatives also ignore the vital role the family plays in countervailing the power of the state, as are they oblivious to the demise of the once-implicit right of parents to raise their children free from undue intervention from the state.

Commenting on the American conservatives' embracing of the liberal "children's rights" movement, Kenneth Anderson discusses how this movement has aimed "to break down the autonomous family into children on the one hand, who are ultimately wards of the state, and parents on the other hand, who are regarded as something like low-level civil servants raising children according to the state's therapeutic directives." The "best interest of the child" standard, notes Anderson, is simply a license for the state to substitute its own judgment for that of the parents.

The behavioral "scientists," who adjudicate the "best interest of the child," are invariably proponents of anti-authority, progressive, child-centered upbringing. Precisely the kind of upbringing that churns out narcissistic, indulged, ignorant, and violent youth who—thank heavens—have robust self-esteems.

With the mother now effectively removed from the family and disallowed unsupervised visits with her children, the Toogoods have been forced to reside separately. If it means getting Martha back, they say they will even consider separation. If the family breaks up, the children will be more likely to suffer poverty, delinquency, drug and alcohol abuse, academic failure, and violent crime, to say nothing of commencing a life of on-and-off welfare dependence. A now-independent family unit could, because of the actions of the state, become dependent on it. Big Bully will have rendered asunder a once intact—if imperfect—family.

55. PARENTS' RIGHTS SCORE SMALL WIN IN LARGER BATTLE

September 28, 2000

The case of the contested use in a British Columbian school district of children's books depicting same-sex relationships wended its way through the courts, culminating finally in the B.C. Supreme Court's muted nod to parental rights.

First was the decision of the Surrey School Board of Trustees to prohibit the use of the books as a learning resource. A host of special interests then decried this as a book ban, taking the matter up as a constitutional challenge. The lower court responded with an argument oh so familiar to Americans: It accused the trustees of using a religious framework in their deliberations. While not quite conceding that the lower court's decision was tantamount to thought control, the Appeal Court affirmed the primacy of parents in the education of the child and, small mercies, the right of people to consult their conscience, even when "marred" by religion.

The issue, however, has only ever been about the frittering away by advocacy groups of the freedoms of a local authority and its constituency. The trustees had faithfully represented the Surrey parents, most of whom wanted to be left to impart their own beliefs about the issue of same-sex families to their tots. The Media's inability to articulate this only compounded the outrage.

In her column, the *Vancouver Sun's* Paula Brook liberally bandies about the book ban accusation, the kind of imprecise thinking that fudges issues and does nothing to prevent the trampling of liberties. Ms. Brook claims that the trustees aimed to purge the books from the District. How they intended to carry out this dastardly deed isn't clear. Was it to be by book burning? Perhaps interception at the borders? A search from door to door, maybe?

The books have always been available in the libraries. What fell within the legitimate purview of the trustees was to guard parental jurisdiction by deciding to keep the classroom free of perceived advocacy. The books were also deemed incompatible with the cognitive and emotional readiness of small children.

To the trustees Ms. Brook capriciously imputes the sinister intention of expunging the books from the District. To the complainant, teacher and gay-activist James Chamberlain, however, she ascribes only the purest of motives. Had he not been swept up in the fight against the forces of darkness, Chamberlain, who instigated the litigation, would have consulted parents, promises Ms. Brook.

Had he indeed listened, Mr. Chamberlain would have heard loud and clear what the trustees told him. Missing from Ms. Brook's account is a news item about a mother whose son was taught by this cherubic gay activist. The mom, an avid volunteer in the class, knew of Chamberlain's sexual orientation, which was immaterial until she saw him on the public broadcaster, where he claimed to have discussed homosexuality with his small charges. Mom then requested a transfer for her child. Did Mr. Chamberlain respect her right as a parent? Not on your life. He ran to an arbitrator. Spared denazification, the mother was still forced into all kinds of humiliation.

Come hell or high water the litigious activist was intent on forcing others to comply with his views. This real danger evades Ms. Brook, who quotes with approval a threat to fire the elected board, made by the education minister of one of the most corrupt and autocratic governments in Canada.

The case typifies the potential for roiling conflict in a public school monopoly that admits of a narrow range of opinion, and cannot satisfy the myriad pedagogic needs in the community. It also showcases how special interests attempt to manipulate the Canadian Charter-besieged courts to override decision-making in local authorities.

The Surrey school trustees are more likely to be mirroring the wishes of local parents than the Gay and Lesbian Educators of B.C., the inbred Teacher's Federation, or the Civil Liberties Association, which seemingly can't discern a book ban from a legitimate exercise of curricular discretion.

The various interests in these and similar cases in the United States advance an obtuse argument designed to diminish dissenting speech: Accepting such books as a resource in schools they equate with a constitutional imperative against discrimination—a fight against a "Charter stomping trend," as Ms. Brook inveighs. Again: utter nonsense. Schools should try teaching instead of pushing the day's dominant doxology. Real knowledge and facts are always more enlightening than propaganda. Knowledge, not politically correct pap, contains the acid with which to dissolve both propaganda and prejudice.

56. ONE DAD, TWO DADS, AND OTHER FAIRY TALES

May 10, 2001

For parents thinking of introducing their kindergarten-aged children to the topic of same-sex families, a couple of book reviews might be helpful.

Asha's Mums, One Dad, Two Dads, Brown Dad, Blue Dads, and *Daddy's Roommate*, are unadulterated advocacy. Scant wonder the books are turgid and cannot be pried from their pitch i.e., that same-sex families are just groovy. What's particularly unforgivable about this pamphleteering is that it leaves children out in the cold. The upbeat little tykes in the books are simply parroting the advocates.

Asha's Mums is the silliest of the three. It tells a completely contrived tale. The two authors must have racked their unsupple minds to come up with a plot that would show the perils from a hostile world to a child with two moms. Since these perils are few, our authors concocted a story that doesn't gel.

Asha is excited over an impending trip to the Science Center. All that changes when the "homophobic" teacher calls on the child to explain why her permission slip sports the signatures of two mothers. You can, after all, only have one mother, reasons the teacher. When the poor child vows never to go back to school, Mom One (Alice) materializes in a flash to upbraid the oppressive pedagogue.

In yet another scene designed to push buttons, Asha's sunny painting of her family, depicting the two moms, initiates a discussion in class. And what would such a discussion be without the progeny of the prototype bigoted parents piping up? "My mom and dad said you can't have two mothers living together…it's bad." No sooner do the angelic kids silence the voice of the dissenting rube rascal than mommies Sara and Alice swoop down to ensure that opinion about same-sex parents remains monolithic. Yes, to sexual diversity, no, to diversity—and freedom—of opinion.

With teacher on the straight and narrow, all are primed for one last lesson. You can have two mommies "just like you can have two aunts and two daddies." It's never too late to start teaching the lessons of moral and intellectual equivalence: everything is the same; no one thing is better or preferable. Judgment must be suspended at all times.

This tale is, of course, a series of sensibility tweaks. Nothing in the permission-slips my daughter brought home over the years ever said, "All sexual partners in the household sign on the dotted line." What's generally requested is a signature of a single parent or a guardian.

Further, unless I don't get the birds and the bees, Asha was conceived with the aid of a man. Whether Asha is a product of artificial insemination, adoption or shotgun, somewhere a man exists with half of her DNA. He might be a deadbeat dad or just a sperm donor. He may even be a poor sod toiling to send The Moms maintenance while they remain mum about him. In this story he has, however, been silenced.

Straining at the seams with condescension, *One Dad, Two Dads, Brown Dad, Blue Dads* is dedicated to "Jacob, who has only one mom and one dad," but doesn't need your sympathy, "because they're both pretty great parents." This bit of comedy lays bare just how indifferent the story is to what children want. Can you honestly imagine a child jumping up and down demanding an extra dad "just like Lou has?" The story has been compared to Dr. Seuss. It shouldn't. *One Dad, Two Dads* lacks Dr. Seuss's delicious sense of the absurd, the kind that tickles kids pink. Absent indoctrination, kids will detect this imposter.

The book starts with a little guy telling of the domestic bliss that comes with having two blue dads. Code Blue is an unfortunate metaphor for gay: the dads are said to be the same as every other non-hypothermic dad except for their hue. How did they get this way? "They were blue when I got them." And that's okay because it seems reasonable to assume that people are born to their sexual orientation. But then comes the clincher: "They are blue because…they are blue. And I think they're wonders—don't you?" It is one thing to suggest the dads were simply born blue, but quite another to declare them wonders by virtue of their tinge. Why impart to children that the value of a person is a function of his sexual orientation? People are wonderful because of their character; because of what they do, not because of whom they bed.

Toward the end, the pigmentally checkered dads begin to multiply and some green dads appear on the scene. Like Oscar Wilde's signature carnation, green is a good deal more festive. However, more than anyone, Wilde, who is often appropriated by the gay community, would have found the attempt to define the Self in terms of sexual preference insulting. After all, the great wit's most favorite organ was still his brain.

Belinda's Bouquet is more honest. One can sense the writer's attempt to adopt a child's perspective. The book does candidly speak to differences. The only hint of the same-sex burden is that the two mothers are the ones who strategically dispense the nuggets of wisdom. If I wanted to be difficult, I might ask why "mama" teaches poor chubby Belinda to chant, "My body belongs to me," every time someone comments about her weight. Wouldn't "Mind your own business," or "You're no oil painting," have been more effective? But one can't hope to divine every bit of feminist affectation.

The themes of adult selfishness, divorce, and same-sex union converge in *Daddy's Roommate*. Published by Alyson Wonderland publications, this story is particularly sad. The little narrator here has no name! This isn't surprising, since children in these books exist to affirm their parents. What's alarming is that educators, who usually stand firm behind these books, and who routinely tout the self-esteem catechism in schools, overlooked the sagging sense of self exhibited by the child in this book.

The nameless narrator tells us his parents have just divorced. With nary a reference to the sadness of the event, he blurts out: "Now there's somebody new at Daddy's house. Daddy and his roommate Frank live together, work together, eat together, sleep together." From here on in it's pretty much *Brown Dad, Blue Dads* all

over again, detailing the good times the dwarfed child spends with
the two larger-than-life men.

Mommy, like the child, is a conduit in the service of the men's
outing. She tells no-name boy that Daddy and Frank are gay and that
"being gay is just another kind of love." "Daddy and his roommate
are very happy together," chants the child, "and I am happy too!" So
long as Dad has found his true self, so will the boy arrange his
feelings accordingly. It's a cruel farce that has a child spouting
homilies in the service of a parent's project.

What would I have considered an honest narrative? "My name is
Ben. I am very sad. My mom and dad are divorcing. Frank is my
dad's new friend. My mom and dad held me tight. I told them I
wanted my old life back and I cried."

57. THREE-STEP PROGRAM TO MORAL
UNACCOUNTABILITY

April 27, 2000

The anatomy of violence in schools runs like this: First, a loser,
who enjoys all the trappings of middle class life—including parental
unconditional approval—and who has no self control, decides to
expand his sphere of misery. The latest prototype in Canada was an
infelicitous 15-year-old boy, referred to occasionally as "Felicity,"
from Orleans, Ontario, who went darting about Cairine Wilson
High, plunging a knife into fellow students.

Next, as was the case in the Columbine affair and in other
incidents around the United States, his compatriots, the children,
commence the ritualistic, exculpatory rhetoric, taught to them by
progressive educators and liberal parents. As one automaton
parroted: "He was poked at and made fun of—the kids in Columbine
felt neglected until their deaths." In a word, the perpetrator, who
suffered from acne, buckled under the psychic pain of overactive
sebaceous glands.

Having been played for all it's worth, the-culture-of-violence causal factor has given way to the more in-vogue bullying theory, so that when the mental health mavens appear on the scene, the narrative expands some to include the popular psychological explanations of how an essentially tender soul was pushed to attempt murder.

The haunting Janice Ian 1970s song "Seventeen" could never have been written today. Because, while skin-deep qualities have always determined the pecking order in schools, angry teenagers nowadays are less inclined to ruminate about their angst, and more likely to act on it. Social justice, they are taught, pivots on redistribution. And redistribution is achieved by making some pay for the lesser fortunes of others. When a youngster is taught to reject the harsh reality of inequality, of not having everything he covets—the anger of entitlement easily bubbles to the fore. Be it popularity or pulchritude, the youth has a sense that someone ought to pay for the pain of his being without.

Furthermore, where once kids might have seen dignity in a brave and stoic face, now, their mentors have declared these to be pathologies, symptoms of repression and denial. Is it any wonder that some youngsters—the bad ones, at least—feel that the culture of share-your-feelings-with-the-group gives them permission to take the rage of entitlement to its deadly conclusion?

Having turned the perpetrator into a *cause célèbre,* society exonerates the youth and his parents from responsibility. In Hillary Clinton's own preferred idiom, "It Takes a Village," and we must all share the blame. Replacing individual with collective responsibility is vital in the grand scheme of things, because blaming *everyone* is like blaming *no one.*

By incorporating rather than expelling the offender from its moral midst, the community further blurs the lines between innocent and guilty, good and bad. This fudging serves to suspend these occurrences in an ethical limbo and make them sufficiently ambiguous to the future offender.

The cry then goes out for more focus groups to educate about bullying and to plump fragile egos. Research, however, indicates that "aggression is more frequently associated with positive self appraisals than with low self-esteem." In her 1997 monograph on Posttraumatic Stress Disorder, Professor Marilyn Bowman points out that, while "every kind of social problem is analyzed as the outgrowth of low self-esteem," and while "treatment programs to teach people how to love themselves are put forward as the means of raising self-esteem," not only is "the relationship between emotion and well being not robust, causal or meaningful," but, on the contrary, there is a dark side to self-esteem. "The prototype aggressor," explains Bowman, "is a man whose self-appraisal is unrealistically positive." Like all efforts to drum up ignorance, this one can be dangerous.

Finally, in order to sustain this self-reverential and self-referential world, and to ensure that, in the words of Allan Bloom, the only enemy that remains is "the man who is not open to everything," the communal will makes one last gesture. Said a pastor on the scene of the stabbing: "You've got to totally accept him, totally forgive him." As in Columbine and Taber before it, a community now prepares to bestow instant forgiveness. People can now begin to speak of being on the mend. Everyone "moves on," until the next time, that is.

58. FAULTING NO-FAULT FORGIVENESS

May 14, 1999

Shortly after the victims of the schoolyard snipers in Littleton, Colorado, and Taber, Alberta, were laid to rest, members of the community, or at least those members that routinely present themselves to the media, indicated their readiness to forgive the murderers.

The spasms of no-fault forgiveness, however, are more a distillation of the mass culture than a reflection of any real religious sensibility. In Littleton, Colorado, the first sign of people adrift in a moral twilight zone was the erection, by a local carpenter, of two symbolic crosses for the killers alongside their victims. "They too had a mom and a dad," preached the carpenter, as if the fact that these sociopaths were born of man and woman entitled them to share a moral plateau with their victims.

The father of a murdered boy, who promptly uprooted and destroyed the crosses raised in memory of the teenage gunmen, was clearly not the hero of this particular news story. The real heroes were the bevy of fresh-faced youths and the adults accompanying them who, following the carpenter's example, spoke of forgiveness. The rationale for instant clemency? "Like, the killers were victims too," and the ubiquitous chant, "We all need to heal."

If in Littleton the killers were embraced, in Taber the moral tempo was no different. Tempered by Canadian gentility, the atmosphere was muted but it bore the same stark elements of moral deconstruction. Close friends of the 14-year-old boy charged in the fatal shooting of a fellow student swore fealty to their friend, and expressed the view that the bullying their murdering friend endured was a license to kill. Their sentiments were reiterated by the poor Reverend Dale Lang, whose son Jason died at the hands of the killer.

In so charitably forgiving and embracing killers, well-meaning individuals and clergy are not only supplanting the power of the God whose mercy they claim to represent, but are showing religious doctrinal failure. "The Jewish perspective pivots on the 'passion for justice,' wrote my father, Rabbi B. Isaacson, in *The International Jewish Encyclopedia*. "Justice always precedes and is a perquisite for mercy..."

This is extremely lucid, because mercy without justice is no mercy at all. By forgiving a killer before he has made amends and paid for his crime, injustice is done to the victim, to society, and inadvertently to the killer for whom redemption can be achieved only by facing the consequences of his actions. If punishment is a declaration of those values we wish to uphold, then to place the memory of a killer posthumously on the same moral plane as his victim is to imperil such values—with each easy act of forgiveness, the sanctity of life is diminished and murder becomes a little less abhorrent.

A Jew is not obliged to forgive a transgressor unless that transgressor has ceased his harmful actions, compensated the victim for damages, and asked for forgiveness. This is both ethically elegant and psychologically smart. It makes the process of asking for and extending forgiveness meaningful, lending it social force. It also upholds the notion of right and wrong. Further, it doesn't mandate the incongruous emotion of compassion for someone who has murdered, raped or committed some other heinous act. One can forgive but one is not obligated to. One is, however, obliged to seek justice.

In their "Orthodoxy" column, Ted and Virginia Byfield of the *Report Newsmagazine* implied that the Christian doctrine is very similar to the Jewish one. Instant expiation flows more from the values of the 1960s than from any doctrinal Christian values, say the couple. Christian forgiveness is thus contingent on the sinner's repentance, and can be granted only by the one sinned against, and not by the various proxies of popularity. "The corollary of the current" practice of minute-made forgiveness is that "it not only abolishes the necessity of repentance; it abolishes sin itself."

Another distinction that has been blissfully botched is the one between private and communal grief. Entire communities are said to be gripped by paroxysms of pain. But can anyone claim to know what is meant by "letting the community grieve and get on with the healing process"? Diana's death gave a peek into the contagion of grief that convulsed the world. Was it genuine? If the showing at her memorial a year later was any indication, then no, it wasn't.

Members of the Taber and Colorado communities can legitimately lay claim to the insecurity that comes with a loss of a previous sense of certitude about the adolescents in their midst. Otherwise, the tribal spectacle of people not directly affected by a tragedy, yet performing rites that should be reserved exclusively for the bereaved is warped and disingenuous.

Members of the community might be shocked, reeling, but the families of the dead alone are grief-stricken. For the family that has lost a child, every day that dawns brings the kind of pain most of us will never know. Members of the community should relinquish their fake grieving process and cook a meal, do the laundry, or simply sit in silence with those whose sorrow is beyond comprehension. That done, they should fade into the background.

59. THE MIDDLE-CLASS FAMILY FROM HELL

January 6, 2000

One truth that has pride of place in the progressive pantheon is that the traditional family is a source of oppression for women and children. Women and children, however, are less likely than ever to have to endure the confines of family. According to author Danielle Crittenden, women today are more likely to be divorced, never married, or to bear children out of wedlock.

Unencumbered by the oppressive effects of marriage, women are also more likely to be poor and to suffer from addictions and sexually transmitted diseases. And their children, a third of whom are being "raised in households headed only by a mother," are paying the price for this emancipation. These children have higher dropout, addiction and crime rates, and are more likely to live in poverty.

Having survived the perils of slavery, the black family, in particular, was still going strong until the 1930s. Then the Welfare State took over and the rest is history. The black American family as a social unit has, to all intents and purposes, been decimated.

What remains of the unit that was once the transmitter of values in society cannot possibly pose a threat to its enemies. Depicted so delightfully in the film *A Christmas Story*, the traditional family has metamorphosed into what Charles Sykes calls the "Therapeutic Family." Having "adjusted itself to the new demands of the social contract with the Self," explains Sykes in *A Nation of Victims,* the modern family has ceased to inculcate values. Instead, it exists exclusively for the ostensible unleashing of "self-expression and creativity" in its members.

The Canadian Broadcasting Corp., always a diligent underwriter of all forms of cohabitation that deviate from the traditional family, must have slipped up when it screened *A Christmas Story*. The film, set in the 1950s, depicts a series of family vignettes through the eyes of nine-year-old Ralphie, who, for Christmas, yearns for that gift of all gifts, the BB gun.

Mother is a homemaker, father is a regular working stiff, and between them they have no repertoire of psychobabble to rub together. No one implores Ralphie to express his feelings, or engage in any form of abreaction. In fact, he is urged to show restraint and is disciplined when naughty. But he sure is not put on Ritalin for daydreaming in class, nor is he diverted into life skills and anger management curricula when he gets into a fistfight. Despite the dearth of therapeutic comfort-speak in his life, Ralphie is a happy little boy.

Perhaps the first to have helped conflate the values of the middle-class bourgeois family with pathological authoritarianism was psychologist Theodor Adorno. Certainly, the literal punishment Ralphie receives for uttering the "F" word, and the ubiquitous reminders he gets of starving children when he refuses his food, fail every New Age psychological commandment. By today's parenting standards, Ralphie would be doomed to an emotional abyss.

Progressives can rest assured: This *bête noire* of a family, with its oppressed mother, therapeutically challenged father, and firm discipline, is being reined in. The Canadian Charter of Rights and Freedoms, which has trounced the Bill of Rights on issues of human rights, has deleted reference to the family. Coupled with the omission of any mention of the family, the Charter includes "age as a prohibited ground for discrimination." With this, writes lawyer Cindy Silver of the Center for Renewal in Public Policy, the Charter "effectively changed the constitutional status of children to one of prima facie equality with adults."

The American Founders intended for the family to be left untouched as "the major source of an orderly and free society," says Dr. Allan Carlson. The judicial trend of the state as *parens patriae* soon saw the family usurped as the primary socialization agent, with a statist ideology ushering in the public school system and compulsory education. The Welfare State and the Supreme Court's radical interpretations as to what constitutes a family and marriage practically dismantled what was once the economic and social backbone of American society. Contemporary America is a society plagued by familial fragmentation, sky-high divorce rates, illegitimacy, and the attendant delinquency—juvenile crime, drug abuse, and illiteracy.

The legacy of the Adorno construct has been carried over into the United Nations Convention on the Rights of the Child. Here too the consensus among rights advocates is that, due to its authoritarian structure, the traditional family is oppressive to women and children. "The solution," explains Silver, "has been for the State to shift the balance in the parent-child relationship through policies that would define and limit the power of the parent while increasing the power of the child."

The state has supplanted family autonomy and parental rights, and kids have paid the price. Yet despite what the state has done to nurture the "Hitler Youth" movement, children still place family above all else. In an exercise undertaken by Elections Canada some years back, an overwhelming number of them expressed a yearning for Ralphie's family. Lucky is the little boy who has such a family. Luckier still is the little boy who has both such a family and...a BB gun.

60. WOMEN WHO WED THE WRONG WAHHABI

May 21, 2003

Just when I thought American victim politics could metastasize no further, Pat Roush appears on the scene. Talk about making the personal political. Roush, a woman whose personal errors have resulted in an international political incident, is asking President Bush to intensify the pressure on Saudi Arabia to rectify the marital mistakes of other American women. She describes her constituents as women who

> ...have married Saudi nationals who were sent to the United States to study in our colleges and universities. Once they accompanied their Saudi husbands back to Saudi Arabia, they soon found out that they lost all civil rights and became prisoners. Their children fall into that same category of slavery and are denied even the basic human rights.

Despite the use of a highly charged word like "slavery," the women she describes were not coerced into wedlock. They were not gulled into romantic entanglements with Saudi men; they entered into the relationships willingly. Like most self-indulgent American females, the women were probably just following their highest calling—their hormones.

Saudi Arabians are adherents of the strictest form of Islam, Wahhabism, which is as austere as the religion the Taliban practiced. A woman who takes up with a man, especially a Wahhabi Muslim, is ultimately responsible for investigating the type of belief system he espouses. What did these gals think he was doing each time he took out the prayer mat and faced Mecca? Yoga? Did they not give a dried camel's hump when their men let slip with the inevitable insult to Christians, Jews or non-Wahhabi Muslims?

The alternative and more likely explanation is that the women simply chose to believe that they'd housetrain their pet Muslim extremist. In the tradition of American insularity, the women Roush speaks for were probably convinced they would turn their Wahhabi paramours into sensitive Westerners, who share the housework, carry the newborn in a papoose, and dutifully grind away at the wife's G-spot at night, just like *Cosmo* Magazine instructs.

Put it this way, back in the days when Pat Roush was experimenting with an Arabian lifestyle, she'd have been far better off taking up with a Ba'athist moderate and emigrating to the secular, pro-woman, and booze-friendly Iraq than to Saudi Arabia. It doesn't get much worse than Saudi Arabia, where uttering a loud Hail Mary can get you in trouble with the authorities.

The women now entombed in Saudi Arabia could have cased the country before moving there. A trip to the library is all it takes to find out about the dismal status of women in Saudi society. I certainly think I would have noticed if the country I was headed to enforced a state religion, and had in tow an energetic religious police, or *Mutawaa'in*. In one incident, the Saudi *Mutawaa'in* caused the death by fire of a number of schoolgirls. The devout cops refused to allow the girls to escape because their heads were immodestly uncovered (the fire, presumably, had incinerated their headgear). A responsible woman doesn't bind the future of her children to such a place.

My now grown-up girl only just survived the perils of the public school system in Canada. Parental vigilance and awareness were key. To detect the corrosive elements of the public school curriculum in North America, a mother has to take pains to educate herself. That's not necessary in Saudi Arabia. Plain for all to see in a Saudi ninth grader's readings is a tract entitled *The Victory of Muslims over Jews.* It's a *hadith*—a statement ascribed to the Prophet Mohammed—and it reads as follows:

> The last hour won't come before the Muslims would
> fight the Jews and the Muslims will kill them so Jews

would hide behind rocks and trees. Then the rocks and
trees would call: oh Muslim, oh servant of God! There is
a Jew behind me, come and kill him...

The very pabulum that nourished bin Laden and other extremists
before him is compulsory for all Saudi students. At least 35 percent
of school studies there are devoted to this kind of "religious"
education.

Some things are facts of life: (1) Saudi Arabia is a ruthless
medieval theocracy. It has been for a very long time. (2) The U.S.
government will rarely protect its citizens in international disputes.
(3) There is no such thing as the Right Wahhabi Guy.

As sad and as hard for a mother to live with as it is, the truth is
that wannabe Wahhabi western women who bind the future of their
children to Wahhabi men are first and foremost responsible for what
becomes of their children.

61. FEMINISTS POLICE THE POLICE

February 26, 1999

Terri Petkau is a sociologist who has been brought up sharp
against the fallacies of the feminist perspective while completing a
tightly argued MA thesis at McMaster University, Hamilton. Ms.
Petkau endeavored to evaluate the perceptions patrol constables had
of the wife assault sensitivity training they received. And what these
front-line workers had to say threatened to overturn her once firmly
entrenched feminist sensibilities. The training, informed completely
by feminism, is doing more harm than good.

Explains Petkau: "I saw the male species as oppressors of women
since time immemorial. I marched, I drew up petitions, and I
camped out at city hall." When told by the men and women of the
force that the feminist training was failing, Ms. Petkau set out to find
out why. "I listened with disbelief to the accounts of the police

officers," she relays. Her study traces and documents the dubious constructs employed in a typical feminist sensitivity training course, the kind of course entrenched in precincts across Canada and the United States.

While the feminist perspective now poses as the truth, in reality it is nothing but a theoretical understanding. Its take on wife assault is just one of many competing perspectives. The feminist orthodoxy, moreover, appeals to carefully selected studies that support its view and overlooks, discounts or ignores those studies challenging it.

How does this perspective ingratiate itself? First, it offers up carefully crafted, mutually exclusive categories of victim and offender: The woman is pure, moral, and blameless, while the male is cast as inherently immoral, deserving only condemnation and punishment. This one-way process in feminist training does not permit shades of gray.

The men and women of the patrol constabulary are also taught to perceive the couples with whom they intervene as being mired in relationships of power, control, and escalation. Feminist trainers speak authoritatively about the triumph of terminating the abusive relationship, the cycle of leaving and returning to the "villain," and the inevitable revictimization by a patriarchal society. These concepts undergird the perspective and are not to be questioned.

The officers are told unequivocally that wife assault exists equally across the socio-economic board. This is a fallacy. On the beat, they encounter a different reality: wife assault is largely a lower-class phenomenon. But feminists, who need people to believe domestic violence is an equal-opportunity offender, would sooner fortify this mythology than direct resources where needed.

By the time they complete this sensitivity training, police patrol trainees have been exposed repeatedly to visuals of rare atrocity stories. This is meant to cause the officers to disregard the difference between the rare cases of extreme brutality and the minor levels of violence they encounter on their patrols. It also feeds into the concept of a continuum of violence against women: If every incident between a man and a woman can be framed as a prelude to an atrocity, then practically all men can be branded as predators. Indeed the slippery slope logical error, which allows feminists to link a wide range of separate attitudes and behaviors, for which there is no evidence of a connection, also allows them to condemn the mild-mannered man given to the occasional caustic comment, to sharing an axis with O.J. Simpson.

Another training totem has it that a woman's deviant behavior, such as drug addiction or child abuse, is a consequence of her victimization, whereas a man's behavior is always his responsibility. The feminist counselor will categorically refuse to hold women accountable for their role in the violence. Plagued by the same dysfunctional patterns over and over again, yet being assured by their helpers that the problem always lies with the man, these destructive women are fated to shuttle from one violent relationship to another.

Anyone who has attended a feminist training course is familiar with its dedicated anti-intellectualism. Dare to venture an explanation for human behavior that doesn't mesh with the feminist credo and one is warned about perpetuating unhelpful myths. Patrol constables in Petkau's sample, however, had a hard time swallowing all this. Is it because the men and women on the shop floor are part of an oppressive system? Not at all. Constables who interface with couples in strife simply don't see what their feminist trainers instruct them to see. They don't report formulaic escalation. They find instead that men and women are equally capable of initiating violent acts.

Patrol constables do have a strong commitment to neutrality and a keen sense of justice. But the policies they must follow are based on extreme examples which do not reflect the complexities of social life. In addition, the feminist dogma acts as a straightjacket, compelling well-intentioned frontline workers to abandon a nuanced understanding of violence between couples and settle for reductive scripts.

Reality is a very powerful solvent: Petkau's officers rejected outright the feminist account of wife assault because they found it inconsistent with what they encountered on the beat. Still, officers in the surveyed precinct were excluded from policy deliberations. Frontline workers are given little credibility because, in Canada and the U.S., the feminist lobby gets to describe and define the dynamics in these relationships as well as suggest solutions.

62. FEMINIST TOTEMS AND TABOOS

June 19, 2001

Veronica Dahl is a professor of computing science at the Simon Fraser University (SFU) in British Columbia, Canada. Computers, however, were not the topic on which she held forth on the local Knowledge TV Network: feminism was (despite her later denials). Professor Dahl opined that boys were falling behind girls in the school system because boys were lazy. But since they believe they are society's "ruling class" (she said in a deceptively dulcet lilt), they know that no matter how badly they perform, their dominant position in society remains secure.

I responded with a newspaper column in which I identified Dahl's fatuous claim as an example of "second wave feminism." By this I mean the view that women are a besieged political class, fighting to unseat a ruling class whose members refuse to let go of patriarchal privilege and power.

Dahl and colleague John Dewey Jones, director of the school of engineering science, protested to the editor that I had failed to divine the laudable context of her message. The gist of Jones' rebuttal: Dahl didn't say what Mercer alleged she said; but even though she didn't say what she is alleged to have said, what Dahl didn't say is nonetheless correct. (No satire of bureaucrats on that old BBC series, *Yes, Prime Minister*, could possibly rival the blather coming from such real-life educrats.)

Though Jones and Dahl denied the meaning I had drawn from her quotation, they went on to reinforce that very message—namely, that girls work hard because of society's expectations; however, boys often don't because males dominate society anyway. Voila: second-wave feminism.

Feminism, in all its nausea-creating waves, is an ideology or theory, and a conspiracy theory at that, since it claims that throughout history men have conspired to dominate women. In this instance, educators, who should know something of the scientific method, were advancing opinions guided not by data but by ideology. History, however, gives scant support to their feminist fairy tale of malevolent male hegemony.

As Barbara Amiel explains in her book *Confessions*, up until the last stages of the industrial revolution, societies were preoccupied with the propagation of their members. It was therefore vital to make the most of man's superior physical strength and woman's ability to bear children. Were women not pregnant or in labor for most of their arduous lives, the tribe would not have endured. For a few children to survive, a woman had to give birth to 10 or 12.

Man's survival would have been equally imperiled had earlier societies pretended, as diligently as ours does, that men aren't stronger than women, or that they don't enjoy an overwhelming advantage in the perception of spatial-geometrical relationships. Professor Doreen Kimura, also of SFU, confirms that men and women differ cognitively in the way they solve problems. Men, on average, are better at spatial tasks, mathematical reasoning, and co-ordination of visual and motor activities.

As Kimura has empirically demonstrated, there is "no evidence for systemic discrimination against women ... and when women do apply for science jobs they get preferential treatment." Her findings, reported in Canada's *National Post*, show that women "self select out of certain science careers." Clearly, women will never be represented equally in the fields of, say, physics and engineering.

The division of labor between the sexes thus has been the culmination of biology and necessity. But while feminist dogma has become a cultural *totem*, discussing the biological differences that separate the sexes has become a cultural *taboo*.

As a result, facts such as those Kimura and Amiel present have done little to stop the spread of radical feminism in the universities, not sparing the hard sciences (as Dahl and Jones demonstrate). Women's studies courses and English syllabi are now littered with the ideology's lumpen jargon. Text is routinely deconstructed and shred. Treated with this academic acid, the reputations and artistry of Shakespeare, Tolstoy, and T. S. Eliot have dissolved: increasingly, they are seen as little more than members of the ruling class of oppressors, their artistry manifesting the alleged power relationships in society.

Secondary schools are also suffused with this stuff. Feminism animates the child-centered, progressive public-school system and the 1960s vision its teachers hold dear. My own daughter was forced-fed a pedagogic diet of pop psychology and politically correct pap, mostly by female teachers. They promoted every mythical, PC orthodoxy that pervades the *Zeitgeist*. At the same time, these women did little to foster content-based learning, something that they deem to be soul destroying.

With their sorry standards and shopping-mall assortment of boutique courses, public schools are ultimately bad for *all* children. But while these schools are intuitively girl-friendly, they are unmistakably unfriendly to boys. Some research indicates that boys thrive in a disciplined, structured learning environment. Child-centered schooling, however, shuns discipline and moral instruction, and promotes co-operative experiences and groupthink over individual achievement. Moreover, boys are biologically predisposed to competition. But when they bubble over with unbridled testosterone, rather than challenge, discipline, and harness their energies, boys are forced instead to conform to the feminist consensus about appropriate male behavior, often with pharmacological aid: boys are far more likely than girls to be slapped with the diagnosis of "learning disabled" and then rammed with Ritalin.

In short, male biopsychology has been demonized, with the result that boys are being made over in the emotional image of woman...or, more precisely, in that emasculated image of man that feminists foster.

The contemporary predicament of men certainly contradicts the Dahl Dogma. Women continue to live longer than men. Five times as many young men as women commit suicide. Men are twice as likely to be unemployed and find it twice as hard to get another job, and they are infinitely more likely to suffer industrial accidents and diseases which may destroy their lives.

Judging from the letters I received from the young men who made it to SFU (boys are also less likely than girls to graduate from high school and go on to college), our devoted faculty are blithely unaware of—or could not care less about—the experience many men have on campus, much less in their daily lives. Wrote one student:

> ...I cannot seem to escape the biases of feminism no matter where I turn. Every female teacher somehow manages to bring the argument around to point out that males overrun everything. If I produce any artwork with any sort of tall thin form in it, I immediately am criticized for producing artwork that involves phallic symbolism. Thus meaning that I obviously am promoting male dominance in society.

The academe, once dedicated to freedom of expression and learning, now allows man-hating zealots to hound males for producing personalized imagery, a reality this young man described so sadly as "wearing of his spirits."

63. ELIMINATE GOVERNMENT-FUNDED EDUCATION!

March 13, 2002

The case of the Cleveland school-voucher program, now affirmed by the Supreme Court, ought not to have been positioned as a state-church issue. At the core of whether parents can receive a taxpayer-funded stipend and spend it in a school of their choice—religious establishment included—is the legitimacy of state involvement in the enterprise of education, not the God-state animus.

But first, getting back to basics means understanding that education is not a right. The only rights people possess are to life, liberty, property, and the pursuit of happiness. The right to go about one's business unmolested and unharmed—and to take the actions necessary to sustain life without harming or encroaching on others— is our only natural right. This right is what government must legitimately protect. By extension, any right that depends for its existence on the labor of another is not a right. To the extent government manufactures and reinforces these non-rights, it is an entity that enslaves some for the benefit and in the service of others.

Where the legislator has deployed the force of the law to transform so many human needs into inalienable rights, he can then declare the thwarting of these bogus rights an actionable violation of "human rights." But just because some service or commodity has, by government fiat, been declared a right, doesn't mean that it will now fall like manna from the heavens. The costs of the commodity or service don't magically dissipate. Someone must be forced to work in order to pay for and supply subsidized housing, health care or education. Rights that rely for their fulfillment on the coerced labor of others are not rights, they are politically counterfeited rights and they violate real rights.

It flows from this that all government programs are immoral, the education monopoly included. To the extent that the Constitution flouts this, it is wrong. Parents have a right to take the necessary action to earn the money with which to educate their young. They don't have the right to compel the childless, the home-schooler, the private school user—nor anyone really—to pay for the education of their young.

Educational vouchers and charter schools are a species of the publicly funded system.

The support for these educational options is understandable. Few systems boast incentives more perverse than public education, where teacher's tenure—not talent—is remunerated, students with an "appetite for destruction" are coddled with therapy, and school failure is rewarded with an increased budget. And these are the least offensive facets of child-centered, progressive public schools. It's a sluggard of a system, and it's turning out bumper crops of ignoramuses, who, all too often, have no more than dangerously inflated self-esteems to show for years of compulsory attendance.

The more sluggish a system, the more likely it is to respond well to competition, which explains why educational alternatives do yield statistically significant, positive results. Introducing market principles to the pedagogic Gulag, however, is not the route! Tweaking a system that is founded on moral quicksand is not the answer! The solution lies in working to replace public with private, consumer-responsive, unregulated, independent education. The home schooling groundswell is the first step; it is a significant and powerful secessionist movement, which signals that, if their tax burden were drastically reduced, American families would likely prefer private schooling.

Bear in mind that where public money is spent, demand for regulation invariably follows. Vouchers allow the financially needy to obtain tax-funded scholarships for private schools. Private education will thus be tainted by money mulcted from the taxpayer. School vouchers will have turned what remains of America's independent schools into politicized, subsidy-seeking wards of the state, willing to replace canon and curriculum with politically correct indoctrination.

Those who object to vouchers because they threaten the hallowed public-education monopoly or because they spawn segregation can rest assured. By improving it, vouchers further strengthen and entrench the public system. As to segregation: egalitarians can rejoice. Vouchers follow the anti-private property, freedom-sabotaging tradition of forced integration.

Right now, many suburban schools are half decent because control over neighborhood schools has devolved to the community. The school will typically reflect the locality in terms of its composition and the kind of values it espouses. The socialist voucher privilege will eliminate local control, as inner-city kids are palmed off on suburban communities. Choice for some, once again, will come at the expense of choice for others, in this case, local property owners who foot the lion's share of the tax bill.

It was the mother of all voucher systems, the post-World War II G.I. Bill, that truly centralized American higher education. Under the guise of educating veterans, the G.I. Bill authorized a massive infusion of tax dollars, creating a coercive plan to entrench social-democratic welfarism, purge "traditional notions of merit and class," and replace academic excellence with "social justice" and political correctness. Strip them of their fig leaf, and vouchers are no better.

64. HARRY'S HOUNDERS AND OTHER VILLAGE IDIOTS

January 23, 2002

Horror of horrors, Prince Harry, the second son of Prince Charles, has been getting plastered and enjoying the odd spliff. It's not quite clear how the unremarkable news reached the press. It would appear, though, that when Prince Charles got word of the wild parties, the drinking and, yes, the inhaling, all hell broke loose in the media. Daddy, it would seem, may have been less than discreet. On the other hand, it could be that Prince Charles' pot plants were wired.

More plausibly, the media picked up the yarn when the boy was spotted visiting a drug rehabilitation clinic in south London. A tad young to be adopting the many fashionable causes his late mother embraced, Harry was not officiating as the new Patron Saint of the Tokers. He had apparently been sent by Prince Charles to study up close "what drugs can do to the lives of young people."

Considering that drug rehab centers are too often full of self-styled addicts (the kind of manipulative young people with a knack for playing the system), this may not have been the best real-life lesson for Prince Charles to foist on his youngest son. The rehab is often the end-of-the-road and the last resort for families tethered by troubled kids. Having reached a breaking point, the family typically is only too eager to outsource a disruptive youngster to a state-sponsored facility. What family would risk trying to get tough with a truant teen, if it means being accused of child abuse by some Sapphic Sister from Social Services?

If not in bad form, Charles' sending our poor "potter" to a rehab center qualifies, at the very least, as melodramatic. Young Harry was soon swept up in the hysteria, with everybody—from the pub owner in Wiltshire where the prince partied, to the headmaster of the exclusive Eton College, to a Home Office spokeswoman, and to the many addiction industry gargoyles—offering up a version of the slippery slope Harry could be careening down. The Wiltshire police joined the rash of recrimination, indicating it would be willing to consider action against Harry if information were to materialize.

Amidst the overreaction, it emerged (run for cover) that Prince Charles had not always entertained himself by chatting to pot plants. While on a school sailing trip, a 14-year-old Charles led a less than teetotaler expedition of boys to a local bar to sample the cherry brandy. As heartless as his mother is alleged to have been, the queen did not pack him off on a cirrhosis-of-the-liver crash course. As a member of a more sober generation, she may have sensed what the addiction industry's hysteria conceals: despite casual or occasional use of drugs, most teenagers don't descend into addiction.

Cool Britannia and the United States share the same insufferable prohibition paranoia. Prime Minister Tony Blair thinks of "drug policy"—the euphemism for the state's interference with what people consume—as a road to "social rejuvenation." "The fight against drugs," wrote Blair, "should be part of a wider range of policies to renew our communities." Indeed, Blair's 1998 Crime and Disorder Act went so far as to enshrine in law coercive drug testing and compulsory treatment protocols.

Here at home, the "Hildebeest" is another believer in the power of legislation to renew communities. If anything, the "philosophy" popularized by Hillary Clinton has the effect of undermining and forcibly stripping families and communities of their powers to keep their members in check, and replacing them with legislation that transfers responsibility for children to the state.

When last did the actions of a legislator serve to renew a genuine community? Public-housing slums? Rent control? In many great cities, rent control has meant that there are more boarded up buildings than there are homeless, because landlords are legally prohibited from recovering the costs of upkeep. Designed to preserve a way of life, enforced inter-provincial wealth equalization programs in Canada have resulted in chronically dependent and depressed regions. And we know how, with welfare policies, government has helped destroy black families: young black women choose to marry the state rather than wed the fathers of their children. Last year, prohibition of drug possession courtesy of government "recharged" the lives of roughly 1.5 million Americans, arrested for marijuana possession.

Clearly, it takes a village idiot to think of government policy as a means to a Renaissance.

Harry's teen pranks, of course, are no more the business of sticky-pawed politicians than they are the business of drug policy advocates. Harry's indiscretion is to have publicly behaved in a manner unbefitting his station. (Then again, his late mother modeled a self-indulgent disregard for royal etiquette and decorum.) His father's indiscretion is to have followed through with a public pop-therapy protocol instead of removing the keys to Highgrove country estate, and enforcing a curfew and some serious pecuniary pain on the boy.

65. WAREHOUSING WAIFS

August 17, 2001

According to the media's hyperbole, Canadian couples don't have enough "high quality" subsidized daycare facilities. As soon as they conceive, these couples are impelled to rush out and place their unsuspecting embryos on daycare waiting lists for fear there will be no placements when the time is ripe to kick the neonate into the harsh world. Apparently, the daycare plight is rife among single parents as well. "Some have just been accepted into school, or have just finally got a job and can't take it because they don't have day care." As one Canadian daycare stakeholder complained, "It's heart breaking."

True, the specter of middle class North Americans waiting in line to warehouse their children in day care centers makes the heart bleed—for the children, that is. Evidently, people are going to work, but are also lugging along gnawing guilt pangs. And a blob of protoplasm like a child should not be permitted to set in motion a self-correcting emotion like guilt. When guilt besieges the nation, it is time for government to assuage it.

I still recall the day I learned my pride and joy had been conceived. Silly me, had I gone out and placed her on a waiting list, my career might look a lot different today. There is a price to pay for that well-adjusted marvel of mine, and I have nobody to blame but myself. I was unable to deposit this personage of my creation to the custody of strangers.

Putting aside my resentment over the lot of moms who remain with their kids versus those who don't, at the heart of the assorted attempts at national daycare in Canada is the government's patronizing belief that parents need "systemic and structured support" in raising their children. Sadly, government is not alone. Fully three quarters of Canadians "welcome a system of day care available to all families that is paid for by government and parents."

Canadians, it would appear, need more than government help with their children—they need divine intervention. The warehoused child certainly does. For her, the daycare internment starts at dawn: it's up with daylight (or before that in winter), gulp down a hurried breakfast, get shoved in the car, and then get ejected at school or nursery school. Then it's get picked up and dropped off at daycare, only to be fetched in the evening by a weary and distracted parent. Children that young cannot cope with such a schedule without forfeiting some of their centeredness, peace of mind, and rightful childhood. Why, Attention Deficit Hyperactivity Disorder is the perfect metaphor for this hectic lifestyle. Any acting out by the child is a reflection of this routine; it is no more than a child's adaptive reaction to a maladaptive life.

A drastic reduction in the scope and size of government and hence in inflation and taxation would lift the burden off families (perhaps even increase the dismal birthrate). Since there's not a hope in hell of that transpiring anytime soon, solutions to this quagmire lie in the personal—not the public—domain. Couples can leave off having children until they are able to give the child the care it needs. Be it dual parenting where father and mother work part time or be it a relative or a stay-at-home parent, there's no reason for societies to collectively retool in order to accommodate parents' perceived entitlement to both career and family minus the guilt.

The various nationalized schemes entrenched across Canada come at a price, as they do anywhere such distribution-based plans exist. Someone always pays. National day care in Britain, says David Conway of the Institute for Economic Affairs, will serve, if anything, to diminish the choices women have. Women who might have opted to stay at home with their children will now be forced to work to fund the system.

Cause and effect pronouncements on daycare and the state of youth today are probably overbroad. But farming kids out so early in their lives, coupled with the intellectual and moral abnegation inherent in progressive parenting and schooling go some distance in explaining the inarticulate, directionless, and angry youth of today. Not even dogs are placed in kennels day in and day out, and even dogs get to have "quiet time" on the rug, interrupted only by the dog-sitter who comes to fulfill the mutt's recreational needs. Doubtless, if children had any say, they would want more of their own parents and less parenting by proxy.

V. The Arts and the Artless

66. MUCH ADO ABOUT CONSERVATIVES AND POP CULTURE

February 7, 2003

Conservatives are "losing a whole generation of students or are severely impairing their ability to speak to them by not being able to speak to students in their own terms," warns conservative-cum-libertarian cultural commentator Paul Cantor in a recent interview for a campus newspaper. Mr. Cantor wants conservatives to stop ignoring pop culture, although he joins with conservatives in choosing moral rather than aesthetic arguments to support his passion for programs like *The X-Files* and *The Simpsons*, the latter of which needs no defense. (*The Simpsons* is by far the finest satire on the satire-starved American TV.)

Still, the notion that conservatives are engaged in a losing battle is hard to sustain, given that they've been barred from the battlefield for so long. How can one lose footing one never had? The kind of teacher the Lost Generation has been exposed to is more likely to have been a progressive teacher. Furthermore, for decades, progressive schools and colleges have made it practically impossible for a conservative tutor to speak to students on any terms other than "their own." It's been some time, for example, since the "damaging" mention of a literary canon has been made around America's curriculum-averse youth. Content-based, top-down education has long been supplanted by pop-culture-friendly, non-hierarchically delivered flimflam.

Besides which, reaching or teaching students by using their frame of reference rather than imparting one is an unmistakably progressive idea. Progressives have always insisted that learning must

203

be made natural, organic. On the other hand, classicists, as E. D. Hirsch Jr. points out, see effective, analytical, and explicit instruction as very definitely not a natural but a highly artificial, often unintuitive process.

The idea that learning flows from the child is vintage romantic nineteenth-century progressivism, the hangovers from which are still with us. Mr. Cantor is probably correct: If they had access to the youth, (evidence for which, as I noted earlier, is lacking), principled conservatives ought not to be at ease with Rousseauan anti-intellectualism.

Like moral arguments, however, arguments that appeal predominantly to cultural context in assessing popular culture are also insufficient.

Cantor points out that Shakespeare in his day was considered popular culture, while today Shakespeare is high culture. To say that in different eras different cultural products were varyingly endorsed or not endorsed is as meaningful as saying Dickens was popular because he was popular. Cultural relativism can end up in just such a tautology.

Moreover, should we ascertain the quality of pop culture from its popularity? I don't think Cantor means for us to do that. When it comes to a widget, high demand would indeed reflect quality. But when the product engages man's higher faculties, arguably not. If Shakespeare was the Seinfeld of his day, could this be evidence not only of changing standards, but perhaps also of a more elevated state among the masses in days of yore?

An insistence on cleaving to cultural context in assessing pop culture might have a chance of working if the cultural products under review are accurately labeled. The Eminem argument, for instance, would move along swimmingly if what Eminem does were labeled as street theatre—Eminem is not a musician. A more impressive form of this art is observed in Africa, where the tradition of a praise singer or a tribal poet laureate still flourishes. The tribal poet is a splendid performing artist. Mr. Cantor prophesies that "the video game is going to be the major art form of the twenty-first century." No doubt there are some very well made video games, and, doubtless, these, like Yoko Ono's concept art, may gain the status of art, but this doesn't—and never will—make them art.

Incapable of systematic thought, lesser libertarians, the kind Professor Clyde Wilson has recently dubbed "dubious hangers-on," are forever poised to turn intellectual dissent into wedge issues. Contrary to the compliance the movement's groupies exact, Mr. Cantor does not appear dogmatic about the interesting themes he wrings from *The X-Files*, among which are globalization, affirmation of Christianity and liberty, and the end of the nation-state.

I would certainly disagree politely with his contention that *The X-Files* is "one of the greatest artistic achievements of the 1990s." I agree with Mr. Cantor that, with a stretch, the program can, albeit unflatteringly, be conceived of as conservative. It is important to recall, however, that the show was chockablock with mysticism and mythical thinking. Those aspects suggest that the show's conservatism is at best a highly idiosyncratic one. It seems very unlikely that liberty could flourish in such an atavistic atmosphere thick with conspiracy, emotionalism, superstition, and a cult-like obsession with the freaky and the bizarre.

Neither is it clear why faith in the free market must require a nearly equal faith in popular culture. Why does it follow that a product produced and exchanged in the process of making a living must inspire faith? More often than not, the marketplace doesn't adjudicate the quality of art or pop culture. Thus one's artistic judgments must be animated by something more, if one thinks that there are objective standards by which popular culture or art can be judged—as the great art critic Robert Hughes seems to think (rather uncontroversially, I might add). The market does no more than offer an aggregate snapshot of the trillions of subjective preferences enacted by consumers. Aguilera (Christina) probably sells more than Ashkenazy (Vladimir) ever did. Britney outdoes Borodin. For some, this will be faith inspiring, for others deeply distressing.

Irrespective of cultural ordination, high and low art have always mingled across time. Hungarian Magyar folk songs are used to great effect in Bela Bartok's music. Hughes points to the influence of jazz on Maurice Ravel, Claude Debussy, and Igor Stravinsky. Andy Warhol may have made a younger generation slobber but, says Hughes, Vincent van Gogh was eighty years ahead of him: "He loved not only Japanese prints, whose color was highly sophisticated, but also the crude, discordant, and even brutal colors of mass industrial printing." And how good would it be if the classical timpanist would finally incorporate the complex rhythms of modern-day drum virtuosos like Neil Peart and Virgil Donati.

Yes, Cantor is right to note that many older conservatives dismiss popular culture and come off as old fogies. But for those of us who are willing to see the good in pop culture, the important thing now is to discuss the standards by which we will judge it. In the words of Hughes, the task has always been and is still to distinguish between the good stuff, the absolute crap, and everything that lies between.

67. JACKSON'S CHILD PLAY

February 26, 2003

What a relief it was when the peerless broadcaster Maury Povich took up the cudgels in defense of pop singer Michael Jackson. The no-nosed Jackson had come short when he set out to charm a hard-nosed British Journalist by the name of Martin Bashir of Granada TV. Bashir had spent eight months in Wacko's World, and came away with some patently obvious and crisply clear conclusions, aired on "Living with Michael Jackson."

This did not sit well with the flighty Jackson. Povich was recruited by the suitably vulgar Fox channel to correct the alleged distortions presented by Bashir. Having fronted a daytime TV freak show, Povich was well qualified for the job, although it is unfair to leading lights like Ricki of *The Ricki Lake Show*, or Montel Williams of the show by that name, or Jerry Springer, to call Povich peerless. (Add to Povich's professional pedigree his marital muse, the legendary Connie Chung, and you get the picture—Chung's verbal swordplay is a match for Larry King's repartee.)

It is not surprising then that in "The Michael Jackson Footage: The Interview You Were Never Meant to See," Povich exposed "truths" such as that Jackson's surgical metamorphosis from a rather nice looking—if androgynous—black boy, to an albino gremlin was just your average adolescent growth spurt.

Bashir, on the other hand, is well respected for his incisive 1995 Panorama interview with the tawdry Princess Diana, and with Louise Woodward, the British nanny who was accused of child murder in the U.S. The insightful comments Bashir spliced into the Jackson documentary narrative showcase his no-nonsense, independent style.

Most Americans, however, were expecting the mind-numbing adulation a Jules Asner, Barbara Walters, or Diane Sawyer would dish up. In interviews that make the flesh crawl, these TV tarts always redeem their subjects, however revolting, with the ever-forgiving vernacular of popular psychology. They may delve into prurient recesses for the sake of ratings, but their liberal framework always absolves the interviewed from personal responsibility.

Bashir's documentary attacks with verve this no-fault therapeutic outlook. He described events plainly and drew reasonable inferences from them. Can anyone argue that Jackson dangled a flesh and blood baby from the hotel balcony? Elizabeth Taylor did, but then she has had half her cranium removed due to a brain mass. Other Jackson buddies and defenders include Uri Geller, the Israeli shyster spoon bender, and his equally off-putting liberal co-religionist, Rabbi Shmuley Boteach, that all-time vulgarizer of the faith.

Speaking truth to power and money is certainly a dying tradition among American journalists. Yet the best journalists rip into their subjects. And Bashir provided plenty corrective feedback to the indulged mega-star. "I'm Peter Pan," Jackson dulcetly intoned. "No you're not; you are Michael Jackson," came Bashir's firm reply. "I let children sleep in my bed not in a sexual way ("It's a warmth thing," joked comedian Jon Stewart), but as a way to heal and spread love,"

Jackson minced, clasping the hairy hand of his very well-developed 12-year-old companion. "You're a 44-year-old man," winced Bashir, offering that he would not want any adult man in bed with his own kids.

Jackson wailed to Bashir about Joe Jackson. Daddy had spanked him and made him feel unloved. Joe was evidently an old-fashioned, therapeutically unenlightened African-American father. He provided his children with an intact family and a wicked work ethic. Proponents of firm discipline, Joe and Katherine Jackson believed individuals as gifted as their kids should be made to realize their potential. Woe is me and what were they thinking?

Povich's contribution is to reveal that bad Bashir failed to air Jackson's afterthought about his old man's genius: When Jackson was through sullying his father, he did offer a weak compliment about the man's intelligence. Perhaps Bashir simply thought that Jackson commenting on intelligence was almost as incredible as Jackson claiming to have conceived his children the old-fashioned fun way, another "truth" Bashir was accused of leaving out.

Did Bashir suck up to the narcissistic star? To get to the guts of a story, a journalist may have to flatter the subject whose entrails he is examining. Jackson gave his consent to the operation, but expected to control the outcomes. It doesn't work that way in the adult world, Peter Pan.

The Fox/Povich production goes one better than Judith Krantz's kitsch with the "candid" confession of Debbie Rowe, Jackson's ex-wife. The lighting is soft, the background music corny, as Debby tells how she did Michael; the kids, apparently, are the "ultimate love children." Michael is shown propped up on a pillow like a little Chihuahua or a Pekinese pooch on show, his concave face turned away from the camera.

"Debbie did it for me," Jackson boasted. The kids don't have their own distinct names. They received Michael's hand-me-down monikers, "Prince Michael I and II." This fits with the disturbing picture Bashir let emerge: No amount of patchwork by Povich can change that Jackson's kids were bred for his benefit.

68. MEDIA MYTH-MAKING

February 27, 2002

In the wake of the slaughter by Pakistani Islamists of the *Wall Street Journal's* Daniel Pearl, CNN news anchors took a break from celebrating the Islamic hajj and turned their short attention spans to celebrating themselves. The better part of the somber day was given over to praising the journalistic endeavor of truth seeking.

Granted, reporters usually manage to convey the minutiae of a story accurately (or so I thought until the War on Iraq). But on the meta-level, they are up to their clavicles in myth making and bias. For instance, since September 11, the media have militantly outshone Muslim leaders in distancing the faith of Islam from the acts of violence perpetrated by Muslims in the name of Islam. This is a new consensus-shaping myth. Any acts of brutality by Muslims are, as the CNN imams are quick to point out, gross perversions of Islam. And every Muslim who kills is in revolt against the genuine Islamic faith.

Such reflexive proselytizing has prompted Bernard Lewis, leading scholar of Islam, to ponder the presumptuousness of "those who are not Muslims," yet are making pronouncements about "what is orthodox and what is heretical in Islam." With so many respected Muslim clerics blessing suicide bombings as a "supreme form of jihad," and with most Islamic nations supporting violent jihad, Islam's inherent peacefulness is not as done a deal as the average TV talking airhead suggests. Writes Matt Kaufman, in an article entitled "The Real Islam":

> Islam has a long history of violence. This dates back to its founder Muhammad in the 7th century; he talked peace at the beginning, but once he gathered enough military power he started launching raids and eventually conquered Mecca. Muslim clerics went on to expand the conditions that justified force, until aggression against

any non-Muslims—justified by the need to create a
single Islamic state—became the norm. So it remained
until the last 300 years or so, when militarily superior
Western powers rendered expansionist *jihad* increasingly
impractical. Today's militance [sic] is no historical
aberration, but a resurgence of the pattern that's
characterized most of Islam's existence.

Why confine the scope of discussion to Islam's true hue? Our
media dunderheads consider almost any person who does bad things
to be in revolt against his essential nature. The journalist's
Rousseauan worldview rejects the reality of evil in human nature.
When people (with the exception of white males) do ghastly things it
is because environmental and institutional contingencies stymie
them. The narrative in the media invariably takes the following tack:
People kill, lie, and cheat because they are poor, unemployed, black,
female, depressed, uneducated, don't live in a democracy or need to
be given what others have toiled to acquire.

The media's depiction of the route to a better world is consistent
with their view that the locus of control over good or bad is not in
the human being's heart and mind but in the external forces that act
on him. Else why would the network folks almost always insist that
mishaps so typical of the human condition be "remedied" with
elaborate social engineering?

Particularly chilling and revealing were the words of Danny
Pearl's widow, herself a journalist. "Revenge," wrote Mariane Pearl,
"would be easy, but it is far more valuable … to address this
problem of terrorism with enough honesty to question our own
responsibility as nations and as individuals for the rise of terrorism."
Note how Mrs. Pearl nihilistically frames punishment as vengeance.
Note how she then proceeds to shift responsibility away from the
subhumans that slit her husband's throat, hinting at larger,
emblematic processes. This truth-deflecting nonsense is insidious
among members of the media.

Mrs. Pearl sums up her sorrow-filled address by calling on "our governments to work hand in hand," and for "love, compassion, friendship and citizenship" to transcend the so-called "clash of civilizations." In journalese, this is generally a clarion call for the staple, governmental, remedial overtures. To wit, central planners must remain nationally and internationally vigilant about rewarding bummery and thuggery with the property of the prosperous.

A great deal must be riding on a recently seeded lie that poverty causes terrorism. Irrespective of thorough refutation from scholars like Daniel Pipes, the media and their political co-religionists are at pains to flog this hobbyhorse. "Militant Islam (or Islamism)," concludes Pipes, "is not a response to poverty or impoverishment; not only are Bangladesh and Iraq not hotbeds of militant Islam, but militant Islam has often surged in countries experiencing rapid economic growth." Suicide bombers and backers of extremism tend to be well educated and well off. Research so far offers overwhelming support for the fact that "the elite flock to Islamist ideology, and that militant Islam results more from success than from failure." Why cast aspersions on the poorest of the poor? Sub-Saharan Africans aren't mounting a global, anti-Western, terrorist offensive.

The libertarian Murray N. Rothbard was careful to steer clear of such cardinal errors: "In dealing with crime," writes Rothbard in Hutus vs. Tutsis, "... liberals are concentrating on the wrong root causes. That is, on 'poverty' or 'child abuse' instead of a rotten immoral character and the factors that may give rise to such a character, e.g., lack of respect for private property, unwillingness to work," and, might I add, an emphasis on immediate gratification. Then again, inversion of the proper moral order to the satisfaction of liberals is achieved when victim compensates victimizer, and when the prudent and risk averse prop up the reckless.

69. BARAKA THE BANAL, ESTABLISHMENT BOOR

October 23, 2002

Leftist writer Maralyn Lois Polak penned an adoring ode to Amiri Baraka, New Jersey's poet laureate, who found himself at the center of a furor over a recitation he gave at a Garden State poetry festival. Ms. Polak describes Baraka's "Somebody Blew Up America" as a "brutally powerful 9-11 poem...messy and sprawling and mesmerizing and incantatory and luminous." Adjective-littered language is bad form for a writer. Polak, however, is not concerned with form in prose or poetry, much less is she concerned with principle.

Art—writing included—is a discipline. Good writing in particular can be about any topic. First and foremost, however, it must be technically accomplished. The kind of art that derives its artistic legitimacy solely from its political message is, however, a decoy for the talentless. As art critic Robert Hughes wrote, art must embody "a love of structure, clarity, complexity, nuance and imaginative ambition," elements that are absent in Baraka. Lacking in mastery, the inept postmodernist will hide behind the bellicosity and counterculture chic of his politics.

Baraka's artless, lazy delivery—not his subversive content—is the problem:

> Who do Tom Ass Clarence work for
> Who doo doo come out the Colon's [sic] mouth
> Who know what kind of Skeeza is a Condoleeza [sic]
> Who pay Connelly [sic] to be a wooden Negro

Other more atavistic lines from Baraka's "doo doo"-bedecked oeuvre include:

> We must eliminate the white man before we can draw a
> free breath on this planet. Nihilismus. Rape the white

girls. Rape their fathers. Cut the mother's throats. Black
dada nihilismus, choke my friends.

Who but the self-appointed intellectual elite likes this verbiage?
Who but the hoity-toity literati think this doggerel is worth
"celebrating"? Polak's indirect derogatory reference to elitism is a
sign of her confusion, because Baraka *is* of the cultural elite. Unless
set to gangster rap, there is no common-man market for his
balderdash. If not for the phonies on New Jersey's State Council on
the Arts (NJSCA), the general public would still presume "Baraka" is
the name of a Hungarian pastry.

Baraka, then, is not a "revolutionary"—a fella that can't be fenced
in—to paraphrase Polak's gabble. He is the banal product of state
ideology that seeks to keep the self-inflicted wounds of minorities
eternally suppurating, so as to give them, through the political
process, a claim to what is not theirs.

Polak is also mistaken about the civilized and civilizing tradition of
the state poet. The state poet survives through political patronage.
Compelled as they are through coerced taxation to support Baraka,
the people of New Jersey can't withdraw their tax dollars from the
NJSCA—and Baraka—without risking retaliation from the state.
Reiterating sociologist Franz Oppenheimer, the late economist
Murray N. Rothbard spoke of "two mutually exclusive ways" of
making a living. When people engage in the process of production
and "voluntary, mutual exchange," they are using "the economic
means" to survive. This is the civilized means. "The other way,"
writes Rothbard,

> Is simpler in that it does not require productivity; it is
> the way of seizure of another's goods or services by the
> use of force and violence. This is the method of one-
> sided confiscation, of theft of the property of others.

This method is "the political means." It's Baraka's way. And,
contra Polak, it's uncivilized. Undeniably, Baraka has the right to

free speech. Here again, Polak misunderstands the ethics of a free society. Can Baraka demand that WorldNetDaily.com give him a hearing? Naturally not. Where private property is concerned, all Baraka has a right to do if he wants his "poems" featured on the site is to appeal to Mr. Farah and his editor, who, in turn, have an absolute right to refuse or accept. Clearly, the dilemma of free speech is a feature of public property alone and of government-regulated, nominally private property. And right now, Baraka's speech is protected and facilitated by coercion: Like it or not, administrators forcibly appropriate funds from taxpayers to support what they call The Arts.

With some exceptions, government-supported art conjures the Soviet Socialist Realism. While the communists forced terrifically ugly, prosaic, state-affirming works on their subjects, our own supercilious liberals labor to trash what's left of Western culture. Think Andres Serrano's "Piss Christ"! As contemptuous as Baraka is, he is merely guilty of being a talentless and tasteless parasite. The real culprits are the politicians who create and fill these positions, then make the taxpayers pay for them.

Disbanding the NJSCA and all such patronage playpens would be the constitutional thing to do. All artists, for that matter, should be removed from the public teat. Barf-making Baraka can become an honest man by seeking his livelihood through "the economic means." Let him pursue his métier on his own ticket.

70. LEWD LEWINSKY

March 9, 1999

After watching Monica Lewinsky's TV debut, I realized who in all this was the real hero. The man who stood bravely between the public and this caricature of a woman is no other than finger-in-the-dyke Kenneth Starr. It is the independent counsel we must thank for delaying the unleashing of the histrionic Monica. Menaces like

Monica are a product of the times, as is the TV-pimp, Bawbawa Walters. These sorry prototypes are carefully nurtured by the education system. Girls are raised to believe that "like" they deserve everything "and stuff." That empowerment means they can abandon reason and realistic self-appraisal because they are "totally awesome." Feelings rule. Venting and pouting are the only ways of being, and if a guy doesn't return your calls, President or "whatever," he's a jerk. Above all, your sexuality, the true meaning of which evades these shallow sisters, is your shrine second only to your self-esteem.

Monica, of course, blamed her woes on a "low self-esteem." What else? Her demeanor, however, was anything but demure. Her admirers chose "self-possessed" to describe her brazen countenance, although "arrogant" was more apt. If anything, this girl suffers inflated self-importance with a touch of grandeur. Monica threw tantrums when the President of the United States shied away from blowing his sax over the phone for her. And the "Pres.," says Monica, should have broadcast their "relationship" to the world had he any decency. From where Monica was perched, the President's men had no right to come between her and her lover. This is a woman whose chunky self-esteem is a match only to her keister.

Next, Monica says "sorry."

Fully 66 percent of those polled thought Monica's apology to the First wife and daughter was a sincere one. What the public now accepts as an apology is another sick sign of the times. Monica said she was contrite yet proceeded to peel off layer-by-layer every scab that ever formed over the sorry affair. This exercise in expiation she carried out in view of millions of people. Apologies have, indeed, become nothing but Oprah-moments, where victims and perpetrators collaborate, under the media's gaze, to belittle the meaning of loss and injustice.

The reactions in the media to Monica are a useful litmus test for the quality of commentary in the press. The Canadian *National Post* came tops, consistently assigning wry descriptions to the "bubble head." Second was the *New York Times*, referring to the interview as "...a giddy Cosmo version of self-realization, a tale told in the psychosexual language of magazine covers that urge their readers to own their sexuality." The *Globe and Mail*, and the *Vancouver Sun* vied for a position on the lowest of reviewer rungs. The Globe and Mail's John Allemang's produced a string of gaseously effervescent superlatives: Monica was "all-consumingly sensuous, frank, lucid, articulate, focused," blah, blah, blah. Even her voice—"High, gentle and firm"—gave this man the hots. The *Vancouver Sun* upped the ante by dignifying Monica's book with a review.

The reviewer called the book "delicious," and offered a sample of Andrew Morton's unwieldy prose, showcasing these linguistic vacuities: Monica is analytical, sharp, brilliant, with a photographic memory...*ad nauseum*. Morton, who told Princess Diana's "story," has popped up under every rock with details about the genesis of Monica's "pain," which could be traced to no other than Tori Spelling's birthday party snubs. Spelling has a lot more to atone for than a bunch of dreadful films.

Monica's heft is no longer upon us, although others will step forward to fill the only impression she ever left on the cultural stage, to paraphrase Sir William Shwenck Gillbert's witticism. But girls like Monica don't get betrayed; they simply star (no pun intended) in their own destructive passion plays. Monica shared her stain-filled affair with anyone who would stand still long enough to listen. And Monica selected her cast, including the sneering Linda Tripp and "Bomber Bill."

71. AFFIRMATIVE OSCARS

March 27, 2002

As a prelude to her pigmentally burdened Oscar acceptance speech, Halle Berry caused an embarrassing scene at the podium. For a good few minutes, we watched the glistening insides of Berry's mouth, as she slobbered, salivated and gave The Heil Halle: a kind of catatonic, repetitive salute in the air. Indeed who can forget the March, 2002 Oscar ceremony.

Berry's performance was incontinent exhilaration at its most undignified. I don't intend to see *Monster's Ball*, the film for which she won Best Actress. A snippet from her performance showed Berry frothing at the mouth yet again. This ought to have translated into a good Humphrey Bogart-type, hysteria-calming slap on the mouth—not into an Oscar award.

The guilt trip about talented black actors being denied recognition due to the incurable racism of mainstreamers (what racism?) is inaccurate, as are all half truths. If black actors *per se* were in great demand among the movie-going public, moviemakers would be rushing to recruit them for more roles. Cultural arousal patterns are more likely involved. Face it, as lovely as she is, Angela Bassett didn't quite get the juices flowing as the love object of Robert De Niro in *The Score*. Perhaps strapping electrodes to a white man's genitals, and shocking him each time Pamela Anderson appears on the screen will turn him on to black actresses for good. Somehow I doubt it. Hormones are politically incorrect. You can take away college placements and Oscars from worthy white guys, but changing their cultural, sexual preferences is a lot harder.

Halle did what Bassett failed to do, but not due to her invisible talent. Whereas Angela Bassett is an authentic, difficult-to-market black beauty, Halle is simply an improved version of the cookie-cut Hollywood chick. She's a sepia-tinted Charlize Theron: a hollow-eyed, marshmallow-cheeked, toothy, Theron-type looker, which is why she sells.

Making history acquires a new meaning when the historical stage is rigged by a subterfuge of Oscar racial politics. Berry and Denzel Washington were imposters in these annals. As is the case with affirmative action, Berry and Denzel's affirmative victories almost obscured that Sidney Poitier's life-long achievements were merit-based. Being black has not stopped Poitier from collecting awards since 1963. Then again, Poitier didn't flog the old race horse. And he certainly rejected the fractured phrases and tortured syntax that come with racial pride.

The snub was, of course, to Russell Crowe. *A Beautiful Mind* won four Oscars, including best picture, yet remarkably, the color-coded Oscar project usurped the leading man. The nuanced and gifted Crowe was made to cede to Denzel in *Training Day*. Crowe would have delivered a fiery acceptance speech. None of the Barbra Streisand and Robert Redford grim sanctimony. Crowe is something of a purist. He talks about art for the sake of art: "long live the narrative" and all that. Unlike Streisand and Redford's political piety, Crowe seems to recognize that he is a performer and no more. None of this "sending a message with my art" baloney.

Calling Redford, who received an honorary Oscar, an intellectual, as Streisand did, is problematic, to say the least. But then Streisand is an insoluble problem. We can argue over whether the Hollywood babes and boys are good looking (I say no, for the most), but there can be few disagreements about the cerebral agility of this crowd, Woody Allen excepted. Let's just say that the presence of Nobel-Prize winning mathematician John Nash in the hall, the subject of the Oscar-nominated film, *A Beautiful Mind*, must have seriously spiked the evening's Bell Curve distribution.

One question: What's with the brutal jaw lines? Is it the Irish ancestry that contributes to the jagged jaws of a Jennifer Connelly? The mandibles of a Jennifer Garner? Sarah Jessica Parker and Sigourney Weaver have some serious competition there. American men certainly don't seem to mind the brutal look. I know men who can gaze for hours at Paula Zahn's face. What are they looking at? Ted Kennedy on estrogen therapy? Jay Leno's female chin twin?

As an archetype of their female beauty, the Egyptians bequeathed us the sublime 1350 B.C. bust of Queen Nefertiti. The French have their ideal of female beauty embodied in the bust of Marianne, their national symbol. What would an American icon of beauty look like? In all likelihood it would combine the flat, coarse planes of J. Lo's large face, with the equally expansive stretches of an Angelina Jolie visage, perhaps with Cher's "mating abalone" phony lips.

Spare me the accusations, I may be premenstrual, but jealous? Only perhaps of the willowy, doleful eyed Angie Harmon, or the exquisite Julie Christie, star of my all-time favorite film, *Dr. Zhivago*. What a perfect face Christie had, but, more important, a kind, warm and generous face—a sensuous face devoid of the snide, come-hither look that so many young American women seem to exude.

72. EMINEM LOSES HIS MALE BITS

November 13, 2002

Trust me; I'd never confuse weeny rebellion with authentic dissent. If fighting state-endorsed political correctness qualifies as dissent, then Eminem, alias Marshall Mathers, was It. I editorialize about why parents—not the state—are responsible for their runts, so why would I complain when Eminem raps a send-up of the same point?

> to the parents of America / I am the derringer aimed at little Erica, to attack her character / The ringleader of this circus of worthless pawns / Sent to lead the march right up to the steps of Congress / And piss on the lawns of the White House and replace it with a Parental Advisory sticker /

Wait a sec, Mercer, you dissed Amiri Baraka, New Jersey's lazy lyricist. How is Eminem different from that appointed poet? Baraka is sponsored by the state: He is of the state and for the state. He pleases The Powers—the self-styled intellectual elite included—by helping perpetuate the *post hoc* myth that black failure is always the white man's fault. The state has a lot riding on that ass. Already emanating from this quarter are the accusations that once again the White Man—Eminem—has appropriated the Black Man's Art, a braying to which H.L. Mencken once put paid: To hold the notion that "any respectable work of art can have a communal origin," seldom survives "scientific investigation." An inspired individual—not an amorphous collective—is the source of good works of art.

Not that I'm pronouncing Eminem a good artist. He is certainly not a musician. His hip-hop poetry, however, is funny and quite skilled. It isn't music, not by any stretch, but it's street theater, and rather good, at that. Whereas Baraka is artistically lazy, dour, and glum, yet dead serious about his stupid stuff, the self-supporting Eminem rhymes with the pace of a machine gun, is entertaining, considerably self-deprecating, and has a sense of irony and satire.

Kudos to him for driving the National Organization for Women (NOW), the Gay, Lesbian and Straight Education Network; The Matthew Shepard Foundation, and especially the Gay and Lesbian Alliance Against Defamation (GLAAD) even more bonkers than they already are. Thanks to these assorted ombudsmen, and to anti-hate crime legislation, which already criminalizes speech and belief because punishment is predicated more on the opinions of the perpetrator than on any harm itself, it's getting harder for a white heterosexual male to get away with an aggressive verbal retort to the Bottom Battalion's hate filled cultural come-ons. Gay political activist Shawn O'Hearn feels "it's our responsibility as gay men… to assist our supposedly straight brothers in the enjoyment of man-on-man sex," or so he wrote in a San Francisco publication. Eminem simply rises to the taunt, issuing a warning, a rejoinder that is far less obscene than that of the establishment-friendly O'Hearn.

> hate fags? the answer's yes homophobic? nah youre just heterophobic starin at my jeans watchin my genitals buldge over… you better let go of em they belong in my scrotum youll never get hold of em

To further whittle away First Amendment rights, agenda-driven social scientists use a form of quackery known as the slippery slope logical error: They typically link a wide range of separate attitudes and behaviors, for which there is no evidence of a connection, and proclaim that violence exists on a continuum, with words on one end. At what point will words erupt or escalate into violent actions, one never can tell. Using slippery slope illogic, Tipper Gore and Lynn Cheney can then with "scientific impunity" blame words for crimes people commit.

A creative permutation of this thinking is deployed in Eminem's debut film, *8 Mile*. The liberal literati reject the view that human beings are responsible agents with free will and see them as incapable of resisting a confluence of biopsychosocial forces. True to this perspective, when a rape occurs in a doomed structure, where black ghetto intersects poor white neighborhood, the film's heroes focus the blame not on the criminal, but on the structure. The mistaken belief that vicious words or dilapidated buildings are conduits to crime explains (metaphorically at least) why the *8 Mile* protagonists respond to the crime by torching the scene of the crime!

Reviewer prolix about the "spirit" of *8 Mile* aside, whether you're white or black, poor or rich—if you grunt, traipse around in troops, and hoot when your territory is invaded, as the characters in the film do, you are more monkey than man. On a positive note, if such menacing people as this film portrays can gather to cheer a battle of wits, where a facility with "lyrics, alliteration, enunciation," and narrative is manifestly evident—this is not all bad.

A bad omen for his anti-PC credentials is that every film reviewer and his dog is embracing Eminem for demonstrating in *8 Mile* that he has a heart, a feature so central to the American esthetic. The Old Em once countered, sure, "there is a positive a message in my music and that's, 'fuck you.'" The New Em is aping Oprah.

73. DUNG AND OTHER OFFAL AT THE GALLERY

October 19, 1999

If I were I to throw the contents of a can of tuna on a canvas, frame it and entitle the thing "A Woman's Angst," I wager that the

National Endowment for the Arts (NEA) would give me a hearing. Who knows? If I add an ethnic twist to my creation, and entitle it "A Jewish Woman's Angst," my none-too-subtle perishable may even end up at The Brooklyn Museum of Art. My splattered fit of pique—the indulged meandering of someone with no talent—projected onto a canvas, would certainly be no different from some of the museum's acclaimed pieces.

A case in point was a show called "Sensation," and also the cause of one. The "Sensation" exhibit had the former Mayor of New York Rudolph Guiliani threatening to withdraw the museum's grant and even evict if the offending exhibit was not removed. A mess, but not nearly as messy as the dubious *objets d'art* themselves, one of which featured a rotting cow's head, another a formaldehyde-suspended bisected pig.

The institutionalized, publicly funded, familiar assault on Catholic symbols coalesced in Chris Ofili's fecal smears. In "The Holy Virgin," Ofili depicts a black Madonna with dung and assorted female orifices cut out and pasted all over the canvas, evidently to affect a play on the word "holy." Ofili, who has been the toast of Britain's artistic circles for some time, joins a cadre of poseurs and purveyors of what is known as concept art, the most notorious of whom is Andres Serrano. Serrano immersed a crucifix in his own body fluid and called it "Piss Christ." Funded by the NEA, Serrano's next sample was a photo of a statuette of the Pope immersed in yet more of the same. You can guess what Serrano called this reflection of his barren soul, lazy mind and prolific bladder.

The capos at the Canada Council for the Arts force their taxpayers to support a fair share of dead-weight conceptualists. Possessing of the same keen eye for talent as the NEA, Canada Council gave us Tamara Sanowar-Makham's creation, the "ultra-maxi priest," which is a vestment gown made of sanitary pads, and intended to express "the oppressive anti-female ideology of the Catholic Church." (If church oppression is what it takes to keep Tamara's creative cramps in check—I'm all for it.) With a grant of $15,000 of the people's money, Canada Council also helped a Ms. Thorneycroft to celebrate "the gloriousness [sic] of putrefaction." The stupid professor solemnized her discovery of the "dust to dust" inevitability by hanging rotting rabbit carcasses up in a forest.

The *Vancouver Sun's* visual art critic—and I use the term loosely— never questioned the art value of the dung n' pee exhibits, but fixed on their power of protest. Michael Scott refused or was unable to distinguish between a portrait composed of the palm prints of children and a jar of urine in which a picture of the Pope has been immersed. Fancying himself the champion of gritty, confrontational real-life art, Scott couldn't discern the act of painting a portrait, however mediocre, from that of producing a sample of urine. And here precisely is the rub: to discern is bad, hence elevating one form of expression above the other garners the pejorative of elitism.

While I may be able to persuade you that my tuna-on-a-canvas has profound personal meaning, I should not be able to convince you that it has artistic validity. For art has to embody both technique and vision. It is a discipline, "indicating a love of structure, clarity, complexity, nuance and imaginative ambition," elements that are absent in the aforementioned pieces.

That concept art is unanimously detested by ordinary folk goes to show that these exhibits are not a populist uprising against "academic art," as the critic Scott would have us believe. Rather, they are by and for the pseudo-intellectuals. It would seem that the very thing that makes art popular, again in the words of Robert Hughes, art critic for the *Times*, is inescapably…"the embodiment of high ability and intense vision."

The same pseudo critics have also wrongly attached an African ancestry to Ofili's efforts: Ofili is said to be connecting with his African roots, because he borrows generously from the magic, and truly creative, little San people of Southern Africa, who delicately dotted their caves with beautiful mystical paintings. Evidently, the use of dung in Ofili's work is also an African thing. I own African art, and I've observed the African artist at work. There is precious little in Ofili's art that is authentically African. The African artist is highly skilled. He achieves glorious sensuality without being

offensive. He would never relinquish his technical mastery for the
ersatz Ofili-type rendition. In its origins, African art was utilitarian:
it was meant to serve a ceremonial purpose. But commercialism has
done nothing to change the deeply reverential nature of what was
once tribal art—the African artist does not create to offend. With
the exception of the blackness of his Madonna, there is nothing in
Ofili's art that is African. He is the product of sloth; the anal-
retentive who prefers to deconstruct, deface and smear. If not for
forced public funding, this *faux* art would fizzle out. Along with it,
says Camille Paglia, should go "the double standard that protects
Jewish and African-American symbols and icons but allows
Catholicism to be routinely trashed by supercilious liberals and
ranting gay activists."

74. WHERE ARE THE ALMIGHTY FENDER BENDERS?

February 29, 2000

The seductive pose the legendary Al Di Meola struck with a nude
lovely on the sleeve of the superb *Kiss My Axe* album was probably
essential marketing, as the appeal of the hot guitar player has never
been so low. Di Meola-like players are rare, but it's good to see
Carlos Santana enjoying a revival, albeit a dubious one. Santana is a
virtuoso. Amidst the cacophony of the first Woodstock, which was
jammed, much like its revival, with the musically inept, Carlos
Santana shone. Here was this guy, oblivious to all else but the
Gibson, rendering a studio-perfect live performance, clearly about
to take the blues scales where only Eddie Van Halen, Eric Clapton
and the late great Stevie Ray Vaughan would tread. And sorry, no
odes to Jimi Hendrix. A fine tunesmith and rhythm man, Hendrix's
picking was sloppy.
    Music might be a matter of taste, but there is no relativism about
technical merit. A career as a classical recitalist would be stumped
were the musician's fingers not sufficiently nimble to render Bach's

preludes and fugues. Or as Glenn Gould put it: "Why do I play Bach so fast? Because I can." And boy, could he. But this demand for "love of structure, clarity, complexity, nuance and imagination" is rare in the pop and rock genres, and has been for some time.

Still, refrain we must from serenading the 1960s and 1970s. While well-crafted melodies were abundant during those years, there were not many worthy axemen, other than Santana, Van Halen, and Clapton. (Incidentally, the only true headbanger of brilliance who won an indirect and posthumous Grammy was Igor Stravinsky for those mountains of sound, *The Rite of Spring* and *The Firebird* ballets.)

Santana's *Supernatural* album is a collaborative calamity. It doesn't hold a candle to *Marathon*, *Abraxas* or the first Santana vinyl gem showcasing the 16-year-old Mike Shrieve pounding the skins. Staging a comeback has meant losing the percussion-driven Latin distinctiveness. What remain are the haunting Santana riffs imposed upon crass, jarring pop tunes that jibe with the likes of Rob Thomas, Everlast or Lauryn Hill. This is the *Zeitgeist's* recipe for success. A recipe that is echoed with less competency in the discordance of Limp Bizkit, Smashing Pumpkins, or Pearl Jam. Listening to musical scaffolding that consists of shoddily executed three chords accompanied, in most cases, by two-note vocal melodies has meant enduring Workers Compensation Board-worthy mental anguish!

Wide Mouth Mason's percussionist demonstrates he can barely manage an eighth note rhythm and that with absolute zero variation. For his part, the guitarist in the band responds with simple strumming, shunning rhythmic variation. Deep breathing technique helped me get down with The Tragically Hip and the song "Save the Planet." Their audile output? The minimalist three chords and a simple drum roll to punctuate the otherwise routine drumming. Rhythmically and melodically the sum total is "Bah Bah Black Sheep."

Singer Sarah McLachlan audaciously claims that her sound had its roots in the music of Cat Stevens. In the genre of pop music, Cat Stevens was gifted. His songs embody rather complex arrangements entirely absent from McLachlan's warbles, which have no melodic progression. On she drones and six CDs later she and her Lilith bosom buddies are still belting monotonous phrases, characterized by little harmonic resolution, and punctuated with a spasm of yodeling. Listen to the Canadian band Rush and you hear harmonic complexity. Interesting chord changes and walking bass-lines combine with the kind of time signature fluctuations that require high-level musicianship and years of practice. Such sonic variety is missing from McLachlan's around-the-campfire sing-alongs, the notes of which are invariably sustained with a distortion pedal, blended into a poorly articulated mess, and superimposed on a drumbeat bereft of fills.

The true finger-blistering, almighty fender-benders remain in the musical closet. These are the neo-classical instrumentalists, and in particular Tony MacAlpine, Yngwie Malmsteen, Eric Johnson, Vinnie Moore, Steve Morse and, of course, Sean Mercer. Recordings of their furious licks will be missing from the stores and the airwaves so long as consumers are willing to pay for stuff that sounds as if it was produced after three lessons with a bad tutor.

75. EYES SHUT TIGHT IN A SNOOZE: A REVIEW

August 9, 1999

Stanley Kubrick's last film, *Eyes Wide Shut*, was not only pretentious and overrated, it was a snooze. This flick is the last in a series of stylized personal projects for which the director became known. Given the mystique Kubrick acquired or cultivated, this posthumous flop is unlikely to damage the legend. For all the film's textured detail, the yarn is threadbare and the subtext replete with clumsy symbolism. The screenplay consists of labored, repetitive, and truncated dialogue where every exchange involves long stares and furrowed brows. "I am a doctor," is Tom Cruise's stock-in-trade phrase. An obscure, campy, hotel desk clerk delivers the only sterling performance. This is cold comfort considering the viewer is stuck with over two hours of Tom Cruise's half-hearted libidinous quests.

Eyes is really a conventional morality play during which Cruise prowls the streets of New York in his seldom-removed undertaker's overcoat in search of some relief for his sexual jealousy. Cruise's jealousy is aroused by a fantasy his wife, played by then real-life wife Nicole Kidman, relays in a moment of spite, and involves a sexual desire for a naval officer she glimpsed while on holiday with her family. So strong was her passion, she tells Tom, that she would have abandoned all for this man.

The confession follows a society party the couple attends in which they both flirt unabashedly with others. Again, the sum total of the dialogue here consists in backslapping, guffaw-inducing genuflection to doctorness. We are treated to an annoying peek at Kubrick's and The Culture's view on the professional pecking order, a view which is reinforced when Cruise makes one of his house calls to a patient whose father has just died. The woman, body writhing like that of a snake in coitus (is this method acting?), throws herself at Cruise. Sex and death co-mingle in one of the many larded symbolic moments in the film. The woman's fiancé, the geek math professor, is depicted as a lesser mortal than the handsome doctor. In defense of the math professor, let me say that he has three degrees done at a well nigh impossible level of abstraction. The general practitioner has, for the most, one degree requiring few leaps of abstraction. I know I am missing the point. This is not about the professional food chain. But neither is it about what Len Blum of the *National Post* described in stream-of-consciousness, indulgent prose: "Attraction. Flirtation. Seduction. Exploitation. Intimacy. Fantasy. Hurt. Revenge." Because if it is erotica you seek, then the movie is as sexy as cold mutton.

Back at the party, Tom is besieged by two models who want him. These females also can't stop wriggling like randy rattlesnakes, their attempts at sexy more phero-moronic than pheromone inspired. Nicole in the meantime is doing her own hormonal hop with a Dracula look-alike. Yes, the film is full of undeveloped characters. As they coil around one another intoxicated, Dracula applies his amorous solvent: "The charm of marriage," he says, "is that it makes a life of deception absolutely necessary." At this point Kubrick is defanged: He becomes a plagiarist who underestimates his audience, as Dracula fails to credit Oscar Wilde for the witty epigram.

No bash would be complete without the doctor coming to the rescue. Upstairs, draped over a chair ever so decoratively, languishes a victim of a drug overdose. She is nude and post coital. Tom runs ears, eyes and pulse checks and then proceeds to sit by the girl's side, sans coffee or an intravenous something, until she is declared saved. The girl pulls through never to forget the good doctor and destined to return the favor in the next hour or two. The Madonna-whore is another wooden symbol in this film.

Tom's journey to sexual and emotional maturation leads him to rekindle an acquaintance with a not-quite-doctor jazz musician. The medical school dropout tells Tom he is on the way to a regular gig where, when he peeks through his blindfold, his peripheral vision is flooded with amazing, masked, naked females. Tom decides to gate crash the orgy. Why Tom becomes imperiled at the orgy is not quite clear. Maybe he annoyed a patron by doing his Überdoctor routine. But to the rescue comes a stranger with familiar protrusions. At this point it must be clear to all that this woman, the Madonna-whore, is toast. In passing boredom I noted that the mask of one of the orgy attendants was a Guernica-like Picasso creation. No doubt the orgy could have done with some Guernica-inspired intensity. (Guernica, painted by Picasso, depicts the bombing of that Spanish town by the Germans.) Instead, it is a fashion shoot, engorged with sexless, perfect bodies, locked in aesthetically pleasing unerotic positions.

Kubrick's morality play reaches an epiphany when, after an unconsummated visit to a friendly prostitute (there goes the Madonna-whore again), Tom learns she has been diagnosed HIV positive. From across the girl's seedy abode, a hood in a trenchcoat stares Tom down. This is a messenger from the orgy society, and the message? The penumbra of sex can kill.

I confess, the only other film by Kubrick I have seen was *A Clockwork Orange*, which I liked. In that cult movie, the delinquent

Alex, inspired by evil and infused with a love for great classical music, does very bad things. The modest moral I took from *Clockwork* was that someone who loves Beethoven's Ninth so dearly could not be all bad. Listening to "Ode to Joy" was certainly more pleasurable than to the minimalist score from *Eyes Shut Wide*.

76. VANILLA PIE-IN-THE-SKY WITH DIAMONDS

January 2, 2002

"The great events of the world take place in the brain," wrote Oscar Wilde in the magnificent *Dorian Gray*. Consistent with the bile Hollywood screenwriters and actors have been churning out for over a decade now, no impressive—let alone great—events or revelations take place in the minds of the protagonists of the film *Vanilla Sky*. To make an exercise in solipsism attractive, the minds involved must be somewhat interesting. Throw together a bunch of pedestrian heads, barely extant dialogue, and an *ad hoc*, make-it-up-as-you-go disjointed plot—and you end up with a poor outcome. Please read on. I won't be divulging the plot or climax of the film, mainly because, although I saw it, I haven't the foggiest what this film is about.

Because the Hollywood landscape has been bleak for so very long, this bit of blandness should not, in all fairness, be the focus of any extra derision. *Vanilla Sky* generally jibes with the staple Hollywood fare. If it's not a special-effects binge, it's a showcase of the toothy, loud and gregarious Julia Roberts-prototype babe, and her assorted male cohorts in a succession of vapid "romantic comedies," sometimes with real men, sometimes with extra-stratospheric beings.

Critics debate with absolute seriousness whether the broom-straddling Harry Potter is an evil or admirable little tyke. Who cares? Why no mention of the disturbing specter of adults en masse flocking to view what is a film for kids? If there is such a thing as mass neurosis, then this is it. The following will no doubt carbon date me, but a "period piece" (joke alert) like the *Teenage Mutant Ninja Turtles* was a matinee to which I took my then-young child and her friends. It was not a cultural event.

The Lord of the Rings was once considered a children's book. It appealed to adults with a proclivity for hobgoblins and gobbledygook. Never would I have predicted that grown-ups would levitate so far above their rational minds as to find this flight from reality worthy of such gush. At some stage it would seem developmentally appropriate for adults to cease craving a steady entertainment diet of fantasy and develop an interest in real people, in relationships and in how flesh-and-blood make their way—and interact—in a complicated world. What has happened to such narratives, to the depiction on celluloid of developed—as opposed to flat—characters? What ever happened to the art of acting? What ever has turned Americans into a stun-gunned audience with the attention span of a nit and an ability to focus only on fast-moving and imploding animated objects, or on relationships that are entirely abstracted from reality? Fact has lately outdone fiction. The need for some escapism can be understood in light of the events since September 11. But the American audience has for some time demonstrated the aesthetic and sensibility of a magpie searching a trash heap for a shiny object.

Into this twilight tradition steps the film *Vanilla Sky*. Remember the collision between William Hurt and Kathleen Turner in that contemporary *film noir Body Heat*? They sizzled. Well, together and apart, Tom Cruise and Penelope Cruz have the magnetism of a wet blanket. A one-watt light bulb generates more heat than this dull duo exudes. The epitome of shallow chic, Cruise plays David Aames, who is a rich and flighty playboy at the helm of a Dad Did It company. Sophia (Penelope Cruz) breezes into his birthday party as his best friend's date. With his mistress (Cameron Diaz as Julie) watching on, Aames becomes captivated by Sophia. I hate to puncture this moment of magic with some un-PC elitism, but when, in response to Tom's request for an introduction, Penelope informs him he has "de plejerrr of Sophia," I somehow heard Penelope shrieking, "Can you buy my fish?" Her shrill voice and locutionary lameness lend Penelope the quality of a fishwife. (Why is the foreign accent such an aphrodisiac? Is it another indication that men don't care what women say, so long as they look good saying it?)

Penelope's smug rat-like grin accompanies the staple behavior that is taught at the Meryl Creep School of Acting—if you wanna appear deep and esoteric, act goofy and erratic. Sophia/Penelope makes facetious little quips that are anything but witty. It is profoundly rude to accost your host right off the bat with the accusation that his empire is not his own, but the doing of daddy. Who is this ill-bred socialist to crash a party and question the manner in which her host has acquired his fortune? How very tacky indeed.

When a couple has very little mental momentum with which to ignite the physical, it is a good strategy to delay the physical. Tom knows this, and postpones bedding the broad. My hackles stood on end when Penelope, in what was supposed to be a playful tease, bellows after Tom, "plejerrr deleyerrr" (should be "pleasure delayer"). Cameron Diaz injects some short-lived life into the film as Julie Gianni, the jilted mistress, whose actions catapult Tom into some parallel universe. Viewers have doubtless seen the forthcoming attraction scene where Diaz drives Tom over the bridge. Admittedly, Diaz is the bad guy, but the words she utters were to me at least very sensible: "When you make love to someone, your body makes a promise to him/her," she insists. Why are you disregarding the emotional consequences that ought to flow from our sleeping together, she conveys to the grimacing Tom, as she careens toward oblivion.

The skin-deep Hollywood perspective, as conveyed in the film, however, is at odds with Diaz's contention that sleeping with someone is not to be treated breezily. Tom's puzzled stare conveys a sense of, "Hey chick, haven't you heard of a one-night stand?" But no, Diaz seems to insist that lovemaking as they had shared has meaning and ought to have been followed with a measure of decorum and care. Irrespective of her reprehensible and irrational action, Diaz makes a good point. At the very least, having made passionate love to the poor girl, Cruise-cum-Aames has no business leaving her off his birthday party guest list or treating her so shabbily.

More evidence of the cutis-deep nature of this film: Cruz and Cruise cook it up so long as they are both "good looking" (not in my opinion, but according to most). No sooner does Cruise lose his good looks than Penelope beats a hasty retreat. Tom's acting, admittedly, is much improved after the accident, when he emerges as a cross between Quasimodo and Elephant Man. On second thought, better rent David Lynch's *Elephant Man*, staring Anthony Hopkins in his pre-Hollywood days and the outstanding John Hurt.

Even better: I mentioned William Hurt earlier. Rather than drift in and out of the *Vanilla Sky* artless maze, try *Gorky Park* on video or DVD. It's a gem of a film with great performances from Hurt and Joanna Pacula. Hurt combines languid and lethal as a Russian detective solving gruesome murders. The film, however, transcends the spy genre thanks to an achingly beautiful performance delivered by Joanna Pacula as Irina. Against the backdrop of Moscow during the communist 1970s, the exquisite Pacula's yearning for freedom is palpable. For Irina, there is neither life nor love without liberty. What would Tom and Penelope know about hitting the viewer in the solar plexus?

77. UNFAITHFUL

May 22, 2002

There are doubtless some good, general reasons to be partial to the appeal of foreign men. From my perspective, American men don't always get the British-type barb or quip. They can become tiresomely preachy, often launching a maudlin mouthful over my kind of expressive excesses. Being understood is nothing to sneeze at. Which is why I'd be sympathetic if the lust the libidinous wife in the film *Unfaithful* develops for the more-relaxed continental man were due to a lack of understanding or tenderness from her spouse. It isn't. So, try as I did, I could not quite grasp her dangerous obsession. Besides which, women's desire for muscle-bound hunks is a curiosity to me, who thinks most sexual activity occurs in the mind.

The lover in *Unfaithful* is a coital cliché. For one, he is French, with all the grating affectations. By casting him as an antiquarian book-dealer, the improbable inference is that Lover is both literate and super stud. Yeah, right. One of Lover's moves is to direct our enchantress to his Seduction Shelf, from which she is instructed to select and read some gibberish. The charm works! The almost-unfaithful wife is so impressed that, as soon as she gets a break from her grueling routine, she rushes back to the quaint, typecast Soho apartment to consummate the relationship.

I liked Diane Lane in the role of Constance Sumner, the cheating spouse. She has an absolutely smashing figure, which I easily forgave, given that she has quite a few more facial wrinkles than I do. As convincing as her sexual delirium was, Lane, who plays opposite Richard Gere as Ed in the role of husband, and underneath—or wrapped around—Olivier Martinez in the role of Paul Martel the lover, cannot escape the stigma of bored, rich, and beautiful.

In one of his books, author Tom Robbins expressed a hilarious, existential disappointment over the fact that the sexual act is something everyone can perform: an act capable of conveying the highest of human emotion is within the grasp of all and sundry! My way around this paradox is to venture that sex devoid of love is reserved for the wild animal and the gay man. To the extent that this is the sex people choose, they are no better than the beast or the gay man. The problem is that marriage itself often breeds some pretty unelevated emotions, the outcome of which is legal but loveless sex. Was this the dilemma facing the wife in director Adrian Lyne's latest film? Although the original incarnation of the film, Claude Chabrol's 1969 *La femme infidèle*, did showcase some relational and emotional nuance with which to flesh out the pure-flesh portions, Lyne's very-much-Hollywood re-make offers none of that. There is not as much as a hint of marital discord to fuel the affair. Rather, what we get is confined to raunchy make-out sessions—sex in Hollywood retains the quality of a *Cirque du Soleil* performance: aesthetic, athletic, and that's that.

Lyne's oeuvre includes *Fatal Attraction*, *Indecent Proposal*, and *9 1/2 Weeks*. In 1998, Lyne was almost caught in *flagrante delicto* with his *Lolita*," the celluloid adaptation of Vladimir Nabokov's great novel about a man's affair with his 12-year-old stepdaughter. *Lolita* is likely to become the least-touted work in the director's repertoire, given the apoplexy over creating any untoward images of Our Children, and given the alleged sexual contagion in the Catholic Church.

Unfaithful has the usual annoying build-up accoutrements intended to convey a regular life. Audience is expected to coo over "cute" kid who pees on the toilet seat, as well as over father-husband who is wooden but warm. Audience is expected to find gorgeous woman homely—rather than unhygienic—because she takes chewing gum from cute kid's mouth and places it in hers.

During the Murder, the culprit's state of mind conjured the murder scene in Albert Camus' 1942 book, *The Stranger*. Then again, I may have just reached a point in this glitzy flick where my mind hankered for inspiration:

> ... all the sweat that had gathered in my eyebrows suddenly ran down over my eyelids, covering them with a dense layer of warm moisture ... That was when everything shook ... I realized that I'd destroyed the balance of the day and the perfect silence of this beach where I'd been happy.

Indeed, murder is never a good idea, as Oscar Wilde reminded: Don't do anything you can't discuss over dinner (settle down, he was kidding). Of this, the director, who apparently went back and forth before deciding on a suitable finale, is not as convinced. Lane settled on a morally inconclusive end. How French!

78. CREEPING PORN AND THE CABLE NEWS
NETWORKS

July 30, 2003

The girl on the screen could have been a Fox News anchorwoman, although she was by far prettier and less vulgar looking than the coarse loudmouths, whose lipstick-dripping mouths deliver, in fog-horn decibels, slogans like: "We Report, You Decide" and "Fair and Balanced."

Appearing on *Your World* with Neil Cavuto, porn star Sunrise Adams attempted, rather touchingly, to play down her cheap hooker looks and sorry syntax with a pair of nerdy spectacles. But while she used the standard, dizzy, woman's magazine self-realization routine to describe her occupation—"this is a pastime for me. This is just something for me to do and enjoy and to grow with"—it was her host, Cavuto, who was responsible for rolling out the welcoming waterbed for the porn star and her pimp, Steve Hirsch, co-founder of Vivid Entertainment.

Don't get me wrong—there should be no legal impediments to entering the adult-entertainment business. Like prostitution, this is strictly a matter for the adults involved. There is no place for federal meddling between consenting grownups. Neither is there room for the paternalistic depiction of women as passive agents, demeaned by male-driven appetites, a humbug shared by conservatives and liberals alike. The large cross-section of porn stars Howard Stern parades on his show makes it clear that these single-minded women like what they do. The sly, lewd glint in the eye, the exhibitionism, and the boundless, primitive sexuality seem to unite them all. (Unlike the Foxettes, porn stars are, however, rather feminine and demure.)

ABC's Diane Sawyer once tried to twist a report about a particularly off-putting specimen in the X-rated business so that it would conform to the angle of Madonna-who-was-turned-into-whore-by-an-indifferent-society. The girl played Sawyer for the fool she is. A shallow, kinky, weird-looking, low-intelligence twit, with few inhibitions and an inability to postpone gratification, the girl was consumed with getting into any limelight, including that of a naked bulb above a dirty bed. She ends up as happy as a porn star in a maximum-security prison, winning a coveted "industry" award. "I can say that I've done pretty much everything there is to do, and I can walk away feeling a little proud about it, you know?" she tells an annoyed Sawyer.

For sure, it takes a "special" person to be able to have sex, often very twisted and unhealthy sex, with thousands of males and females. The fact that porn star Jenna Jamison is treated like a celebrity, even being respectfully interviewed on Fox News, doesn't change what she is. A person who chooses to sell sex for a living, rather than work at a supermarket or teach school, used to be called a whore in civilized society! A porn star is a hooker with a camera crew and a contract—a prostitute with a penchant for exhibitionism.

Cavuto referred to her enterprising pimp as "the king of porn," but for Sunrise Adams he reserved the honorific "successful film star." The pornographer and the prostitute are, I venture, far more honest than the dishonest lot that pervades Fox. "The Fox effect" has come to denote the network's journalistically wanton rejection of objective news coverage. The news the network hustles is indeed more drama than data.

But Fox is "sexing up" more than just news. It's customary to see the skanky Jamison as a commentator on the E! Networks programs, but the news cable networks, with Fox in the lead, are not far behind. These faux-conservatives are certainly helping to mainstream society's more dubious members. The class act that is Martha Stewart, for instance, is routinely derided on Fox. Their choice of "Lifestyle Guru"? The rotting flesh that is Gene Simmons of the band Kiss.

Ranked third among cable news channels, MSNBC and its country bumpkin Joe Scarborough are pedaling hard to keep up. Doing his bit to juice up his show, and in the process to challenge Fox, Scarborough sojourned to the fleshpots of Hollywood, for a week billed misleadingly as a confrontation. It was nothing of the sort. This was an affirmation of slut and celebrity.

The perceptive viewer ought to have taken from the show that humanity's detritus can be graded. Hollywood madam Heidi Fleiss and pornographer Larry Flynt were the upstanding citizens in the Scarborough lineup. These straight shooters, who've been so horribly persecuted by the law, are nowhere near as loathsome as Ashley Judd is. Rather than put her own money where her shrill mouth is, Judd's idea of "charity" is to use her prominence to steal from the burdened American taxpayer and give to African governments to fight AIDS. The fleecing Judd thinks this immoral and coerced wealth transfer will stop Africans from fornicating into the afterlife. Her own countrymen and women can eat tortillas, for all she cares.

Scarborough shares with the liberals he lambastes the same underlying assumptions about human nature—he sees pornography as "degrading to women and society." The Bush acolyte's clunky mind has it upside down. Hugh Hefner is not the problem. The problem lies with a society whose members have made him an icon. American young women are as brazen, brash, and cocky as any porn star. They aren't Hefner's victims; Hefner simply created a market for females who can think of nothing more elevated than being photographed with their legs about their ears. When Hefner told Scarborough *Playboy* magazine is an American "lifestyle magazine," he had a valid point.

Had he wanted to make a statement about class, beauty, and talent, Scarborough could have. But there was no place on Joe's stump for Grace Kelly look-alike Gwyneth Paltrow, or for actress Jill Hennessy, an alert, keenly intelligent, and delicate-looking gamine of a girl. Instead, Scarborough's co-host was a dim, scantily clad actress by the name of Heather Tom. An abundance of pasty flesh, bleached candyfloss hair, a plump thickset mug, and a bulbous mouth all conspired to entrench the Fox-anchor porn star look and apparel.

VI. Twenty-First-Century Voodoo

79. BROKEN BRAINS?

January 16, 2002

Andrea Pia Yates methodically drowned her five children aged six months to seven years. Accepting responsibility for her actions was not a proposition—certainly not a legal one—so the Houston woman pleaded innocent by reason of insanity. On hand to second Yates' innocence was the dog-and-pony psychiatric show—the very witch doctors whose livelihood depends on diseasing every aspect of bad behavior; the same people who have no qualms about junking free will and responsibility for an unproven biological determinism, riddled with logical, factual, and moral infelicities.

The general consensus among members of the psychiatric profession who belabored the Yates case in the media is that Yates' brain was "broken" at the time of the murders. She was, said one Dr. Tribal Bones, no different than a person who has had a heart attack. A heart attack is a physical event. The tissue damage is palpable. Consider, moreover, that a person suffering a heart attack endures an involuntary—emphasis on involuntary—coronary thrombosis, and you get the idea of how utterly incorrect this analogy really is. Consider also that there is no credible scientific, peer-reviewed evidence for the organic basis of aberrant behavior, and you grasp the chicanery that surrounds the claim that strange or bad conduct is caused by "chemical imbalances" in the brain.

Psychiatrists don't have a test that can prove that a so-called mental illness is actually organic in origin. For this reason, they seldom engage in testing. Say they ran an assay on Yates, and the tests yielded an elevated level in her brain of this or the other neurotransmitter. Such results are invariably statistically insignificant. But for the sake of argument, let's pretend they are not. There is seldom a way to conclusively demonstrate that, in this instance, the drudgery of drowning the kids, the prison ordeal, and decades of devouring medication did not cause such test results, rather than a pre-existing condition. On the face of it, our shameful shamans are demanding that the rotten behavior itself be accepted as proof for the organic nature of evil conduct. Sounds remarkably like a circular argument to me.

The more rigorous and honest clinicians concede that drawing a causal relationship between "mental illness" and "chemical imbalances" is impossible. That prescription medication often helps misbehaved or unhappy individuals is no proof that strange behavior is an organic disease. One can chemically castrate a pedophile. But does this demonstrate that molesting kids is an organic disease? Never. It proves only that chemical castration can at times reduce recidivism in people who have chosen to victimize children.

Roughly 75 percent of the value of "antidepressant" drugs is due to the placebo effect. And talk therapies—cognitive-behavioral therapy in particular—can have equal or better results. Veracity permits only that we limit our causal conclusions to saying that assorted treatment modalities sometimes help people with behavioral problems, nothing more.

Philosopher and psychiatrist Thomas Szasz has delivered a deductive death knell to this house of cards, pointing out that, unlike medicine, where the same principles are used to explain health and disease, the pseudo-science of psychiatry uses one set of principles to explain rational behavior; another set to explain irrational behavior. When a person does something ghastly, it is surmised *post hoc* that he has ceased being a morally responsible agent, and herewith acquired a disease. Do we ever seek chemical causes for the positive and extraordinary actions of a Bill Gates? Because Gates does good things, we attribute his actions to *choice*. Because Yates' actions were evil, we attribute them to *causes*: to a diseased mind or an inattentive mate.

A genuine organic brain disorder, like the Parkinson's Michael J. Fox suffers from, causes very specific behavioral deficits, tremors, for one. Even if it were for real, the chemical abnormality our voodooists allude to cannot cause a series of complex, coordinated, and purposeful actions. No brain disease can cause the following sequence: Seize a baby girl. Ignore the tiny thing's whimpering and thrust her underwater until she ceases it. Pick the next in line. Submerge, until the victim's convulsions subside. Fasten your deadly grip on the next tot. Let go once the throes of death are over and the small body goes limp. Repeat until all five little charges are dead. No alleged chemical abnormality can explain away and account for the components of choice, planfullness, and resolve so salient in these actions.

Morally and logically bankrupt, this thinking is also adopted by the terrorist's exculpator. A mass murderer is suddenly no longer a morally culpable agent, but an inchoate entity whose diseased mind or stark surroundings caused him to commit the crime. The murderer weaseling out with the classic excuse, "I was only following orders"—in Yates' case, the voices in her head; in the terrorist's case, Allah—does not change the fact that he is an active agent—a victimizer, not a victim—who has opted to obey an evil authority, imaginary or real. Ever wonder why the voices Yates may have heard never impelled her to do something good? We would hardly have to invent a fictitious disease if Yates had heard voices instructing her to cuddle her babies, now would we?

80. TRADING MORALITY FOR MUMBO-JUMBO

March 20, 2002

The people who monopolize the narrative of right and wrong in the culture were not pleased when a jury found Andrea Pia Yates guilty of murdering her five children. So they swung into action: The lawyers, mental-health agitators, academics, and journalists had a go at the jurors, denouncing them as Texan troglodytes. At the same time, the cultural cognoscenti continued to refer to Yates tenderly as "the Houston mother," something that is both technically incorrect and morally reprehensible, considering Yates' self-inflicted childless status.

Next came an attack on the Texas insanity defense. The law says that it's insufficient to show that a person is "mentally ill" to render her not guilty of murder by reason of insanity. It's necessary to also demonstrate that, at the time of the crime, she did not know right from wrong. The premise of this law is lucid—it bears the hallmark of natural law. Natural law is law arrived at through reason and not through the self-serving drive of special-interest groups, and certainly not with the aid of a science that is as valid as the practice of table turning by spirit mediums. By parity of reason, the natural law is immutably just. At times the law of the state coincides with the natural law. More often than not, natural justice has been buried under the rubble of legislation and statute.

By stating that "mental illness" is a necessary but insufficient condition for finding a person not guilty by reason of insanity, Texas' insanity defense acknowledges an unyielding truth: An individual's essential nature does not change because he suffers behavioral or mood problems. Most "mentally-ill" people choose never to commit murder. Why? Because mental peculiarities don't rob people of their moral nature. Texas law concurs by implying that even under extreme mental duress, a person is not without the capacity to reflect on his actions and thoughts and make choices. In every situation, no matter the constraints, one can exercise some free will, even if only to decide how to respond to a hopeless predicament.

This is what his experience in Auschwitz taught philosopher and distinguished psychiatrist, Viktor E. Frankl. "In the camps one lost everything," Frankl reiterated in a *New York Times* interview, "except the last of the human freedoms, to choose one's attitude in any given set of circumstances, to choose one's own way," a reality that makes

Yates all the more contemptible, because many choices and supports were available to her. Despite that, mankind and his dog have decided that since Yates rejected her many privileges and options, and acted contrary to reason, she had no reasons for her actions.

Yet more nonsense. Yates explained that she had defiled her children with her devilish mothering. She decided that rather than, for instance, terminate herself—the source of all the evil—she would terminate the little people whom she had allegedly tainted. Is that not a decision? It's a terrible one, but it's a conscious decision. Yet people are too squeamish to stare into the maw of evil—they refuse to take Yates at her word.

Enter the insanity plea. It capitulates to the mistaken notion that, when crimes are too horrible to comprehend, medical concepts must replace moral concepts. The implications of the insanity plea are very odd indeed: To find her not guilty by reason of insanity, the jurors would have had to accept that it was not Yates, but her "disease" or some separate alter ego that tortured those children to death. Yates, moreover, would have been cast not as a victimizer, but as the innocent victim of her "affliction."

Rejected, thankfully, by the good Texan jurors, this bogus bifurcation flouts the Law of Identity: A person can't have done the deed, yet simultaneously be innocent of it! The 19th-century American philosopher Lysander Spooner put it thus: "Guilt is an intrinsic quality of actions, and can neither be created, destroyed or changed by legislation."

But not if the judicial activists have anything to say. They are now complaining that the law's standard for legal insanity must be broadened so that even on a determination that Yates knew right from wrong, it would still have been possible to find her innocent. In other words, a history of behavioral problems will suffice to render a killer not responsible for his actions.

The real bedlam lies in a society that allows the psychiatric articles of faith to replace morality.

81. COLLIDING WITH REALITY—POST-
TRAUMATICALLY

First published on December 14, 2000
Updated after September 11

If I were to tell you that the incidence of stress-related disorders among war veterans, civilians in war zones, Israeli children subject to bombardments, and Holocaust survivors is not significantly higher than in comparable populations which have not been exposed to these stressors, would you believe me? I'll go one better: Clinicians warned that the cataclysmic events of September 11 would coincide with an increase in the use and need for mental health services. Yet it didn't happen. The specter of the ubiquitous crisis-intervention team descending on a community following a tragedy doesn't help my case—my claim that these services are unnecessary if not downright harmful is at odds with their popularity.

On September 11, agents from Crisis Management International (CMI) galvanized a nationwide network consisting of 1402 therapists and psychologists to tend to the New York workforce. Charles Fishman, editor of *Fast Company,* reported that it was not unusual on any given day to find a corporation employing dozens of these agents to administer a protocol known as "critical-incident stress debriefing." "Even after two weeks," marveled Fishman, one firm "was still using between 10 and 20 CMI counselors a day" to administer both group and individual sessions. At a cost of $250 an hour per counselor, some companies were spending upwards of $35,000 daily on stress-debriefing services.

The common perception that there exists a direct connection between extreme events and disordered behavior is firmly ensconced across our communities. All told, the incidence of "toxic" events in the lives of people in western democracies is very high. In Third World countries it is virtually universal. Yet paradoxically, the lifetime prevalence of Posttraumatic Stress Disorder (PTSD) is very low. "Very few directly exposed individuals develop distress disorders," writes Marilyn Bowman, professor of psychology at Simon Fraser University, British Columbia, and an expert on the subject of PTSD.

Still, the crisis-debriefing protocol, administered by intrusive strangers, now routinely accompanies any upheaval in the workplace, in schools and elsewhere. With the psychiatric profession's *Diagnostic and Statistical Manual of Mental Disorders* stipulating that merely hearing about a "toxic" event may cause mental damage, is there any wonder that such intervention has become an imperative?

Yet most of the data supporting these flawed assumptions are derived from biased clinical samples and rely on controversial self-reports. A patient presenting for treatment is already unrepresentative of the general population. She will typically tell of an event and implicate the incident in her symptoms. The clinician then erroneously concludes that there is a causal relationship between the event and the patient's symptoms. This *post hoc* or backward reasoning contaminates most studies on PTSD. Controlled studies though, show that well-functioning individuals tend to report as many pathological experiences as do people who don't function well. The same faulty reasoning must lead us to conclude that their trauma caused their successes.

The findings of Robert Rosenheck of Veterans Affairs certainly confirm that the deluge of dispatched therapists following September 11 was likely redundant. In a paper in the *American Journal of Psychiatry*, Rosenheck documented only small increases in mental health service use in New York among veterans with PTSD following the attacks of September 11. These increases differed only slightly from those of previous years, and were, in fact, slightly smaller than the increases observed in other large American cities. This led Rosenheck to conclude that, "Although the events of September 11 were profoundly traumatic for those directly involved and clearly distressing for others, they are not necessarily medically significant."

So what am I missing here? Toxic events are rife in people's lives, yet stress-attributed disorders are not common? Clearly the toxic event in and of itself doesn't cause PTSD. In her book on individual differences in PTSD, and in a 1999 paper in the *Canadian Journal of Psychiatry*, Bowman demonstrates that whether those exposed to traumatic events will suffer mental repercussions is determined by certain stable temperamental styles. Intelligence confers a protective benefit, as does an individual's belief system. The relatively unchanging tendencies to feel helpless and to attribute responsibility to others are predisposing personality traits. Another good predictor of PTSD is a history of psychiatric and personality disorders.

Despite such evidence, mental health professionals continue to expand their jurisdiction. Tooled up with Freudian constructs like "denial" and "repression," they insist that if you are not "venting," you are "in denial"; if you are stoical, you are likely "repressing." Evidence that contradicts the clinician's theory is enlisted as evidence for the theory's correctness—every behavior the post-trauma individual shows—adaptive or not—is said to be a consequence of the trauma and proof of it.

Therapy itself is based on the premise that "expression of negative feelings is essential," to quote Bowman. Venting, moreover, is regarded as a moral virtue, helping to explain not only the camera-friendly grief chic cultivated by people many times removed from a tragedy but also the pressure to undertake counseling. But the evidence indicates that denial more often provides an adaptive benefit. Individuals given to emotionality fare worse than people with a stiff upper lip. And when therapy is undertaken, clinical outcomes are in fact improved when it focuses on problem-solving strategies instead of on the excavation of emotional agony.

The pressure from many PTSD-advocacy groups notwithstanding, the American Psychological Association's clinical division reports that *zero* out of 255 treatments for PTSD meet criteria that are well established. Evidence for the efficacy of treatments is indeed scant if non-existent. No surprise here. The faulty assumptions underlying this clinical diagnosis dovetail with a general emphasis on subjectivity and relativism in psychological research and the culture at large. It's all part of our contemporary aversion to objective inquiry and a fascination with the emotional and the histrionic. Bowman contends that we have regressed to an unenlightened, premodern—not postmodern—era, paralleled in some of history's less evolved periods.

Chimeras such as repressed memory therapy and multiple personality disorder, which not so long ago received the nod from many mainstream mental health professionals, bear this out. Sustaining the adversity-distress model, however, requires the willing collusion between "professional guild interests" and groups of individuals who prefer to attribute their difficulties to anything but themselves.

82. ATTENTION DEFICIT DISORDER IS ALL IN THE HEAD

December 28, 1999

Disease labels are now being slapped on an ever-wider range of behavior. Members of the psychiatric and medical professions and their patients have all taken to the idiom of disease like ducks to water. The twin evils of reductionism and the pathologizing of everyday behavior are at work here. Complex behavior, once considered the function of morals, choices, and yes, character, is now routinely reduced to the basic components of genetics and biochemistry and outsourced to the "expert." In the process, the thief is now more appropriately called a kleptomaniac; the arsonist a pyromaniac; and the promiscuous a sex addict. This is both poor scientific practice as well as morally and intellectually impoverished.

It has not stopped Dr. John Ratey, a Harvard associate professor and a well-respected, prominent psychiatrist, from claiming in his 1997 book *Shadow Syndromes* that quirky behaviors are actually mild mental illnesses resulting from brain dysfunction. The lout who is appropriately obsequious with the boss because he knows where his bread is buttered, but who is less dainty with the wife, even thumping her occasionally, would be a candidate for compassion. He is after all doing battle with what Dr. Ratey terms "Intermittent Rage Disorder." And the dad who dotes on his children while they are with him, but fails to mail them child support money as soon as they are out of sight, is simply afflicted with "Environmental Dependency Disorder": He remembers his kids only when they are around.

Is there proof for these *sub-rosa* disease categories? None whatsoever, although this has not prevented Ratey and many like him from coating their pronouncements with a patina of scientific respectability—and then cashing in. If Ratey is up the creek without a paddle, then he is up there with the best of company. *The Psychiatric Diagnostic and Statistical Manual* (DSM-IV), the Rosetta Stone of the profession, has grown since its inception in the 1950s from 60 categories of abnormal behavior to about 410 diagnostic labels today and counting. Many of the disorders described in it are a matter of trend and niche.

One of the diagnoses Dr. Ratey is particularly fond of is "Attention Deficit Hyperactivity Disorder" (ADHD). So fond is he of the label that he diagnosed himself with it. The reason this seemingly competent person decided he had a learning disorder is because he was unable to free associate during psychoanalysis!

Indeed, ADHD is the focus of a growing industry. The Canadian Attention Deficit Disorder Foundation says this learning disorder is likely genetically transmitted, affecting six to seven percent of the population. There are pervasive efforts underway to pronounce ADHD a disorder of the brain, although the evidence for this is poor. Driven by advocates and special interests—among them former U.S. Vice President Al Gore's wife Tipper and a slew of medical professionals and peddlers of pharmaceuticals—U.S. legislators have gone ahead and pronounced ADHD a brain-based disorder. This is most curious because the flagship American National Institutes of Health (NIH), led by a panel of independent scientists, concluded that there is as yet "no independent valid test" for ADHD, and that "further research is necessary to establish ADHD as a brain disorder."

The treatment protocol for ADHD is another aspect of this controversial diagnosis that gives the NIH pause. Children with ADHD are often given powerful psychostimulants. Yet there are no long-term studies of either stimulants or psychosocial treatments, and certainly "no information on the long-term outcomes of medication-treated ADHD individuals in terms of educational and occupational achievements, involvement with the police, or other areas of social functioning." But what must surely put the advocates to shame are the NIH's consistent findings that treatment for ADHD yields little improvement in academic achievement and social skills. Treatment, it seems, doesn't do what it is supposed to do.

If nothing else, it is an interesting exercise to scrutinize the DSM-IV-based ADHD diagnostic criteria. Who doesn't know a child who "has difficulty sustaining attention, doesn't seem to listen when spoken to directly, loses things necessary for tasks, fidgets, or is on the go constantly"? Come to think of it, most adults at some point or another conform to such a description. Couple such subjective diagnostic criteria with the fact that boys outnumber girls with the condition by nine to one, and ask yourself whether the ADHD diagnosis is not inadvertently targeting typical male exuberance.

The ADHD experts claim that children who take these drugs are better liked by other children and experience less punishment for their actions, which, in turn, improves their self-image. Considering that the adverse effects from prolonged use of medications for ADHD can range from cardiac arrhythmia through to seizures and liver damage, this is some price to pay for popularity.

83. ADDICTIONS ARE ABOUT BEHAVIOR, NOT DISEASE

June 22, 2000

When it comes to thinking about addiction, opinions converge. Social progressives and conservatives alike share the same ideological hangover from the Prohibition era, with a twist of AA sadism. All are religious about abstinence, and all accept as bible from Sinai the wisdom of coercing addicts into treatment regimens. (Incidentally, the success the proponents of coerced treatment claim for it is no argument in its favor.) But perhaps the greatest error made in the attempt at humane formulations about addiction is to cast as a disease what is essentially a problem of behavior.

The dangers of gathering more and more behaviors under the disease label is not something pharmacology moguls, politicians or health care professionals ruminate about, despite the ramifications for a society already committed to a morality lite and to diminished personal responsibility. In his book *Diseasing of America,* addiction researcher Stanton Peele breaks with this tradition. Disease conceptions of misbehavior are bad science and morally and intellectually sloppy, argues Peele. "Once we treat alcoholism and addiction as diseases, we cannot rule out that anything people do but shouldn't is a disease, from crime to excessive sexuality to procrastination."

Aggravated by the media, the misconception that these behaviors are brain based and linked to a genetic vulnerability persists in the absence of scientific evidence. There is no genetic marker for alcoholism or drug addiction; there is no inherited mechanism that leads a person to be unable to control his substance use, to go on tremendous binges, or to leave off his connection to people and environments in order to consume a substance. Neither are there genetic markers that distinguish the addict from the moderate user or the nonuser. Brain-based theories of addiction are simply baseless.

Show your typical media reporter a color-coded PET scan of a user in action, and he'll rush out to report to millions of equally ignorant viewers that here's proof that addiction is a disease. Always on hand to back up self-serving errors, the "experts" will concur: When people take drugs, their brain functioning changes. This, they take as proof for the brain-based theory of addiction.

Of course, all a PET scan conveys is that when people take drugs, changes occur in brain metabolism, nothing more and nothing less. When they have sex, cuddle their infants, or eat chocolate, similar changes occur in the same brain centers. Do changes in the brain tell us anything about the person's behavior or its motivation? Hardly. Can we infer an addiction from the fact that certain centers in the brain of the sexually preoccupied perk up when he has sex? Of course not. Then again, when people recover from addiction—by any means at all—their brain functioning also alters. By no means is this evidence that addiction is organic or biological in the sense that appendicitis or diabetes is. Everything we do involves our brain, and the brain alters its physical structure and functioning in response to the environment. We could just as well say that learning French is a biological accomplishment, though most of us would rather call it an intellectual achievement.

Identifying activities as stimulating the cerebral pleasure centers fails to explain, then, why people find different things pleasurable and why different people react in destructive, addictive ways to some of these stimuli, while others incorporate them into a balanced overall lifestyle.

Unlike genuine organic diseases, addictive disorders are known only by the behaviors they describe. In the absence of the ongoing behavior there is no way of telling whether the person is or will be addicted. "By claiming that alcoholics are alcoholics even if they haven't drunk for fifteen years, alcoholism is made to seem less tied to drinking behavior and more like cancer," writes Peele. "A person," however, "does not get over cancer by stopping a ... behavior" while "the sole and essential indicator of successful remission of alcoholism is that a person ceases to drink."

Despite its intellectual dishonesty, the rationale for using the disease model to describe and think about addiction is that medical treatment is effective. Yet another deception. An overview of controlled studies indicates that "treated patients do not fare better than untreated people with the same problems." Of particular note is a 1996, 4500-subject-strong epidemiological study conducted by the National Longitudinal Alcohol Epidemiological Survey. Treated alcoholics, it was found, were more heavily alcohol dependent on average than untreated alcoholics. Behavioral problems more often than not don't respond to medical intervention.

While the application of the medical disease model to addictions has served to "remove the stigma from these behaviors," it is not clear why this is a good thing. The disease conception of addiction acts to isolate the noxious behavior from the person. Thus when we claim that drugs, much like the flu, "get a hold" of one, we conveniently deflect from that which mediates human action; when we persist in deferring to the drug to explain everything the user does, we forget in the process of this circular argument that the person predates the drug. There is no sense in which opting to shoot up for the first time, then doing it again, then stealing or breaking and entering to get some, mimic the organic disease process in cancer or diabetes.

Try as the egalitarians do to whittle down the differences between people to simple schedules of reinforcement, they invariably fail. Not being laboratory rats, human behavior is mediated by—and cannot be explained without reference to—values, conscious choices, and probity of character or lack thereof. Not surprisingly, heroin addicts are highly disposed to having social problems even before they become addicted. Equally, truancy and smoking behavior serve as good predictors of future drug use. An honest look at drug use means we cannot pry it from personal predilections.

84. DIAGNOSTIC DISORDERS

January 13, 2000

The love and concern for their children is one of the most powerful driving forces in the lives of parents. We want them to succeed in what is an increasingly competitive world. Attention Deficit Hyperactivity Disorder (ADHD) touches on our fears and aspirations for our children. It also puts to the test the manner in which we accept their imperfections and the effect of those imperfections on us. This is why, understandably, the topic of ADHD causes such distress to parents.

When I queried this catchall diagnosis, giving voice, incidentally, to a robust and ongoing debate underway in the scientific community, readers objected. I was accused of neglecting to do "research," although talking to ADHD stakeholders was usually how readers defined research. Let me say that while the human story is emotionally powerful and makes for good copy, in isolation, it is an anecdote with little research validity beyond that of a case study. I would hope, however, that people use their critical faculties to question medical orthodoxy. Arguments must ultimately be judged on their merit, not by the authority or the qualifications of those who make them.

In 1997, Robert Sternberg, a prominent Yale professor of psychology, told *The New Republic* magazine there was no medical evidence to support the view that children who are labeled learning-disabled have an immutable neurological disability in learning. A year later the flagship American National Institutes of Health (NIH) confirmed Sternberg's pronouncement. In a Consensus Statement on the Diagnosis and Treatment of ADHD, prepared by a non-advocate, non-Federal panel of experts, the NIH cautioned that "further research is necessary to establish ADHD as a brain disorder." This paper offers a distillation of the relevant research to date in the field.

There are persistent concerns in the research and clinical communities regarding the psychiatric *Diagnostic and Statistical*

Manual of Mental Disorders (DSM) from which the ADHD and many other fashionable diagnoses are culled. The latest critical examination of the manual is entitled *Making Us Crazy DSM: The Psychiatric Bible and the Creation of Mental Disorder*. Written by two American academics, it received a nod from the British *Times Literary Supplement*, whose reviewer ventured that the DSM is an American invention, unique to that culture. The DSM, wrote social psychologist Carol Tavris, represents a "brilliant orchestration of pseudo-science, marketing and promotion," which has "succeeded in transforming the normal difficulties of life into mental disorders."

The book points not only to the shabbiness of scientific evidence inherent in the DSM, but to the hundreds of diagnoses created which are vulnerable to misuse. Conditions like "Oppositional Defiant Disorder or "Conduct Disorder" harbor Orwellian possibilities. Such diagnoses were likely the bailiwick of the mental health professionals in the former Soviet Union, when they needed to dispose of dissidents. For real double-bind value, look no further than a DSM condition called "Non-Compliance with Treatment." Disagree with the medical demiurge, and he slaps you with a diagnosis. Not only are "most of the DSM labels circular," cautions Tavris, but they "confuse labels with explanations." Ultimately, they aim to give the public a psychiatric explanation for the pain in their lives, in the hope that a pill will eradicate it.

There are now approximately five to six million children on Ritalin in North America, up from one million in 1990. Most of the children being medicated are boys, with minority boys 11 times more likely to be on this stimulant. Ninety percent of Ritalin, which is supposed to help children focus, is marketed in the U.S. One can't help but wonder why American and Canadian children don't score very well on international scholastic tests. Perhaps there isn't enough Ritalin going around?

By masking the pain of living with a pill, mental health professionals are abnegating their responsibility and traditional mandate to explore and improve the many psychosocial factors that influence a life. In the process, vital interventions are overlooked and control over and responsibility for our lives forfeited in favor of the inaction and resignation inherent in a biological determinism. Finally, by allowing emotional life to be homogenized through pharmacology, we are passing up on what it means to be human.

85. RANK INTERNET RATINGS

June 18, 2003

In short order, you'll hear some compelling reasons to doubt the popular Alexa Internet ranking system. But first, don't fret: WorldNetDaily's cyberspace status is indisputable. The site is among the top 500 most visited Internet sites. It ranks 517th on the more popular—and seemingly more pliable—Alexa, and 434th on Ranking.com.

While few regular Internet users likely know or care about the Alexa Internet ranking system, clusters of enthusiastic users toot the toolbar and for very good reason. In ranking website popularity, Alexa purports to use site statistics (when it can get them), "snapshots of the Web" (whatever that means), and related links to rank order the popular Internet sites. But, as Alexa.com readily concedes, the Alexa toolbar is the most important source of their information. "The toolbar," says the site, "is a program that users install into the browser," and which gives information about "the usage paths of the collective Alexa community."

The Alexa toolbar does much more than that. Once installed, it inflates website ranking, an effect that is most pronounced for smaller, less-frequented sites. Download it, and your Alexa website rank begins like magic to improve in leaps and bounds, even when your site's traffic remains constant, which is what I discovered when, curious, I downloaded the toolbar. The rating for IlanaMercer.com was already unrealistically high, but from then on it only improved, even though the site's statistics remained constant for at least three consecutive months.

Fore sure, IlanaMercer.com is a great site. Personally, I think it deserves to be rated among the top 70,000 sites in cyberspace. But as someone who is not prone to mythical thinking or self-aggrandizement, I know better. Put it this way: The message of peace, an unfettered market economy, limited government, and individual freedom is just not as popular in the welfare-beset and warring America as one would infer from the rank Alexa gives my site.

I had a good idea what was happening. My theory was confirmed when I posted Sean Mercer's domain name to a venerable list, many of whose members are Alexa devotees. As a consequence of that one posting, Sean's website rank improved an order of magnitude! Again, Sean is a superb guitarist and musician. I recommend his CD. But in the era of Shakira, Kid Rock, and a sea of incompetents, it's silly to imagine that the sudden spike in the popularity of his website reflected a growing interest in complex, well-executed, progressive-rock compositions. The truth was that the well-tooled list members had helped Sean's ratings rocket, even though his total monthly hits only went from 10,000 to 10,020.

The Alexa service doesn't always know how many unique hits a site gets. What Alexa most probably does is to work out a likely distribution of toolbars in the general population of Internet users. Hypothesizing that one in every X Internet users downloads a toolbar, Alexa will then assign a relative rating to a website, based on toolbar data. Alexa thus has no idea (or so goes my theory) that the spike on SeanMercer.com correlated with a meager 20 additional hits to the site. What they see is the activity coming from 20 toolbars. The odds that 20 individuals, most with toolbars, strike at once are clearly not that high. Sure enough, after that statistically insignificant surge, Dr. Rock went for a while from three millionth to 460,000th or thereabouts, based on a traffic improvement of 20 hits!

I've not seen graphs that plot a site's traffic alongside its alleged ranking, but, in addition to the site's total traffic, which is indisputably the best gauge, a consistent performance on separate rating systems is probably a good way to approximate an authentic rank. In addition to its 30 to 40 million page views per month and close to five million unique visitors, WorldNetDaily ranks consistently on the gauges. Both Ranking.com and Alexa attest that NewsMax.com, Townhall, and Jewish World Review are trailing badly.

Naturally, the larger the sample of Internet users, the less likely distortions are to slant outcomes, and, hence, the more accurate the results. Indeed, Ranking.com and Alexa.com are in general agreement on the position of the huge news sites. Ranking.com has CNN at 15th; Alexa has it at 20th. MSNBC lags a little at 23rd and 29th respectively. Fox News is 171st on Ranking.com and 135th with Alexa, and the *New York Times* manages 121st to Alexa's 51st. The "Newspaper of Record" is still very popular.

Excessive discrepancies between rating systems ought to raise suspicions about realistically unintuitive popularity claims, especially when clusters of obsessive users all download the tool and massage one another's rankings.

You read this space to get a dose of reason, not rubbish. Alexa says IlanaMercer.com is the 68,000th most popular site on the World Wide Web not because it is, but because an abundance of people with toolbars are hitting the site, including myself, while working with the comprehensive links page. Alexa records the continuous toolbar bustle on the site, and *voila*.

VII. The War for Western Values

86. SAFARI SCHOLARSHIP REINVENTS HISTORY

March 1, 2001

Hollywood is good at peddling historical fiction, the kind the public doesn't hesitate to accept as Bible from Sinai. But for some time now, Tinsel Town has been getting stiff competition from unexpected quarters. Coming to an African Studies department near you is some startling information: The venerable Greeks, the fathers of Western Civilization, stole their philosophical and scientific know-how from Egypt. Egypt, and not Greece, is the fount of Western tradition. In an unchronicled trip, Aristotle is said to have sojourned to Egypt with Alexander the Great, smuggled books out of the Alexandrian library, and slapped his name on these books, promoting them as his own. He wasn't alone. Socrates, Pythagoras, and Plato were plagiarizers in their own right. Is there no end to the antics of those White Bad Boys?

You may never have given much thought to the skin color of the ancient Egyptians. Artifacts at least indicate that they were a diverse people, more Benetton than black. That the Egyptians were actually Black Africans, then, must come as a surprise. Elizabeth Taylor had no business playing Cleopatra. The Macedonian of the Ptolemaic bloodline was really a long-limbed Black woman. Even the Sphinx had Negroid features. That is until it fell prey to one of the first "documented," racially motivated acts of vandalism—the facial crater the Sphinx stoically bears comes from being socked on the nose by Napoleon's racist troops. There go those anemic lads and their antics again.

You heard right. This mythistory is called Afrocentrism. It's promoted by a number of undistinguished African academics and taught to students across North America from grade school through to the university level. Accordingly, Africans have an ineffable claim against Europeans. For how does one put a price on the mugging of a civilization? Unlike the equally nonsensical Holocaust denial, which immediately raises establishment and media ire, this remedial revisionism has been met with little objection. For the most part, rebutting this bunk has fallen to a Greek Classicist by the name of Mary Lefkowitz.

To this end, Lefkowitz would have had to mine Afrocentric books such as *Black Athena* by Cornell's Martin Bernal, *Stolen Legacy* by George G. M. James, and the school tracts known as the "Portland African-American Baseline Essays." "The Science Baseline" Essay claims, no less, that "thousands of years ago Egyptians-cum-blacks flew in electroplated gold gliders, knew accurately the distance to the sun, and discovered the Theory of Evolution." According to a Senegalese Afrocentrist called Cheikh Anta Diop, Africans invented everything from Judaism to engineering, to astronomy, to dialectical materialism. (Although Marxism is no cause for inventor's pride.)

One nagging question: Afrocentrics claim that practically every reprehensible occurrence in history is the doing of the Great White and his linear thinking. Why, if Eurocentric culture is so horrible, would they want to lay claim to it? By coveting it, aren't Afrocentrists providing Western Civilization with the ultimate validation? Furthermore, entire civilizations are not typically the kleptomaniac's item of choice. As Lefkowitz points out in *Not Out of Africa*, "If the Greeks had learned their philosophy from a large theoretical literature produced by Egyptian writers, surely some trace of that literature would have remained in Egypt."

Alas, there is no point searching for sense where only African chauvinism is evident. Nor need one look for methodological coherence. For scholars whose mission it is to promote a view of African superiority, Afrocentrists are doing a poor job. The methodology of the Afrocentrist consists in neglecting chronology, treating myths as history, and using citations fraudulently. In Afrocentric works, hypothesis morphs into fact, authorities that don't bolster a thesis are recruited in its service, and an absence of proof becomes evidence of conspiracy. And always, the fabulous fabrications are followed up with vicious *ad hominem* attacks leveled at the few scholars who dare confront the evidence.

An example of one jarring deception is a reference to the Egyptian Mystery System whence the Greeks allegedly stole their philosophy. The reference comes not from an authentic historical text, but from eighteenth-century French fiction and Freemasonry. Also amusing is that the city of Alexandria was founded only after Alexander's conquest of Egypt, and the library from which Aristotle allegedly pilfered his genius was founded after the philosopher's death.

Such myth making thrives and is nurtured in a culture that eschews objective truth. Where once there was an understanding that there exists a reality independent of the human observer, students are now taught that truth is a social construction, a function of the power and position—or lack of them—a person or group holds in society. Casting fact and objective truth as no more than a perspective is a handy bit of egalitarianism: If nothing is immutably true, then all positions are but a matter of preference and can vie for equal validity.

The public school system is the perfect medium for Afrocentrism. The reason pedagogues haven't rejected Afrocentrism outright is because it's seen as a means to increase self-esteem among young Africans. Self-esteem no less than multiculturalism is a prized project and an article of faith in the public school system; it is the very embodiment of the therapeutic state. Self-styled victim groups, notably natives and women, have had their suppurating historical wounds similarly tended with curricular concessions, so why not Africans? Of course, this line of reasoning lends itself just as well to teaching Holocaust denial in order to allay the guilt that plagues students of German descent.

Adapted to the public school system's mission, history must be made palliative rather than faithful to fact.

87. HONK AN APOLOGY FOR HONKY

October 30, 2002

They pursued the police tenaciously. They called in with tips about the murders. They even postponed scheduled executions in order to try and pierce Chief Charles Moose's resistant mindset. "Check out Montgomery," they counseled. When a mere mention of "Montgomery" failed to get Moose's antlers moving in the right direction, well, they spent a dime on another call, this time providing explicit directions to the Alabama local. Silly snipers; not knowing that homeless Africans are a protected species, they loitered in parking lots in their Chevy Caprice, hoping to get noticed, and all but flagged down a police car. Hell, they even penned their notes in Ebonics.

The serial slayers went beyond the call of duty in trying to get caught; Chief Moose, on the other hand, did his best to adhere to the Look Away Doctrine, now imperiling American lives. When eyewitness reports about dark complexions began to surface, the lachrymose (or should I say lachrymoose) Chief moved quickly to stem them. With his long anti-racial profiling pedigree, Moose refused to unfairly "paint some group," unless, of course, the group was white. "I'll talk to the devil himself to keep another person alive," the Chief promised, but forgot to specify that unless the devil was a lone, can't-get-laid, loser white male, then he—Chief Moose—would have no truck with him. Moose simply refused to consider that Beelzebub might not be white, and adamantly steered the investigation away from any Black Muslim and in the direction of "white guys with guns."

Still, people in DC are honking happily for The Moose, and the serial profilers in the media concur. "They were wrong on all counts," wrote WorldNetDaily's Paul Sperry: "Number of suspects, physical description and motive." So, why, for crying out loud, are they still at it? Their textbook abstractions were as colossally stupid as the anchors and producers who solicited these. Yet, no sooner was their folly exposed than the media cognoscenti, confidence unshaken, continued unapologetically to dilate on this or that pop-psychological aspect of the case. Never had the commentators been willing to view the deadly duo's religious and racial composites as any more than superfluous white noise.

The question remains, how did such an investigation fail to take into consideration the larger geopolitical context? Bill O'Reilly of the Fox News Network was certainly waylaid by political correctness when, following the snipers' arrest, representatives of the Council on American-Islamic Relations appeared on The Factor. The two men proceeded to aggressively brand any apprehension about Muslims in mainstream communities as an expression of racism. O'Reilly, unfortunately, accepted their rendition.

It's quite possible that the violence in our midst and abroad is all Honky's imperial, racist fault. By all means, examine to your heart's content the school of thought that claims that wherever and whenever the proverbial Noble Savage is restless, it's a sign Honky messed with his biorhythms. But for Pete's sake, separate your theory of culpability from the common cause civilized people must share: Preventing the loss of innocent lives.

In so doing, one cannot flee from reality. Regardless where one's sympathies lie, regardless of how one views the cause of Muslim insurrections the world over, one must surely recognize that, for whatever reason, they are at the center of practically every bloody conflict in the world today. Is it possible that Muslims are right and that the "infidels" in Lebanon, Israel, India, Russia, Sudan, Indonesia, The Ivory Coast, Kenya, Nigeria, all deserve to be visited by Jihad? Sure it is. But here on *terra firma*, the reality remains that Muslims are more prone to beheading reporters, making snuff movies, stoning women or blowing up innocent people as they go about their daily chores.

Allow me further to inquire whether it's at all possible that without sniper John Lee Malvo—the murderous muse who allegedly picked off many of the victims—some of the deceased might have had a sporting chance? Is Brimelow wrong when he wryly points out in *Alien Nation* that criminal aliens "accounted for over 25 percent of the federal prison population in 1993," and that "they represent its fastest-growing segment"?

Here's another piece of the puzzle: Whatever your theory about difference in the propensity for crime among racial groups, the fact is that, while "blacks make up only 12 percent of the American population, they make up 64 percent of all violent arrests." Brimelow and I might be traitors to the politically correct crowd, but we are faithful to the facts. You must be too; your very survival hinges on it.

In the hunt for a mass murderer, it is rational, not racist, to take into account the higher propensity for crime among certain groups, the combustible larger geopolitical context, and the extent to which high-crime communities have embraced radical ideologies and conflicts. Moose's investigation left out this context.

88. ROUSSEAU'S NOBLE SAVAGE—NOT ON THIS CONTINENT

September 14, 2000

There are certain narratives that come to dominate the marketplace of ideas to the exclusion of competing perspectives. The narrative of justice in society is one example. Like any successful monopoly, the monopoly over cultural discourse is won through government privilege. The Canadian native cauldron is an example. While ordinary Canadians are fair-minded to a fault on aboriginal affairs—they like and respect diversity—they do long to interact with natives as equals before the law of the land. Silently, Canadians also question the native industry's version of justice in which they must now acquiesce.

In partnership with government, native leadership, the lawyers, consultants, and academics get to decide who is on the side of the angels and who must burn in purgatory. With hefty incentives at stake, these special interests work particularly hard to relieve Canadians of their decision-making rights, while at the same time continuing to indenture them in the funding of their agenda.

Before being effectively silenced, Canadians spoke loud and clear on aboriginal privilege. They delivered a resounding referendum-No to the 1992 Charlottetown Accord, which proposed to entrench special rights for Indians. The battered—and might I add, Western—principle of equality before the law still has its adherents. Alas, government found other legislative tricks with which to undermine the Accord, forging ahead with its agenda and overriding the will of the people.

The cultural script concerning all things native has become indisputable. Buoyed by the perverse principle of collective guilt, native readers often inform me that my ancestors were land thieves, as am I. "I'm innocent," I plead, "my people have an alibi. At the time of the crimes against natives, Jews were being persecuted in Europe for being Jews." No matter: according to orthodoxy, all Eurocentric folk stand in the dock accused (falsely) of stealing the land from natives, who, of course, had only ever lived in harmony with it.

Natives are nature's custodians—there's another fallacy popularized by Jean Jacques Rousseau's panegyric on the *Noble Savage*. Voltaire was in the know when he said that Rousseau is to philosophers as the ape is to man. Rousseau certainly was uninformed by facts when he described natives as living in unity with nature. Less forgivable are the many present-day authors and excavators who, despite the corpus of research on the lack of conservation among natives, persist in describing pre-Columbian America as "a pristine natural kingdom."

Before the decimation of its population, largely via the white man's diseases, the Americas had a sizable population of natives that exerted a considerable ecological footprint. For one, native tribes engaged in bi-annual forest burning. According to an article in *Environment* by B.L. Turner and Karl Butzer, "The forests of the Americas, from Canada to Argentina were so highly disturbed or modified by Amerindian use by 1492 that it is surprising that even the popular literature missed this point. The species which the Indians most wanted to hunt...were found most easily in areas of recently burnt forest, which is why they burnt the forest over and over again."

Then there was the practice of stampeding during a hunt of animal herds over a cliff. Used repeatedly, some buffalo jumps hold the remains of hundreds of thousands of animals, with patterns of local extinction being documented. Where agriculture was practiced in the central and southern parts of America, evidence from sediment points to severe soil erosion, already widespread before the arrival of the white man.

While we're on the topic of fraud, who penned the famous words, "The flowers are our sisters...the eagle our brother...Whatever we do to the earth, we do to ourselves..."? Chief Seattle's famous 1854 New-Age speech, deployed by environmentalists to buttress native conservationism, was written in 1972 by a Hollywood scriptwriter by the name of Ted Perry.

The myth of the purity of primitive life juxtaposed to the savagery of Western Culture is even less justified in light of archeological findings. The Americas are scattered with evidence of routine massacres, cannibalism, dismemberment, slavery, abuse of women, and human sacrifice among native tribes. Why, the Northwest Territories Yellowknife tribe eventually disappeared as a direct result of a massacre carried out as late as 1823. The same justice that asks westerners to pay for posterity for the sins of their fathers should demand that remaining native "nations" pay reparations among themselves.

In no way do these realties mitigate or excuse the cruel treatment natives have endured. They serve, rather, to cut through the "rhetoric of moral superiority" and challenge the cultural consensus.

89. HOLD THEIR FEET TO THE FIRE!

May 29, 2002

Condoleezza Rice was unblushing in her dismissive treatment of the critical mass of intelligence pertaining to impending terrorist attacks. The distinction she made between analytical reports and specific intelligence information was especially specious. According to Rice's official blather, a 1999 report by the Library of Congress stating that suicide bombers belonging to al-Qaida could crash an aircraft into U.S. targets belongs to the realm of analysis. It wasn't "actionable intelligence."

It's essential that she and President Bush not be allowed to fob their responsibilities for the World Trade Center catastrophe onto their underlings or onto previous administrations. It's essential to both question the manner in which she characterized the information, as well as her remorseless flippancy.

Is Rice claiming that the mental capacity for deduction is not part of her job description? (President Bush might get away with that.) Can't Americans expect the thousands of agents they employ to possess the rudimental capability for drawing inferences from data and moving to verify or refute information? Can Rice not be expected to execute a simple algorithm, like instruct her subordinates to canvass and screen certain targeted suspects?

Incredible doesn't quite describe what Condoleezza calls intelligence "specifics." The National Security Adviser will move to act only if she gets word of time, place, and method of attack. What next? A gilded, personalized invitation to attend the crime scene?

Yet more official White House noise designed to downplay government culpability is the delegitimizing of blame and finger pointing. No surprise here. The premise of blame is responsibility. I can blame you only if you are entrusted with a responsibility to do—or refrain from doing—something. One only has to hint at presidential culpability, and Bush swings into Chance Gardener mode: The simpleton whose moral clarity is his stock-in-trade. The fact that he intended no harm and would revive the dead if he could, really only means that we can allow some extenuation in passing judgment on him. As the president himself said, his most important job "is to protect our homeland." His responsibility for the task is not cancelled by an, "I didn't know."

Talk about a reformation of Washington's atrophied alphabet soup of intelligence agencies is yet another decoy. An overarching agency exists. What, pray tell, is the National Security Council headed by Condoleezza Rice? It's an office created by the National Security Act of 1947 to advise the president on "integration of domestic, foreign and military policies relating to national security and to facilitate interagency cooperation." If suspicion existed— analytic, synthetic, prosaic or poetic—Rice should have put the squeeze on the system she oversees.

In the past year, we've seen how financial fiascos in the private sector resulted in bankruptcy, indictments, and a loss of reputation. However, when it comes to malfeasance in government, neither the laws of man nor the laws of nature apply. Wrongdoing and incompetence in government are not punished, but are rewarded with budgetary increases. "We in the civil service don't have profits and losses," explained Sir Humphrey, top bureaucrat in the brilliant BBC satire, *Yes, Prime Minister*. "Success in the civil service is measured by the size of our staff and budget. A big department is more successful than a small one." And a government department accretes through inefficiency. Such perverse incentives explain why the wicked Bureau of Citizenship and Immigration Services, now recruiting, is also one of the fastest-growing departments. Failure translates into ever-growing budgets and powers.

It gets worse. By now everyone knows of the Phoenix FBI agent who, in July 2001, wrote a memorandum about the bin Ladenites who were training in American flight schools. Agent Ken Williams' report was very "specific." Over and above the standard sloth the memo met in the Washington headquarters, it transpired that the FBI was also concerned about "racial profiling." With good cause. The pending, bipartisan End Racial Profiling Act of 2001 is the model victim's legislation. It'll allow the U.S. government or the investigated racial or ethnic minority member to sue the taxpayer if there is a remote sense that law enforcement has engaged in an investigation that has "a disparate impact" on a minority's ever-oozing emotional wounds.

His ability to construct mental categories of danger and use them as a predictive—and protective—measure may have allowed our prehistoric ancestor Homo erectus to stick around long enough to turn into Homo sapiens. But that's of no consequence to legislators. Our masters have no qualms about outlawing this natural in-built survival mechanism nor do they fret over emasculating law enforcement, especially where the common man's safety is concerned. Their own taxpayer-funded security details, after all, are not confined to frisking old ladies. And in the event that the unthinkable occurs, it won't be a politician who will be left holding a Taser gun.

90. OSAMA'S SNICKERING AT OUR MILITARY

July 24, 2002

President Bush's first National Strategy for Homeland Security gives the principles of federalism lip service. The recommendations are for the creation of a tiered national response system, which will further consolidate powers in the central government. As part of the game plan, the armed forces may be unleashed on U.S. citizens.

Exposed are a couple of new trends. The president promises to review the United States' obligations to international treaties and law. It's unlikely the president is assuring us of his commitment to continue shunning illegitimate forums like the International Criminal Court treaty. What he's probably hinting at are the prospects of signing some of the dubious global-government treaties that will allow the administration to further corner Americans, block off all the exits, and steal more American property. The administration has been especially eager to clamp down on tax havens. Under the cloak of fighting terrorism and money laundering, it's not impossible that Washington will sign on to the contemptible EU, OECD, and UN tax-harmonization schemes, which seek to outlaw low-tax jurisdictions.

Then there's the president's intention to "engage" the private sector as "a key homeland security partner." It may not amount to outright nationalization, but co-opting business in the service of The War as a matter of policy certainly has the flavor of fascism.

Most foreboding is the talk about deploying the law—not the existing law, mind you—to "enable our country to fight the war on terrorism more effectively." The premise underlying the development of new "legislative actions" is that we lack laws to help deal with the new threat. That's twaddle!

We have immigration and deportation laws, as well as laws against treason, hate crimes, murder, and conspiracy to commit murder. Not counting state and local government laws, authors Paul Craig Roberts and Lawrence M. Stratton tallied 56,009 pages of laws in the U.S. Code, 134,488 pages of regulatory laws in the Code of Federal Regulation and more than 68,107 pages of laws in the Federal Register. "The Federal Law is further augmented by more than 2,756 volumes of judicial precedent," they write in *The Tyranny of Good Intentions*. And that was back in 2000! Want to tell me there aren't enough laws to take care of business?

The biggest *faux pas,* however, in the National Strategy is the failure to listen to Sulaiman Abu Ghaith's loud jeers. Abu Ghaith is Osama bin Laden's spokesman. He recently gave an interview to an Algerian newspaper in which he mocked the American campaign to dismantle al-Qaida, calling it a "Hollywood script." The new Pentagon-endorsed VH1 series entitled *Military Diaries* makes Abu Ghaith's characterization difficult to dispute. Touted as a "powerful firsthand look at our heroes, their stories and the music that gets them through," this "militarytainment" should strengthen OBL's resolve.

Welcoming the viewer are the thrusting pelvis and swaying breasts of a recruit by the name of Charlie, followed by Laurie, Danielle, Paul, and Jimmie, among others. These poster-girlie recruits want us to know that their "real duty is to provide humanitarian aid to the Afghans." They share with us their dreams of being "self-help authors." And they impart the joys of manning posts like "Diversity Awareness Officers" or "Drug and Alcohol Counselors." Suffice it to say that the "human face" of our coed men and women of the armed forces exudes mush, not mettle. If ever there were a U.S.-style motivational video for OBL and his ascetic Islamists—*Military Diaries* is it.

The military has, of late, also been preoccupied with the kind of waste-management problems that al-Qaida operatives are free of. Incontinence and urinary tract infections are plaguing our military lasses, screamed a news headline. In addition to their documented inferior physical resilience and elevated propensity for neuroses—to say nothing of the sexual dynamics they bring to the military— women have also accelerated welfarism in the forces. According to whistleblower Catherine Aspy, "The Army is a vast day-care center, full of unmarried teen-age mothers using it as a welfare home."

In fairness, women are not solely to blame. The VH1 series reveals the mentality that pervades the military, including the top brass. Instead of being ashamed of the let-it-all-hang-out credo, the Men at the Top are parading emotional whimsy like they would a Purple Heart. Somewhere in the National Strategy there ought to be a plan to dismiss all the women, including those with the Y chromosome. *Esprit de corps* in the military may be high, but morale doesn't reliably reflect effectiveness or lethality.

91. RAISING TODDLERS FOR THE TALIBAN

December 10, 2001

Progressive parents have done it again. They've unleashed their progeny on us. The breezy bubbleheads that gave us the prototype schoolyard mass murderer, whose petulance and sense of entitlement led him to pump his peers with lead; the same loopy parents have again handed us their life's work—a son who joined the Taliban.

John Walker Lindh, alias Abdul Hamid, the wounded 20-year-old American who was picked up by U.S. Special Forces in Afghanistan, is the precious progeny of such parents. Walker was a combatant, fighting for the Taliban. His ordeal was the end stage, the culmination of a process that was indulged, even facilitated, by his parents. Yet to listen to his dad Frank Lindh, you'd think he was nothing but a sweet kid, returned from a summer camp gone terribly wrong.

The warp and woof of this permissive upbringing begins with Lindh's conversion at age sixteen. The dropout who was named for John Lennon was not content with merely practicing the rituals of Islam or confining himself to a mosque in San Francisco. With the blessings of his Catholic father and Buddhist mother, Lindh traveled to Yemen to study Arabic. At this stage, no bells went off for Mr. and Mrs. Bozo. They were wholly supportive of Abdul's "spiritual quest," allowing the boy to journey to Pakistan for the supposed study of Islam.

Dodo dad conceded, in retrospect, during the staple stump interview with Larry King, that he'd like right now to give sonny boy "a little kick in the butt for not telling" him "what he was up to." But at the time, "Other than a kid who ... had converted to a religion that" dad respected, "and that seemed very healthy and good for him," Mr. Lindh saw no reason to exercise parental propriety. The beatific Frank Lindh might as well have been parroting Kahlil Gibran's *The Prophet*. Lindh's ideas about parenting echo the silly riffs delivered in that obscure text; words that became—and seemingly still are—a catechism for the progressive parent and his hip children:

> Your children are not your children.
> They are the sons and daughters of Life's longing for itself.
> They come through you but not from you,
> And though they are with you, yet they belong not to you.
> You may give them your love but not your thoughts.
> For they have their own thoughts.

Indeed, the questionable wisdom of the child-centered school of parenting lingers in every cultural crevice: the schools, the mental health profession, and the media. Like Rousseau's noble savage, the child is regarded as a naturally good being, whose only requirement is unconditional love. Formative figures are no more than facilitators; catalysts for the child's "growth." The belief is that, if left to his devices, free from adult poisoning, this spontaneous learner will interact with his environment and, in the fullness of time, glean the necessary moral and intellectual lessons.

The self-esteem talisman is another creation of progressive parents and pedagogues. Accordingly, every child, irrespective of his qualities and abilities, must be helped to develop a gargantuan self-esteem. There is a price to pay for encouraging in kids a Nietzchean celebration of self. We now know that dangerously inflated self-esteem, the kind that is endemic among Americans, is associated with the psychopathic behavior that erupts regularly in schools and other arenas. It certainly seems pertinent in the case of John Walker Lindh.

With their "It Takes a Village" creed, the official liberal literati have also collectivized accountability for "Our Children," to use Hillary Clinton's confiscatory term. Consequently, parents behave as if Taliban toddlers or schoolyard assassins just land on you, courtesy of some amorphous social force. Shirking responsibility for his *laissez-faire* parenting, John Walker Lindh's father duly not only deflected from his role in his son's downfall, but hinted that the young man was brainwashed and should have been "debriefed by the government," and sent home.

John Walker Lindh's actions, however, were premeditated and intentional. While we are certainly shaped by an upbringing, we are not determined by it. The ability to exercise a measure of free will in practically every contingency in life is what separates human beings from animals, whose actions are instinctive. All the same, Lindh senior could have made it easier for his son. When the boy came home with a cap, a Koran, and a prayer mat tucked under his arm, Frank Lindh should not have palled about. Instead, he ought to have thanked his lucky charms that the boy wasn't waving a Wicca wand or riding a broomstick. Then and there he ought to have dropped the ever-so-mod habit the progressive parent has of paraphrasing a child's every utterance and extending him endless Socratic invitations to respond, and explained to his cherub that it's natural for impressionable youth to romanticize unknown beliefs, but that this temporary infatuation could lead him down a dangerous path. "No, you cannot worship at a nearby mosque, and no, so long as I pay your way, the University of Medina is not going to be your alma mater," would have been appropriate responses.

The Lindh case should be a warning to American parents to keep a firm grip on reality. Despite President Bush's assurances, the letter and spirit of Islam evade us: some scholars vouch for the faith's peacefulness; others controvert it. Mindful of this, parents should avoid blessing a sudden run by a son on the Islamic seminary or extracurricular trips to view the stalactites and stalagmites of the Afghan caves. It's safer to stick with Sunday or Hebrew school.

92. ENTERTAINMENT INTERRUPTUS

November 28, 2001

The film *Spy Games* reaches a crescendo as retiring CIA officer Robert Redford transfers $282,000 of his life's savings to an account in the Cayman Islands. The money is supposed to help pay for the rescue of Redford's bureau protégé Brad Pitt, who has been "burned" by his employers at the CIA for going solo. Pitt turns rogue when he has a revelation. He discovers that working for the CIA is a dirty business.

For years, Pitt manages to swim in some very polluted waters until he becomes romantically entangled. The object of his affections is a bitter British bit, herself no stranger to blood sports. In one of her varied incarnations as a human rights activist, this gentle soul blows up a building. In the process, she kills the son of a Chinese diplomat. Unbeknownst to Pitt's love interest, the CIA offers her up to the Chinese in exchange for a captive American operative. No great loss, says I, but not according to Pitt, who attempts to rescue the girl from this infernal pit. In the process, Pitt is captured, tortured, and is about to be put to death, when Redford pulls a clever stunt.

As the Cayman Islands transaction is playing out on the screen, my mind becomes tangentially—but necessarily—preoccupied. I confess, I can easily become bored during a film, and am wont to tug at the sleeve of my better quarter and, not unlike a two-year-old, ask questions. "I'm not sure," I tell the wincing man, "that Redford would be able to complete such a transaction now, not with the new anti-terrorism laws." "Can't you leave me in peace," comes the poor man's tortured reply, a line he has commandeered from Basil Fawlty of *Fawlty Towers*.

Back home, I attempt to search for the relevant information among the sea of "Legislation Related to the Attack of September 11." The contagion includes nine "Bills and Joint Resolutions Signed Into Law," nine "Other Resolutions Approved," fifteen items of "Legislation With Floor Action," and dozens of "Legislation Without Floor Action." Sure enough, the protagonist—not to mention the screenplay writer—in *Spy Games* would have found his style cramped by the USA Patriot Act. Banker's secrecy agreements notwithstanding, Redford's broker would probably be wise to "file a report of a suspicious financial transaction." In fact, an amendment to this act makes it mandatory for a registered broker to submit a suspicious activity report. By the time the transaction was approved, Pitt would be toast.

The bills that have already been signed into law have been exposed many times over for their assaults on liberties, assaults that are not necessarily commensurate with safety. The banking subterfuge is no different, and neither is it new. As Veronique de Rugy of the Cato Institute wrote, "Financial transactions and bank accounts in the United States have been monitored for some time now." Unfortunately, this monitoring—a spying game that the American Bankers Association pegs at roughly $10 billion a year—didn't detect the nine SunTrust accounts used in Florida by the terrorists involved in the attack on the World Trade Center.

The USA Patriot Act is indeed supposed to provide "Appropriate Tools Required to Intercept and Obstruct Terrorism." In theory, the Act could certainly make an alien with terrorist affinities "ineligible for admission or deportable," that is if such ties were readily traceable. Realistically, The Act cannot void of vipers the many U.S.-based Jihad nesting grounds, set up for the purpose of funneling ideological trainees into the terrorism trade, just as "French laws monitoring bank accounts and illegal activities don't stop Algerian terrorists living in France from regularly murdering people by placing bombs in subways," writes de Rugy.

If the existing votes-for-visas immigration policy were not bad enough, Bill S1424 proposes to grant officials "permanent authority" to confer an "S" visa on an alien if he can supply critical information with respect to criminal or terrorist organizations. The thought of bureaucrats freely using visas as bait to recruit operatives for the intelligence community is chilling. Still less confidence inspiring is the intention to release into American neighborhoods individuals who are in a position to rat out an al-Qaida member.

Many—if not most—bills have deceiving titles. The "Air Transportation Safety and System Stabilization Act's" appellation masks a bailout bill for the airline industry. Other bills like the one proposed by, wouldn't you have guessed, the "Hildebeest" are worse than useless. Sen. Clinton spearheaded an increase in funding to "mental health providers serving public safety workers affected by the terrorist attacks of September 11." The therapy used to treat such workers would be crisis intervention and debriefing, a therapeutic modality that is useless as far as efficacy goes, and may even be harmful to its recipients.

A cursory perusal of the legislation related to the attack serves as an intemperate—and much needed—reminder of how fatuous the "work" of the legislator is. What were these people thinking when they issued "a joint resolution encouraging every United States citizen to display the flag of the United States? Or one "condemning any price gouging with respect to motor fuels during the hours and days after the terrorist acts of September 11"? To paraphrase journalist Barbara Amiel's memorable words, government is keeping out of our bedrooms, but what is it doing in every other room? No callousness intended, but being blown up by terrorists is no reason to give victims awards for valor. The deaths are a result of horrible happenstance; they are not conscious acts of bravery. Yet Congress conferred the highest of honors on "civilian employees of the Department of Defense who are killed or wounded by a terrorist attack."

Fido has not yet been given the Purple Heart for his olfactory contributions to the September 11 rescue efforts. But one giddy Rep. by the name of Benjamin Gilman wanted Congress to recognize the Furry Brigade "for their service in the rescue and recovery efforts in the aftermath of the terrorist attacks on the United States on September 11, 2001." (What can I say? "Blessed Be the Cheese Makers for They Shall Inherit the Earth." See *The Life of Brian*.)

Advance such consistently puerile notions in a private sector job, and you stand to be fired, or at the very least examined for the presence of a brain infarct. Here's an idea for our parochial parasites: Stop groping obscenely for the "Stimulus Package" in order to revive the economy. Instead, resign. In pirate parlance, "walk the plank"! Get a real job! Do your patriotic bit for the nation.

93. ISRAEL BELONGS TO THE JEWS

July 3, 2002

The far-left, pro-Palestinian Israeli newspaper *Ha'aretz* recently reported on an extensive survey of Palestinian school textbooks. The books are bizarre. They all but expunge Israel from the map of the region, referring to the territory between the Jordan River and the Mediterranean Sea as "Palestine." There's no mention of "Israel," much less the promise of "peace" in exchange for Israel's retreat to the pre-1967 borders. The books also teach that the Palestinians have first rights to the country. Accordingly, the "Arab Canaanites were there before the Jews, therefore the zionistic [sic] claim of rights to the land by virtue of forefathers is a lie."

Other than among its Arab adherents, one would expect such loony-tune historical revisionism from crackpots like members of the Institute for Historical Review. (The IHR is a motley of discredited oddballs, poseurs and pseudo-historians, whose members are dedicated to proving that Jews lied about the Holocaust. Intellectually, the IHR is a sort of malevolent version of the Flat Earth Society.)

The Palestinian textbooks also describe Zionism as "a movement of which the seizing of land is foremost among its tenets." This is a strand that sadly runs through many libertarian sophomoric scripts about "Zionist imperialism." Once again, this level of sophistry is rare even among the Left. When it's forthcoming, it hails from Noam Chomsky's dank corner.

Why so many libertarians share the Arab world's unstinting commitment to fabrication on this front is a puzzle. The defensive wars Israel has been forced into belie this sloganeering. A glance at a map of the region—a speck of Israel surrounded by a sea of Arabs—renders the "imperialism" shibboleth positively hollow.

Libertarians err in mistaking the 2,000-year-old Jewish right to the land for a biblically-based, religious claim. The claim is first and foremost historical, although naturally, the Hebrew community's claim to its ancient homeland can't be reduced to a title search at the deeds office. Jewish rights to Israel proceed from the original ownership of the land: The original and rightful owners were Jews. The fact that they were killed and exiled by the Romans doesn't nullify their ownership.

Despite their dispossession 2,000 years ago, Jews clung to life in Israel throughout the centuries, never relinquishing their claim to the occupied territory. Enduring the ruthlessness of the Byzantines, the massacres of the Muslim dynasties, and the onslaught of the Crusaders, the Mongols, and the Ottoman Turks, Jews struggled to maintain a continuous presence in Israel since the exile.

Theirs is a tie that has never been severed. If anything, by maintaining over the centuries a purposeful, continuous, and heroic presence in the conquered land, the Jew's claim to Israel has been affirmed and seared in the annals of time. No subsequent hegemonic regional power, like the Ottomans, ever had the right to deny them their right to re-enter or to repurchase land titles from those willing to sell them. (For this point I am indebted to British philosopher, David Conway.)

The land of Israel is omnipresent in every facet of the Jewish identity and culture; it has been since time immemorial. Clearly, the right to the land can't be understood without reference to the concept of nationhood and national identity, something libertarians often dismiss or confuse with statism.

By comparison, the Palestinian project is a recent one. It's a pan-Arabic undertaking, candidly discussed in the Arab world during the crucial years of propaganda shaping. Not wanting to leave the international community with the (true) impression that a hundred million or so Arabs aimed to destroy the tiny state of Israel, Arab leaders deployed the Palestinians' "cause" to achieve the same end. One of the *coups* in this strategy was the demand that the Palestinians be given the "Right of Return" to Israel. The "Right of Return," now a staple in the Bush administration's negotiations rhetoric, will allow any self-styled Palestinian refugee to settle in Israel proper. Since Israel is a democracy, and since the birth rate of Palestinians is many times the birthrate of Jews, the "Right of Return" will guarantee that within decades, Palestinians will outnumber Jews in Israel. Israel will cease to exist as a Jewish State.

It's worth contemplating that for centuries the Near East has been a cultural backwater. "The Mohammedans"—to quote the delightfully archaic Ludwig von Mises—have for hundreds of years failed to produce so much as a "book of significance," much less any scientific or other advancement. The catalysts for creativity and prosperity are the ideas of individual freedom and freedom from the state. As Mises noted, these ideas are inimical to the cultures of the East, and the Islamic world in particular. Considering that the continued survival of Israel may well depend on her ethnic composition, it is hard to understand why lovers of liberty view a Palestinians takeover so favorably.

Leftists, understandably, have no particular love of individual freedom and its attendant economic system of capitalism. But why are libertarians so eager to see Israel cease to exist as a Jewish homeland, and as a relatively thriving place? This is indeed an enigma. It certainly calls into question their commitment to liberty and western civilization.

Given the extent of Jewish homesteading in Israel, all the international community was doing when it begrudgingly granted Jews the permission to rebuild their despoiled homeland was to recognize the Jew's natural right to the land—to recognize that Jews have a right to self-determination and political autonomy in their national homeland, and that that homeland is Israel.

When Jews commenced what must be the most remarkable modern-day national revival, Israel was a wasteland. Palestinians had done precious little for the land they purport to so love. In fact, in 1948, the invading Arab armies instructed the Palestinians to vacate their holdings in Israel until the Jews were exterminated, after which they would return to inherit the land. Palestinians duly scuttled, abandoning the land with nomadic ease.

Contrast that with the Jews: Modern-day Israel was "born in battle." The fledgling nation was then only 600,000 strong when the neighboring Arabs attacked. And continued to attack: The 1948 War of Independence saw the death of more than 6,000 Israelis. The Sinai Campaign followed, and then the 1967 Six-Day War, the War of Attrition, and the 1973 Yom Kippur War, with all their casualties. And always, on top of these defensive wars, the never-ending war against terrorist infiltration.

The conquering Romans slaughtered 580,000 ferocious Jewish soldiers and erased 985 Jewish villages before defeating and exiling the Jews. The Jews were forced to give up their homeland then, but will never so do again.

94. DID MOHAMMED INVENT PROFILING?

January 9, 2002

When it comes to the sensitive topic of racial or ethnic profiling, Muslims, historically, were innovators in their own right. The Nazis were not the originators of the yellow cloth with which they tagged Jews. The tagging rag has its origins in the laws of the Charter of Omar—a set of vicious anti-infidel rules that were applied to Jews with extra vim. These laws were introduced by the caliph who succeeded the prophet Mohammed.

Prior to the prophet, Jews and Arabs did indeed live in relative harmony, but when Mohammed failed to convert the Jews to Islam, the proselytizing prophet of peace exterminated at least one Jewish tribe, etched the Holy Koran with anti-Jewish vitriol, and launched centuries of brutality against Jews. Arabs also preceded the Nazis by centuries when they devised the Jewish ghetto, that dwelling demarcator known in Arabic as the *hara* or *mella*. Following the Arab conquest in the seventh century, Jewish life in the Islamic world became fraught with massacres, blood libel, and plunder. Synagogues were regularly torn down, and Jews were impelled to pay special head and property taxes.

Meticulously sourced accounts of Jewish travails over the centuries under Islam are detailed in Joan Peters' seminal, *From Time Immemorial: The Origins of the Arab-Jewish Conflict over Palestine.* These reveal a population subject to the whim of the particular Muslim ruler, and the degree to which he was committed to implementing the anti-infidel laws of the Holy Koran and the Charter of Omar. Under Islamic religious law, for instance, if a Muslim murdered an infidel, he was liable only for a fine. But even this "blood money" was rarely forthcoming, because the testimony of an infidel was invalid against a Muslim.

In the land that was once Babylonia, the Jews of Iraq weathered the vicissitudes of a daily life without rights but with endless indignities. Some particularly murderous landmarks stand out: the A.D. 1000 expropriation of Jewish property, the 1333 destruction of their synagogues, and the 1776 Basra slaughter, leading up to mob killings in 1941 and numerous public-square hangings between 1969 and 1973.

The chronicles of Jewish life over the centuries in Aden, Algeria, Tunisia, Morocco, Syria, and Libya are similarly marred. As one 19th-century observer recounted, the ancient community of Yemenite Jews was "in a position of inferiority, and is oppressed by a people which declares itself holy and pious but which is very brutal, barbarous and hard-hearted." Of particular note is the murder in 1032 of thousands of Jews in Fez, Morocco, followed, in 1146, by the Almohad atrocities in which hundreds of thousands of Jews and Christians were massacred by the Muslim Almohads.

As Palestinian and Arab propaganda would have it, Muslim hate for the Jew is a contemporary phenomenon, caused entirely by the tiny "Zionist state." While the contempt for the *dhimmi*, as the Jew was derogatorily termed, has evolved over the years—drawing on "traditional Koranic slurs," as well as gathering vintage Nazi debris along the way—the hate boasts a pure Islamic pedigree.

"In 1940," writes Peters, "the mufti [a kind of rabbi] of Jerusalem wrote to the Axis powers requesting the right of the Arabs to settle the question of the Jews along similar lines to those used to solve the

Jewish question in Germany and Italy." Egyptian Minister Anwar
Sadat's touch was somewhat comical. In 1950, Sadat, who may have
confused Hitler for Houdini, published an open "Dear Adolf" letter,
commending Hitler for "saving the world from this malignant evil."

In 1964 a "scholar" from the University of Damascus issued a
warning to the Syrian public to refrain from "letting your children
out at night, lest the Jew come and take their blood for the purpose
of making matzot for Passover." (My mother's matzo balls,
incidentally, are nowhere near that labor intensive.) Such a
sentiment is still very much within the realm of respected political
and intellectual discourse throughout the Arab world.

An anti-Semitic czarist canard and fraud like "The Protocols of the
Elders of Zion" has been adopted as Arab lore. Last year, UN-funded
Muslim pamphleteers handed out The Protocols at the "anti-racist"
conference in Durban. The charge that Jews are taking over the
world joins the deicide charge and the denial—and justification—of
the Holocaust, among Saudis, Egyptians, Palestinian...you name
them.

Before Arab leaders realized they had won the propaganda war
and could relax, they had frenetically and cunningly been extending
specious invites for Arab Jews to return to their homelands. You see,
the approximately 1.5 million Jewish refugees from Arab lands could
have become a considerable obstacle to the Palestinian propaganda
machine had Israel been as conniving as her enemies. Imagine the
kind of trump card Israel might have wielded had she, like her
uncivilized neighbors, kept these legitimate Jewish refugees in
camps, refused to settle them, fomented hate among them for the
Arab, and turned the fugitives into political pawns—as Arab nations
have so masterfully done to their so-called refugees.

In 1976, these Jewish refugees, represented by the American
Sephardi Federation, responded to the cynical invites with a full-page
advertisement in the New York Times. The ad entailed a news service
photo that showed a mob of Iraqi onlookers surrounding two bodies
suspended from a scaffold. The dangling bodies were those of Sabam

Haim, and David Hazaquil, both Jews, hung in Baghdad. Beneath the photograph the organization responded: "Invitation declined."

95. TO BE OR NOT TO BE BLOWN UP

November 27, 2002

An editorial in the Egyptian government paper *Al-Akhbar* celebrated the killing of "11 Israeli terrorists" and the wounding of dozens in "a martyrdom operation in occupied Jerusalem." The Egyptian government's mouthpiece credits "Palestinian martyrs" for the "brave ambush," and blames the "terrorist state of Israel." "It is the Jews who are behind every calamity," hissed the editor of another such state organ, *Al-Gumhuriyya*. And this from a government Israel is officially at peace with.

Among the "Israeli terrorists" murdered were four children—two 13-year-olds, an eight-year-old boy who died along with his grandmother, and a 16-year-old boy whose mother was also killed. Reporting on what has become an unremarkable event in the lives of Israeli civilians—Palestinian homicide bombers have killed 309 Israelis over the last 26 months—the Associated Press went through the motions: Bomber boards an early morning bus in a Jerusalem neighborhood. The blast shatters the humdrum of children on their way to school and the elderly off to market for early-morning shopping. The AP cursorily mentions dismembered body parts and limbs littering the pavements. The clean-up operation consists invariably in gathering and matching bits of anatomy—a foot here, a hand there, a piece of hair—to give the victims a Jewish burial.

In this instance, 47 people were also wounded and at least nine are in critical condition. Although the networks rarely cover this aspect, the task facing Israeli medics has become a routine. Surgeons must slice open the surviving victims of these fiendish devices, picking from the flesh and burrowing in the bone for embedded shards of shrapnel, ball bearings, and nails. The rat poison is a diabolic touch, intended to intensify internal bleeding. If they survive, victims are left maimed and wracked with life-long disfigurement and pain.

Few commentators, Alan Keyes excepted, have had the heart and spine to express the existential meaning of painstakingly—almost lovingly—packing parcels of shrapnel, ball-bearings, nails and rat poison, to lodge in the bodies of Israeli civilians. Keyes, whose MSNBC program was axed shortly after a magnificent display of outrage, was man enough and moral enough to point out that this premeditated evil—supported by a majority of Palestinians— bespeaks the will to exterminate Israelis, and creates a deep and dark reality in the human heart.

Contrary to what the various pop-analysts claim, these bombs aren't a response to hopelessness. In the words of Howard Jacobson of the British *Independent*, "It is fanaticism of sympathy to grant the power of life and death to those who are dissatisfied, as though unhappiness were a sort of absolution that wiped out every other human obligation."

This fanaticism of misplaced sympathy is what those on the Far Left and on the Old Right consistently display. With a welcome exception. The paleoconservative scholar Paul Gottfried is unable to figure out what one does with enemies who try to blow you up even when you offer to give them back what they had lost in war. Gottfried advises that "the most the Israelis may be able to achieve in the present unsatisfactory situation is making those who are blowing up their families pay a high price."

To be fair, belittling Israel's survival efforts is not the sole purview of the far left and the Old Right. The neoconservative Jewish lobby does a dandy job of it. Of late, it has intensified the bid to hitch the legitimate Jewish struggle to the fight against global terror. This terrorism tag-along diminishes half a century of defensive wars, fought for survival—Even if Israel and the U.S. are indeed at war with the same enemies, Israel has been warding them off for decades and should not stoop to tailor life-and-death self-defense to the broader unholy neoconservative agenda.

Israeli leadership, moreover—and this is Sharon's instinct—must defend the right of an ethnically homogenous people to live free of aggression. Instead, her lobbyists persistently pretend Israel is a pluralistic melting pot, made in the image of the U.S., the kind neocon globalists want to see replicated worldwide. "The neocon attempts to compare an ethnically specific Jewish State to the multicultural toilet that the U.S. is becoming" makes professor Gottfried bristle. Israel's ethnic coherence has not prevented the integration of "a large Palestinian minority, who in Israel proper exercise the rights of citizens," he notes. Gottfried also observes that the absence of pluralism has not precluded the establishment in Israel of "parliamentary opposition parties, a free press and the rule of law"—unique in the neighborhood.

If he were living in Israel, Gottfried says, he'd vote for Sharon: "He's a blood-and-soil nationalist, like the old Afrikaners, and won't do anything to endanger the security of his nation to please Barbra Streisand or Joe Sobran."

96. ARAFAT: A MAN OF THE PEOPLE

November 15, 2004

Absolute and entire ugliness is rare, observed the Victorian author John Ruskin. He did not have the pleasure of meeting Yasser Arafat.

In his last photo opportunity, Arafat, whose soul reflected his countenance, wore pajamas and a fur hat. As he clasped the hands of members of his entourage, sporting a syphilitic grin, he made an obscene attempt to raise an aide's hand to his grotesque, giant lips. The Arab on whose hand Arafat had orally fixated pulled away persistently, embarrassed, as though a hound had mounted his leg.

But Arafat's mug and manners were the least of his obscenities. The Egyptian-born representative of the Palestinian People began his campaign of violence against Israel well before the 1967 war—his official pretext.

One of his first acts of terror within Israel was in 1965—a failed attempt by the Fatah to bomb the National Water Carrier, the country's irrigation and reservoir system. One of the last atrocities to have been carried out by Arafat's Fatah and *Al Aqsa* Martyrs occurred in March. Fatah and Hamas collaborated in a double-suicide bombing in the port of Ashdod. Ten Israelis were killed and 16 wounded.

Officially, Arafat stopped claiming responsibility for acts of terror in 1988. The West ignored the body count and took him at his word—his English word.

In Arabic, however, Arafat persistently promised to maintain the struggle to "eliminate the state of Israel and establish a purely Palestinian state," in the words of a 1996 speech delivered in Stockholm. It was a vow he repeated often, most notably in the same year at a rally near Bethlehem: "We know only one word—jihad. jihad, jihad, jihad. Whoever does not like it can drink from the Dead Sea or from the Sea of Gaza."

Or, as he prated to *Al-Hayat Al-Jadeeda*, newspaper of the Palestinian Authority (PA): "O my dear ones on the occupied lands, relatives and friends throughout Palestine and the diaspora, my colleagues in struggle and in arms, my colleagues in struggle and in jihad … Intensify the revolution and the blessed intifada … We must burn the ground under the feet of the invaders."

My fear and loathing of Yasser Arafat was born of personal experience as an Israeli. In 1974 Arafat sent the Democratic Front for the Liberation of Palestine (DFLP), an offshoot of the Palestinian Liberation Organization (PLO), into northern Israel. They infiltrated a high school in Maalot, killing 26 people; 21 were children only a little older than I was.

In April of that year, PLO terrorists attacked Kiryat Shmona, murdering 18, including eight children. The pathologist who performed the autopsies on the Maalot and Kiryat Shmona children was a close family friend. He arrived at my father's home distraught and later suffered a nervous breakdown.

In March 1978, Fatah terrorists took over a bus on the Coastal Haifa-Tel-Aviv highway (on which I traveled daily—in a bus—to school and back), killing 21 Israelis.

The committee for accuracy in Middle East Reporting in America has provided a potted history of Arafat's mass murders from 1965 until 2004. Some of the most ghastly acts on his rap sheet are the slayings of 47 people on a Swissair flight in 1970; nine pupils and three teachers in an attack on a school bus from Moshav Avivim, also in 1970; 27 religious pilgrims at Lod Airport; 11 Israeli athletes in the 1972 Munich Massacre.

Also bearing Arafat's signature were the hijacking of an Air France plane that ended with the Entebbe rescue and the pirating of the Italian cruise ship Achille Lauro, during which a wheelchair-bound elderly man, Leon Klinghoffer, was shot and thrown overboard. This cold-blooded killing Arafat coordinated from his headquarters in Tunis, to which he had been expelled from Lebanon. And before that from Jordan.

That the Left grieves over Yasser Arafat is not surprising. This is another manifestation of the coffeehouse humanitarianism of the folks at CNN, the New York Times, and the U.N. and its terrorist arm, the United Nations Relief and Works Agency for Palestine Refugees in the Near East (UNRWA).

A correspondent (and a writer in his own right) puts it better than I ever could: "Theirs is a seeming Rousseauan sympathy for the Symbolic Savage, any savage, wherever he may be, whom they fantasize as fighting nobly against the stifling strictures of Civil (and civilizing) Authority."

Indeed, what does one say about a commentariat, and for that matter, about kings and heads of state, whose "notion of 'freedom,'" as my correspondent points out, "is better symbolized by alienated rebel figures, such as Arafat and other terrorists—stateless malcontents answerable to no one, whose chief enemies are soap and razors"?

Especially misguided were the debates over Arafat's wealth—an estimated $1.3 billion in personal holdings. The proverbial man from Mars would be forgiven for thinking Arafat was an entrepreneur, rather than a grubby thief.

Fortunately, Forbes's Nathan Vardi audited Arafat, discovering that he used this vast fortune, including "the $5.5 billion in international aid that has flowed into the PA since 1994," to maintain an "elaborate patronage system"—corruption was the byword of Arafat's administration. The Palestinian Legislator Hannan Ashrawi, however, preferred to characterize such nepotism as "being fatherly"—a characterization MSNBC's Joe Scarborough failed to challenge.

Joe Scarborough, who usually likes to dish it straight up, also claimed that Father Arafat walked away from Ehud Barak's two-state solution, brokered by President Bill Clinton, because he feared assassination by the extremists who had—and still have—the run of the Palestinian Authority (PA).

Wrong. Arafat believed that by resorting to violence, he could achieve a one-state solution. How else, asks writer Maurice Ostroff, does one explain the dramatic rise in terror attacks during 1993 and 1994 while peace talks were still in progress?

As a master of triangulation, Arafat was able to string the Israeli and American camps along while working diligently to reach agreements with the most extreme Arab leaders and factions in the PA and beyond. If anything, it was Arafat and his Fatah and *Al-Aqsa* Martyrs' close contacts with Damascus and Tehran, Hamas, and Islamic Jihad that secured his safety for so long.

Considering their newly found, elections-spurred affinity for faith, Arafat's liberal fans ought to acquaint themselves with some facts. Particularly pertinent is the Palestinian fabrication about Islam's—and Arafat's—attachment to Jerusalem.

"Yerushalaim" is the Hebrew biblical name for the city that was sacred to Jews for nearly two thousand years before Muhammad. Not once is Jerusalem mentioned in the Koran. Muhammad was said to have departed to the heavens from the *Al Aksa* Mosque, but there was no mosque in Jerusalem. The Dome of the Rock and the *Al Aksa* Mosque were built on the Jewish Temple Mount. This usurpation was subsequently justified by Muslim theologians by superimposing their relatively recent fondness for Jerusalem upon the existing, ancient sanctity of the place to Jews.

Samuel Katz, in *Battleground: Fact And Fantasy* In Palestine, poses this question: What would the Christian reaction be if the same Muslim theologians had chosen to appropriate the Church of the Holy Sepulcher, re-name it, declare it Muslim property (which means killing for it), and demand Arafat be buried in it?

Israel's justice minister Yosef Lapid provided a wonderfully apposite response: "Jerusalem is the city where Jewish kings are buried and not Arab terrorists."

Amen.

97. PINOCCHIO'S PALESTINIAN PROBOSCIS

May 15, 2002

About his people, the late Palestinian intellectual, Ibrahim Abu-Lughod, said this: "We're mediocre, and in the end maybe that very mediocrity is what's going to beat the Israelis, for all their brilliance." Uncharacteristically candid, the professor was, however, understating the issue in a manner even less typical of his people's habit. In the war of words, the Israelis have, sadly, been thoroughly defeated. The clod's strategy has been effective—a victory lap is more in order.

"Arafat's obsequious, clownish posturing," as Edward Said— another Palestinian intellectual—described the chairman, is now ameliorated by a bevy of slick propagandists. Professor Abu-Lughod might have agreed, however, that their delivery is still more brawn than brains. Be it chief Palestinian Authority representative in the U.S., Abdel Hasan Rahman, or the beguiling legal adviser for the PA, Diana Buttu, the strategy they deploy is the same: unflinchingly repeat the staple lies again and again, while retaining a shot-with-botox facial expression.

And so the canard of a massacre or atrocities in Jenin was repeated even in the face of the discovery by Kadoura Moussa, the Fatah director for the northern West Bank, of 56 battle casualties. Not included among the dead was a corpse which—while being lugged by a group of Palestinian aspiring movie extras (staging one of those perennial "funerals" for the benefit of the uncritical, leftist media)—was dropped from the stretcher, only to rise from the dead and scurry away.

The Palestinian Jenin joust is reminiscent of the 1948 Deir Yassin libel. Deir Yassin was a village turned Arab base, where a fierce, Jenin-like battle ensued between the Israelis and the attacking Arab forces over the route to Jerusalem. As in Jenin, writes Samuel Katz in *Battleground: Fact and Fantasy in Palestine*, Arab fighters barricaded themselves among the villagers. One-third of the Israeli force was injured—some killed. Tragically, and in contrast to Jenin, many civilians did in fact perish in the crossfire.

Then, as today, Arab leaders were aided by British propaganda, with the result that the lie—according to which the Israelis had committed a massacre—grew over the decades like Pinocchio's proboscis. Jews have expressed deep sorrow over the tragic events in Deir Yassin, something a local villager recorded in a Jordanian daily. Yunes Ahmed Assad recounted that, "The Jews never intended to hurt the population of the village," and that "the Arab exodus from other villages..." was caused by "the exaggerated descriptions spread by Arab leaders to incite them to fight the Jews."

Has there been any expression of regret from Palestinian leaders, the UN, and the news networks the world over—all of which orchestrated the massacre libel? Have the networks stopped indulging—and giving credence to—the embellishments of the Palestinians?

More obfuscation than lie is the mantra that the "occupation" is responsible for the homicidal bombers. Nowhere does Hamas (or, to the best of my knowledge, any Islamic militant group, including the factions sponsored by and operating under Arafat) promise to swear off violence when—and if—Israel retreats to the indefensible borders of 1967. These grisly killers are very clear about their agenda.

The 1988 Covenant of the Islamic Resistance Movement (Hamas) states:

> The Islamic Resistance Movement believes that the land of Palestine is an Islamic Waqf consecrated for future Moslem generations until Judgement [sic] Day. It, or any part of it, should not be squandered; it, or any part of it, should not be given up.

And:

> There is no solution for the Palestinian question except through Jihad. Initiatives, proposals and international conferences are all a waste of time and vain endeavors.

The Hamas seals The Covenant with a foreboding, pan-Islamic promise that "Israel will exist and will continue to exist until Islam will obliterate it, just as it obliterated others before it."

To use that cliché of in-betweenness, Israel is caught between murderous militants and a hard place. In their own words, "occupation" of the West Bank and Gaza is not the cause of the militants' murder sprees—Jewish life in the land of Israel is. And nowhere do the militants, who have the run of the PA, promise to cease exploding innocent people if and when a retreat from Gaza and the West Bank is finalized. The Islamists tell us they will rest only when they conquer the land of Israel in its totality.1

According to the Hamas Covenant, nothing less than the destruction of Israel as a Jewish State will do. So when Raghida Dergham, the bonny propagandist from the newspaper *Al Hayat*, repeats for the umpteenth time on Hardball that the depredations of the "Israeli occupation" are responsible for Hamas' detonating of Israelis, she lies. Hamas' own manifesto contradicts her.

98. IMMOLATION BY IMMIGRATION

March 5, 2003

There has been some fuss about the qualifications of Eduardo Aguirre, President Bush's newly appointed head of the Bureau of Citizenship and Immigration Services. Much of the fuss, however, misses the mark. Mr. Bush hasn't appointed an unqualified man as much as he has, characteristically, used this appointment to make political hay.

Other than being part of the administration's ongoing public relations battle for the Latino vote, Bush's choice of a Latino immigration success story as his immigration pointman is intended to shamelessly signal that speaking authoritatively about immigration is the prerogative of an immigrant of ethnic descent. To make immigration-related decisions for the nation, you should, at the very least, be a minority.

A minority is certainly what my family was at the American Immigration and Naturalization Service headquarters in Montreal, as we waited to complete the final leg of the immigration odyssey. It was hard not to notice—and the PC Patrol will hit the roof because I did—but we were, as far as I could see, the only family of European descent in that room. We were immigrating to the United States of America, but the room was a linguistic tower of babble minus the English language.

The lopsided ethnic mix at the INS processing point was no coincidence; it is a consequence of American immigration policy starting in 1965. Had we been legal immigrants during the 1950s, we would have formed part of an inflow of new arrivals of which over two-thirds would have hailed from Europe or Canada. Similarly, during the Great Wave of immigration from 1890 to 1920, immigration policy guaranteed that newcomers reinforced the ethnic composition of native Americans; they were from the traditional northern and western European sources.

This policy persisted until 1965, when the Amendments to the Immigration and Nationality Act took effect, repealing the national-origin criterion and replacing it with a worldwide egalitarian quota that invited each country to contribute equally to the influx. The policy triggered an unparalleled, unselective, relentless human tsunami.

It was then that immigration policy also became predicated on family reunification rather than on skills relevant to the American economy. Unless American companies are recruiting wizened elderly people and small children who speak in foreign tongues, most of the immigrants assembled with us were the extended family of citizens. My spouse's "outstanding researcher" designation was very clearly not the rule in our intake.

Coupled with the allure of a generous welfare system, this change accounts for the generally poor quality of immigrants since 1965, and their unsustainable never-ending numbers—one qualified individual is a ticket for an entire tribe.

The 1965 Act radically transformed the U.S.'s original ethnic mix. Since its implementation, immigration to the U.S. has indeed been predominantly from the Third World. As Patrick J. Buchanan notes in *Death of the West*, this is the largest population transfer in history, with mass immigration from Africa, Asia, and Latin America destined to displace the American historical majority. Bill Clinton's glee gives an indication of what's ahead. Thanks to state-orchestrated immigration policy, he told a cheering high-school audience, "In little more than 50 years, there will be no majority race in the United States."

Implied in Clinton's jubilation, and in that of "the permanent government of bureaucrats, mediacrats, educrats, assorted policy wonks and intellectuals," to use Peter Brimelow's taxonomy of the toxic classes, is the following: 1) The American European historical majority was a bad thing; it needed to be cut back through state intervention and centralized oversight. 2) Immigration to the U.S is a universal right.

The soon-to-be-dispossessed historical majority never got to debate these empty assumptions.

Shoring up the immigration tyranny is yet another myth crushed with courage and candor by Brimelow in his *Alien Nation*. As the fable goes, America is a multicultural nation of immigrants, and nobody whose ancestors arrived as immigrants can possibly oppose mass immigration without falling into self-contradiction. Against this, consider the foolishness of supporting for purely nostalgic reasons a policy that was turned toxic.

Furthermore, the nation was never founded as a multicultural nation, at least not in the manner in which the term is enforced nowadays. The U.S. was biracial: Roughly 19.3 percent were black, but the people who established the political order, described by Thomas Jefferson as "a composition of the freest principles of the English constitution, ...derived from natural right and natural reason," were white, overwhelmingly British Christians.

While illegal immigration is logistically vexing, it should pose no problem of principle. Every sane individual agrees that the roughly 12 million illegals have no right to be here, and that repelling invaders who may endanger the lives and property of nationals is an uncontested function of government. It's as obvious as the Pope is Catholic to all except loony liberals, willfully misinformed utilitarians at the *Wall Street Journal*, and utopian libertarians, who get hopelessly lost somewhere between what *is* and what *ought* to be.

By focusing exclusively on the illegal immigration no-brainer, however, most media scribes and immigration watchdogs are providing a useful diversion from the crux of the immigration problem. And playing into the hands of an administration that wants us to forget that legal immigration is the real catastrophe.

99. DISPLACING AMERICANS

July 2, 2003

In making their case for a free-for-all immigration policy, open-border libertarians usually confine themselves to insipid sentimental arguments. This manipulative fare is easy to dismiss. After all, saying that immigrants are only seeking "a better way of life" in our country or that immigration is an American tradition hardly constitutes a valid justification for laws that are manifestly antithetical to the welfare and rights of Americans.

Immigration lawyer Gregory Siskind is one such specimen. Siskind, who claims his work is inspired by his libertarian beliefs and Jewish faith, to boot, traffics in H-1B visas. These are temporary work permits, which are also a route to acquiring legal permanent resident status. The out-of-control H-1B visa program has become an example of crony capitalism in action—it's tantamount to a taxpayer subsidy for hi-tech corporations.

Siskind claims his work benefits the economy. As his immigration muse, he touts the man who monkeys with our money, Alan Greenspan. Predictably, Greenspan is as hip about immigration as he is about inflating the money supply. That Siskind credits the Fed chairman with "ensuring that America thrives" ought to cast doubts on any judgment he makes about the value to the economy of his H-1B work, much less on his libertarian *bona fides*.

Far worse is Jim Rogers' paean to open borders published by the Future of Freedom Foundation, an organization that generally doesn't countenance falsehoods. In support for his open-border position, Rogers claims falsely that the United States has huge shortages of computer specialists, software and other engineers. Our Mr. Siskind, for his part, hazards that advocates of limited immigration or a moratorium on work visas wish to "shut down the country's borders to protect the economic well-being of the few."

As few as 172,000? That's the official number of unemployed high-tech professionals who are, if we are to believe Siskind, acting as spoilsports. Computer software engineers lead the way with 62,000 unemployed! Indeed, these figures, available from the Bureau of Labor Statistics at the U.S. Department of Labor, put paid to the untruths spread by immigration fetishists. Unemployment among electrical and electronics engineers reached seven percent in the first quarter of 2003!

Yet the current cap of H-1B visas stands at 195,000, and immigration lawyers like Siskind are lobbying Congress to keep the new arrivals coming. In 1992, the allowable number of H-1B visas was 65,000, but due to pressure, Congress increased the number of incomers first to 115,000 and then to its current level. "Since the H-1B cap was raised to 195,000 visas a year in 2000," reports the Institute of Electrical and Electronics Engineers-United States of America (IEEE-USA), unemployment among American engineers and computer scientists has jumped from 65,000 to 114,000 in 2001 to 166,000 in 2002 to its current unequalled high.

Yes, correlation is not causation. But you have to admit the correlation is a strong one. And it is further strengthened by the fact that during the same time span, the Immigration and Naturalization Service, cheered on by the likes of Siskind and the cockroaches in Congress, had approved a total of "529,000 new and renewal H-1B visa petitions from U.S. employers." Talk about treason! American governments are unique in their efforts to displace their own population, while at the same time training it in the art of silent suffering—the locals are guaranteed to go quietly into the night, mouthing mad mantras about immigration's blessings.

The sheer volume of unemployed, highly skilled people in the fields of science and engineering must give pause. This "may not be a short-term cyclical phenomenon," ventures Dr. Ronil Hira of the IEEE-USA Institute of Electrical and Electronics Engineers-United States of America, but a result of much more fundamental changes in the U.S. economy. Even theoreticians who refuse to adapt abstracted economic models to reality must concede that America's best and brightest young people will be unlikely to pursue careers in science and engineering anytime soon, not if they want to eat.

Professionals like electrical engineers and computer scientists have an added problem. Most of these fellows make their living via the economic means. The political class and its sycophants— immigration lawyers and activists—utilize the political means to earn their keep. As libertarian economist Murray Rothbard reminded, these "are two mutually exclusive ways of acquiring wealth"—the economic means is honest and productive, the political means is dishonest and predatory...but oh so very effective.

100. LOVE-IN AT THE BORDERS

July 9, 2003

The ethics of private property ought to guide all libertarians on the matter of immigration. And an essential attribute of property and ownership is the right to exclude or include—the right to discriminate is an undisputed feature of property. In the absence of a state, or in the presence of a limited government where almost all land is privately owned, migration would be a very restricted affair. It would depend on the graces of private property owners. A newcomer may be invited over by a propertied person, who would shoulder the costs. If he wishes to venture beyond the invited sphere, the newcomer would seek consent from the private property owners with whom he wishes to interface. The more the status of property approaches the libertarian ideal, the less free migration would be.

The libertarian theorist Professor Hans-Hermann Hoppe has brought to my attention his excellent *Natural Order, the State, and the Immigration Problem* journal article. It comports well with my description of the abuses of the H-1B visa program as part and parcel not of the law of the free market, but of the law of the state.

In a free society based on absolute private-property rights, the natural tendency of men—a tendency that is most conducive to peace—is to live among their own, but to trade with any and all. In such a society, commercial property owners will tend to be far more inclusive than residential property owners. As Hoppe notes, owners of retail establishments, like hotels and restaurants, "have every economic incentive not to discriminate unfairly against strangers because this would lead to reduced profits or losses." Still, they will have to consider the impact of culturally exotic behavior on "local domestic sales," and will impose codes of conduct on guests.

Seeking low-wage employees, employers would also be partial to foreigners but, absent the protectionist state, the employer would be accountable to the community, and would be wary of the strife and lowered productivity caused by a multiethnic and multi-linguistic workforce. All the more so when a foreign workforce moves into residential areas.

In short, reasons Hoppe, in a natural order—absent government—there will be plenty of "interregional trade and travel," but little mingling in residential areas. Just as people tend to marry along cultural and racial lines, so they maintain rather homogeneous residential neighborhoods. This is how the chips fall in a highly regulated society, so much more so in a free society, based on absolute property rights. Is this contemptible? To the left-libertarian open-border purist it is—else why would he be lending ideological support to the state's efforts to upset any semblance of a natural order and to shape society in politically pleasing ways?

His tentative grasp of property leads the leftist libertarian to forget that public property is property funded by taxpayers through expropriated taxes. It belongs to taxpayers. Yet at least a million additional immigrants a year are allowed the free use of these taxpayer-supported amenities. Every new arrival avails himself of public works such as roads, hospitals, parks, libraries, schools and welfare.

This is why the H-1B visa program, as I pointed out in "Displacing Americans," is tantamount to a subsidy to business at the expense of the taxpayer. And Hoppe concurs: "[E]mployers under democratic Welfare State conditions are permitted by state law to externalize their employment costs on others" and will "tend to import increasingly low-skilled and low value-productive immigrants, regardless of their effect on all-around communal property values." Here, the rightful owners of public property do not get to vet the newcomers—the state and big business do. Yet when faced with such economic fascism (government-business collusion), open-border libertarians exalt business' every move.

Perpetually suspended in some kind of third dimension—or on a collision course with reality, as the libertarian Roy A. Child put it—the best open-border libertarians can come up with is, "There should be no public property or Welfare State." Well there is, and levitating in la-la land is not going to change this fact of life. To which the immigration enthusiast's only response is to propose a kind of chaos theory—let the multitudes come, the Welfare State will buckle under and collapse. Out of the chaos, a free order will emerge (sigh).

Back on *terra firma*, state-administered immigration continues undisturbed. Its egalitarian, multicultural impetus guarantees that a quota is divvied among the nations of the world, irrespective of the sentiments of Americans or their own cultural affinities and origins. Government's laws, moreover, make avoiding this compulsory integration impossible. A Middle Eastern immigrant enters the country. Despite post-September 11 jitters, and a desire to protect his tenants, an apartment-complex owner cannot by law refuse to lease to the new arrival. The law prohibits property owners from exercising the right to exclude applicants from housing—civil-rights legislation and affirmative action circumscribe hiring, firing, renting, selling, and even money lending.

All told, government is vested in emasculating Americans. Remove their guns, their right to defend their property, force multiculturalism and cultural relativism down their gullets, control their property so that it is not their own, and then import millions of new constituents who'll further enforce welfarism and statism. Open-border libertarians are on board with the state for this last leg of the journey.

101. TRADE GOODS, NOT PLACES

February 6, 2002

Libertarians agree that forced distribution of wealth from those who create it to those who don't is categorically wrong. Yet in his support for unfettered movement of people across borders, you'll repeatedly hear the garden-variety libertarian open-border enthusiast say that, "Libertarians don't care if immigrants use a disproportionate amount of social services." Why this liberal "generosity" with funds not his own? "Because," as one such advocate dilettantishly declared, "we believe all social programs should be junked."

Talk about a petulant *non sequitur*.

Notwithstanding that nationals pay taxes, from the fact that taxpayer-funded welfare for nationals is morally wrong, why does it follow that extending it to millions of unviable non-nationals is economically and morally negligible? Or that it remotely comports with the libertarian goal of curtailing government growth? How is this stock-in-trade, truncated argument different from positing that because a bank has been robbed by one band of bandits (welfare-dependant nationals), repelling or arresting the next (welfare-dependent non-nationals) is unnecessary because the damage has already been done?

Besides, the existence of taxpayer-funded services like roads, education, and health care makes immigrants *de facto* free riders. Anti-discrimination and affirmative action laws further give immigrants legal rights to the property of nationals. As libertarian economist Murray Rothbard put it, this is the quintessential "swamping by the central state of an existing population for political ends."

Pat Buchanan, then, is mostly correct when he accuses the typical libertarian of being devoted to limitless immigration, and thus to the further enlargement and empowerment of the state, with an exception. Among us are a few who implacably oppose free immigration, on the grounds cogently posed by economist and libertarian *extraordinaire*, Hans-Hermann Hoppe.

As Hoppe points out, proponents of restricted immigration tend to be advocates of protectionist economic policies; advocates of free and relatively non-discriminatory immigration policies are invariably proponents of free trade. Pat Buchanan fits the former category; his leftist economics and national and cultural conservatism combine in a vehement opposition to *laissez faire*. Most libertarians fit the latter mold, habitually chanting that free trade is commensurate with the free flow of people across borders.

But it is this tie-in that Hoppe rejects out of hand. Free trade is not only perfectly compatible with restricted immigration, but restricted immigration and free trade are "mutually reinforcing policies," he says. What the Love-In at the Border libertarian recommends amounts to invasion and forced integration against which government must legitimately protect its citizens.

If we apply the principles undergirding free trade to immigration, then restricting immigration becomes essential. Right now, explains Hoppe, "someone can migrate from one place to another without anyone else wanting him to do so," but "goods and services cannot be shipped from place to place unless both sender and receiver agree." This distinction seems almost mischievously trivial, but it penetrates the core. Trade is always invited, consensual and, hence, mutually beneficial to the private property holders that are party to the transactions. When government restricts trade, it violates—not protects—the rights of private property owners to exchange goods and to enjoy freedom of association.

Free immigration, on the other hand, "does not mean immigration by invitation of individual households and firms, but unwanted invasion or forced integration." When government restricts immigration, it is actually protecting private households and firms from these perils.

Matters would be simple if all libertarians agreed that a constitutional government has an obligation to repel foreign invaders. They don't, not if they are anarchists. Both open-border and closed-border libertarian anarcho-capitalists posit that an ideal society is one where there is no entity—government—to monopolize defense and justice functions. In a society based on anarcho-capitalism, where every bit of property is privately owned, the reasoning goes, private property owners cannot object if X invites Y onto his property, so long as he keeps him there, or so long as Y obtains permission to venture onto other spaces. Despite their shared anarchism, limited-immigration anarcho-libertarians and free-immigration anarcho-libertarians arrive respectively at different conclusions when they make the transition from utopia to real life.

The latter believe the state must refrain from interfering with the free movement of people despite the danger they may pose to nationals. The former arrive at the exact opposite conclusion: So long as the modern American Welfare State stands, and so long as it owns large swaths of property, it's permissible to expect the state to carry out its traditional defensive functions. This includes repelling incomers who may endanger the lives and livelihoods of locals.

The open-border libertarian will claim that his is the less porous position. He will accuse the limited-immigration libertarian of being guilty of, on the one hand, wanting the state to take action to counter immigration, but, on the other hand, because of his anarchism, being at pains to find a basis for the interventions he favors. Not being an anarchist, and hence not having to justify the limited use by government of force against invaders, I hope I have escaped these contradictions.

In sum, so long as the U.S. remains a high-wage area, with a tax-funded welfare system, it will experience migratory pressure from low-wage countries. Protectionist policies immeasurably worsen this pressure, because, when people are prevented from selling their wares into foreign markets, they're more inclined to relocate in search of better economic conditions. Unhampered trade can diminish this pressure.

Real-life immigration, then, can be made to imitate the art of free trade. "By advocating free trade and restricted immigration, one follows the same principle: requiring an invitation for people as for goods and services," says Hoppe. Or else, it's Return to Sender.

102. DO OR DIE DIVERSITY

February 13, 2002

Open-border immigration enthusiasts suffer from frequent brain events. One such unlucky stroke is the theory behind their "revolving door" policy recommendations. Accordingly, many immigrants don't really want to settle in the United States, and if not for the ostensibly closed borders, people from Mexico, the People's Republic of China, the Philippines, India, and Vietnam would make their stash and head straight back to their bucolic motherlands. According to this position, the problem is not in the easy entry, but the blocked "escape" routes: once in the U.S., illegals can't exit without being apprehended.

Open-border advocates want to see the implementation of a "revolving door" policy, one that allows documented foreign workers to come and go freely. Realistically speaking, "a revolving door" is a euphemism for open borders. Furthermore, the immigration enthusiast's convictions about the self-regulating nature of the free flow of people across borders rest entirely on liberal paternalism! To the liberal, foreigners are exotic beings, who can't wait to resume their tourist-friendly, ethnically distinct lives back home. The facts contradict such piffle. If the swelling number of legal and illegal entrants is a hint, few of those lucky enough to enter the U.S. ever consider leaving, even if they own rice paddy real estate back home.

More significantly, even if we accept (incorrectly) the immigration liberal's unfounded assertion that this influx is an economic gain for all, material considerations may not be the most important in the immigration quagmire. In *Alien Nation*, Peter Brimelow calls attention to the need "for some degree of ethnic and cultural coherence" in order to safeguard the free market and freedom itself. Like Pat Buchanan, Brimelow alerts to the alarming consequences of an immigration policy that has ensured that 85 percent of the 16 million legal immigrants arriving in the U.S. between 1968 and 1993 hailed from the Third World. Once conferred with citizenship, each and every immigrant may lawfully sponsor more relatives who, in turn, can do the same. For an illegal, it takes no more than procreating on U.S. soil to acquire an American relative—baby is automatically a citizen.

Post September 11, Americans may be wishing with a vengeance that the country did not harbor a fifth column of legitimate immigrants, rooting—perhaps even actively working—for the destruction of the United States. Americans may be longing for the coherence that was sundered beginning with Ted Kennedy's 1965 Amendments to the Immigration and Nationality Act, when national-origin restrictions were repealed.

The immigration dilemma is indeed not reducible to dollars and dimes, although, as it so happens, the gains from immigration to the U.S. economy as a whole are small. George Borjas, professor of Public Policy at Harvard University, documents in detail how, since the 1965 Amendments, "the United States has been granting entry visas to persons who have relatives in the United States, with no regard to their skills or economic potential. Immigrants today are less skilled than their predecessors, more likely to require public assistance, and far more likely to have children who remain in poor, segregated communities."

The libertarian immigration proponent is fond of blaming the welfare state for the quality of the newcomers. Abolish the welfare state, he typically excoriates, and immigrants will become more productive. The causal sequence is wrong! The starting point is the quality of immigrants entering the U.S. For the kind of immigrant that is given preference under current policy, welfare is a magnet. Once again the open-border enthusiast's thinking is striking in likeness to the liberal central planner's beliefs. Both see the social environment as the main determinant of people's behavior, a conviction that undergirds the liberal's energetic social engineering. For his part, the immigration liberal's convictions give him license to ignore the rapid acculturation of post-1965 immigrants to U.S. largess: The longer these immigrants reside in the country, the more likely they are to receive welfare. This was not characteristic of pre-1965 immigrants, even though welfare benefits were a constant back then, just as they are now.

The politics of petulance is another aspect to which post-1965 immigrants have been quick to acclimatize. In previous decades immigrants assimilated. Now they are encouraged by politicians and identity-politics activists to cling to an almost militant distinctiveness. The state-enforced ideology of multiculturalism and diversity has thus become a double-edged sword, deployed by government at once to make newcomers more subversive and the local population more submissive.

Indeed, Americans no longer so much as protest when their lives are jeopardized by imported thugs, and have by now been thoroughly convinced that this danger is the price of living in a free—more honestly, a free-for-all—county. When he admonishes ordinary Americans for their "ethnic mistrust and xenophobia," the immigration liberationist has joined the state and its lickspittle toadies in the media and in academia in brandishing multiculturalism to justify the importation of potential constituents.

Open-border types are usually egalitarians. Perhaps they even mean well when they insist that we be forced to "share" the fruits of our labor with newcomers. The same cannot be said of government-spawned immigration policy. Rumored to be underway is an attempt to give "amnesty" or legalize roughly 12 million illegal immigrants.

Since the nation's personal income tax burden rests unfairly on 32 million people—most of them of the "pale, patriarchal, penile" variety, or whatever the current multicultural pejorative is for the besieged white male—they will be footing the bill.

103. THE REAL WAR IS AT HOME

July 10, 2002

Most people don't know who Haim Sapir is. Had he been an American, Sapir would have been declared a hero. Had he been an American, Sapir would be clamoring for his halo on the talk-show circuit. He'd have a gooey-lipped Fox News ditz, bubbling with questions like, "What went through your mind when you killed the non-terrorist Hesham Mohamed Hadayet at the El Al ticket counter, in LAX, on the Fourth of July?"

We came to know about the slightly built Israeli, who tackled and shot the Egyptian, not from the laconic Israelis, but from an American eyewitness, who suctioned himself to a television camera at the first opportunity.

Americans have a tough time distinguishing real from phony heroes. Sapir was just doing his job. He was trained to take out the enemy in 30 seconds, and he probably thinks he didn't quite measure up. But for Americans, who live in a world festooned with symbolism and sentimentality, such matter-of-fact realities may be difficult to grasp.

When you're given to emotional flights of fancy, your leaders are better able to obscure the reality on the ground. For one, they can hide the fact that the military is no longer doing anything that will advance the good of its countrymen or punish the enemy. Leaders can, moreover, give The War its own momentum, as this administration has done, by hyping it as a symbolic war.

For example, facts and common sense indicated should not have been attacked. If anything, threatening to attack a nation that had not aggressed against us was bound to make a dormant but dangerous Saddam Hussein act recklessly. To disguise these hard specifics, the administration whipped up a frenzy, framing its unprovoked aggression as a metaphoric battle of good against evil, and launching the U.S. on a figurative, wild-goose chase.

There is, however, a real war—its battlefront is in our midst. With the July-Fourth murders of Victoria Hen and Yaakov Aminov, we got a lesson on how semantics can conceal the slow war of attrition here at home—where the citizens are the unwitting warriors, the leaders their mortal enemies. The other lesson gleaned was that no administration will ever allow Americans to defend themselves by singling out and ejecting the fifth columnists living among them.

At this juncture we find Hesham Mohamed Hadayet, who lived in the U.S. quite comfortably. On July Fourth, 2002, politicians moved like lightning to depict Hadayet as a perpetrator of a random attack. The fact that Hadayet was a semiautomatic, sword-wielding Islamist, whose family departed mysteriously for Egypt a week prior to the Los Angeles International Airport attack, was, apparently, sheer coincidence. Or so claimed Ari Fleischer, the FBI, state politicians, and almost all the pointy-heads on television.

If this performance is anything to go by, the tack is to convince Americans that their enemies at home are simply lone lunatics. Isolated incidents, after all, don't adequately support demands for culturally compatible immigration policies, for profiling, or for large-scale deportations—all of which need to happen if lives are to be safeguarded. In the absence of a cause for drastic change, Americans will be forced to accept their lot and…die silently.

And so it was that a speedy amen was given to the "isolated incident" theory. Americans had to be convinced, and fast, that the war effort needed to grow just enough to support Bush's worldwide faith-based offensive but not quite sufficiently to allow Americans to protect life at home. That is, to convince them Iraq had to be attacked, but also impress upon them that they must continue to open their borders to enemies like the Hadayets of the world.

No surprise then that the Debka*file*'s Counter-Terror Sources had information about Hadayet that is at odds with the random-event humbug. It appears that Hadayet was an al-Qaida plant, member of a sleeper-cell, a fact backed by no less than the gray eminence of the Arab press, the London-based *Al Hayat*! As a member of the Egyptian

Jihad Islami, al-Qaida's primary operational arm, the Egyptian gunman likely met twice in California with one of the Jihad Islami chiefs, Dr. Ayman Zuwahri, also Osama bin Laden's deputy.

The man fits the profile of the kind of terrorist who has plagued airlines and terminals for the past twenty years. But with a trick of the tongue, he was declared a mismatch, nothing but an artifact.

VIII. Western Values Versus Imperial Ambitions

104. SAVE AMERICA FROM THE WAR PARTY

September 19, 2002

By agreeing to allow the unconditional return of weapons inspectors, Iraq had done well to expose—sadly, not halt—the Bush administration's unstoppable agenda. This gesture by Iraq was not so much a "stunning turnabout," but a culmination of a plain and reasonable attempt by an economically desperate Iraq to tie the return of inspectors to the lifting of sanctions. It failed. Washington's predictably disgruntled response confirmed that George W. Bush never wanted Saddam Hussein to roll over, but wanted, very plainly, to sock it to him.

In the process of promising to wage war in the name of cherished American values, President Bush forgot a pesky little detail: The U.S. government is beholden to the Constitution, which prohibits the president from declaring war (something he had, to all intents and purposes, already done by ordering bombing sorties over Iraq). It is Congress that declares a war; the president wages it.

Rather than go the constitutional route, Mr. Bush began by declaring his commitment to topple the regime in Baghdad, believing somehow that such a prerogative was a policy privilege he commandeered on being elected. The unconstitutional implications of his audacious imperialism never really hit home with Americans.

Flouting his obligation to get "the consent of the governed," to quote the Declaration of Independence, Mr. Bush ended up seeking approval from the United Nations, a body entirely unrepresentative of—even hostile to—the American people. The president then went on to bully a clearly corrupt Congress to authorize war against Iraq before the November midterm elections. Congress's vote was no more than a formality. War was declared, to all intents and purposes, by executive order!

By acquiescing on inspectors, Iraq must have hoped to unfurl the lattice of lies that served to propel Mr. Bush's war. The president's swirl of rhetoric before the UN was not even tangentially related to the original indictment against Iraq: that it had a hand in September 11 and directly supported Islamic fundamentalist terrorism. Iraq was a secular dictatorship profoundly at odds with Islamic fundamentalism. No less an authority than the former head of the CIA's counterterrorism office, Vincent Cannistraro, stated categorically that there was no evidence of Iraq's links to al-Qaida. Even the putative Prague meeting between Mohamed Atta, the ringleader of September 11, and Iraqi intelligence, turned out to be bogus.

What remained for Mr. Bush then was to pirate the old, pre-Gulf War narrative for his UN address. Lacking proof of Iraqi links to al-Qaida, Mr. Bush fixed on accusing Iraq of reacquiring chemical, biological, and nuclear weapons, as well as long-range ballistic missiles. Essentially Iraq was convicted based on a rehash of its record during—and prior to—Desert Storm, not based on the current threat she posed to the United States and the region.

Enter Scott Ritter, true American patriot. Mr. Ritter is a 12-year Marine Corps and Gulf War veteran. He is also a Republican. Most pertinent, Mr. Ritter is a former UN weapons inspector in Iraq, and much less cavalier than Mr. Bush about sending Americans to die in Iraq. Equally grave were Mr. Ritter's misgivings about killing innocent Iraqis.

Mr. Ritter's case against such an attack was founded in reason and fact, not in political expediency. He understands the technology that goes into making, acquiring, and detecting weapons of mass destruction. Having spent seven years inspecting and turning Iraq inside out, Mr. Ritter said Iraq had been 95 percent disarmed and had no weapons of mass destruction, an assessment backed by many experts in strategic studies. Iraq, Mr. Ritter pointed out, is a Third World nation, whose military prowess is now a fifth of what it was when hobbled during the Gulf War. It has no navy or air force. It was never a threat to American national security.

The attack on Iraq defied the very foundations of international law. There was no moral argument for attacking a nation that had not aggressed against the United States. Judging from the bipartisan slobbering the president's moral preening elicited and continues to elicit, Mr. Ritter's morals are like pearls before swine.

105. AXIS OF ILLOGIC

December 18, 2002

Publicly available CIA reports offered no fresh incriminating evidence against Iraq, but a lot of innovative variations on the Bush Bafflegab. To wit: "Saddam will probably"; "Give him time and he will eventually"; "With sufficient weapons-grade fissile material, he'll doubtless"; "He doesn't have the capability to develop enriched uranium or plutonium to fuel a nuclear bomb, but hang in there …"

This is obviously not the letter of the text, but close enough to its spirit. How the CIA cobbles evidence for an "interest in acquiring" or "an effort to procure"—considering that these purchases never seem to materialize—isn't clear. What proof do we have that they were even initiated? CIA language is manifestly intended to exempt the writer from having to substantiate much of the claims.

What a relief it was, then, when a real incriminating event finally occurred. A North Korean vessel was not allegedly—but actually—apprehended in the Arabian Sea, carrying 15 well-concealed Scud missiles. All in all, Baghdad Before Bush was suspected of hiding about 60 Scud-variant missiles. Here we had the equivalent of one-fourth of the entire Iraqi arsenal on one ship!

While Iraqi palm dates were subject to U.S.-enforced trade embargoes, it was comforting to know that North Korean Scud missiles were not. About the North Korean commitment to free trade, Donald Rumsfeld effused: They "continue to be the single largest proliferator of ballistic-missile technology on the face of the Earth, putting into the hands of many countries the technologies and capabilities which have the potential for killing hundreds of thousands of people." Joy!

Nothing is more admirable, however, than a nation that uses its trading advantage with discretion: North Korea didn't sell missiles to Iraq—it only sells them to "friendly nations" like Pakistan, Syria, Egypt, Iran, Libya, and Yemen, to which its latest shipment was headed.

Iraq, as the administration insisted, may have been jam-packed with Jihadists, but Yemen doesn't exactly have to outsource for its Islamist assassins. Like America, it has plenty of homegrown homicidal talent. Recall the Yemeni port of Aden was the site of the attack on the destroyer USS Cole, which killed 17 sailors. Off the coast of Yemen, a bomb, not so long ago, damaged a French oil tanker, killing a sailor. British Special Forces even conducted searches for Osama bin Laden in Yemen, where al-Qaida was said to be regrouping.

The North Korean missile crisis must have left Saddam bitter about the favoritism that has allowed said nation such generous maneuverability on the axis of evil. (Although his initial frazzled reaction was probably: "Could this be something I ordered for the New Year celebrations and forgot about?") North Korea has been welcomed out of the closet with its ongoing uranium enrichment program. And, evidently, the North Koreans are permitted to trade openly in deadly weapons, albeit with peaceniks like the Yemenites.

At the time, honorary axis member Iran, a gaily open supporter of terrorism, remained unhindered by threats of a U.S. invasion, as did the rogue states of Saudi Arabia, Syria, Libya, and Sudan. While the CIA was adamant it had no Iraqi smoking gun, evidence for these other nations' hospitality to terrorism abounded.

As luck would have it, under the Bush Iraq Doctrine, evidence against a theory constitutes evidence for a theory. No smoking gun means there's a hidden gun somewhere or a plan to acquire a gun, or a hidden plan to acquire a gun and hide it.

Whichever is the case, it was reason enough for an attack. Never mind that Saddam's visibly antiquated and crumbling infrastructure was being crisscrossed and closely watched by weapons inspectors. And no matter that the U.S. was bombing him illegally—and immorally—over the unilaterally established No-Fly Zone.

More poignantly, Saddam was by then acutely aware of Washington's not-so-secret Nuclear Posture Review. The NPR was crystal clear about this administration's willingness to use lower-yield, precision nuclear weapons on Iraq if Saddam attacked the U.S. with nuclear, biological or chemical weapons. Washington clearly hasn't been as dyslexic about the lessons of history as it would appear—at least implicitly, there was an acknowledgement that Cold War restraint is no folly.

Why then did this president behave as if Saladin the Second was scheming to do what the former Soviet Union didn't dare do with its more than 10,000 strategic nuclear warheads; 30,000 nonstrategic nuclear warheads; 6,000-plus ready-to-go nuclear warheads mounted on more than 1,000 intercontinental ballistic missiles—not to mention thousands of submarine-launchable nuclear weapons and more than 1,000 nuclear bombs carried by long-range jet aircraft? (The tally is courtesy of the Independent Institute's Robert Higgs.)

Could Saddam really have been hell-bent on doing what the many times more evil and powerful former Soviet Union avoided at all costs? Was Saddam suicidal? The facts suggested not. Given the administration's re-embracing of the deterrence principle as articulated in the NPR, Bush's lockjaw on Iraq didn't make sense.

And neither was it meant to. It was meant to radically change the way we think. This was an exercise in "consciousness-raising," befitting the permanent revolution one can expect from the ideologues in this administration.

106. TUNED-OUT, TURNED-ON, AND HOT FOR WAR

January 15, 2003

Come to think of it, there was a discrepancy between Washington's treatment of North Korea and its treatment of Iraq only if one was searching for a just principle behind the actions. Abandon *principle* and settle for an abiding *pattern*, and it becomes clear that what animated the administration's assault on Baghdad was what also puts the spring in the step of every schoolyard bully: the smell of vulnerability.

There's more. War is beneficial not only to Fox News' ratings; it's good for the presidency too. The dynamic behind war as a vehicle for political popularity is quite simple, even primitive. Anyone of the Fox News anchors makes a good case study, and the other network personnel soon caught up. The writing was on the wall well before hundreds of embeds officially slipped between the sheets with the military.

At the best of times, Fox anchorwomen are an aggressive amalgam of furiously gyrating facial muscles and staccato Pidgin English. But to watch these women doing the Countdown to Obliterating Iraq segments was like watching bitches on heat. One anchorwoman's memorable Freudian slip was to express disappointment that there was as yet no "evidence that'll give us an excuse [her words] to attack Iraq."

Since the Bush war whirl began, the intellectual climate has changed so rapidly that such *faux pas* didn't even register with viewers. The American people had taken this war, its propaganda, and its prosecutors to their hearts—perverted warpath patriotism was what was getting the folks hot. People who are in a constant state of heightened emotional arousal tend to want to remain that way; the emotions are self-reinforcing. The president and his advisers knew that to keep the people tuned-out, they had to keep them turned-on.

Simpler than the Stay On Heat principle is the bully convention. It explains why the impressive display of aggression by the North Koreans was a winner that kept Bullyboy at bay. It was not Iraq that raised the specter of a "Third World War," after announcing its withdrawal from the world's foremost nuclear arms-control treaty. And it wasn't Saddam's relatively subdued rhetoric that sent U.S. Assistant Secretary of State James Kelly scampering to consult with China, Singapore, Indonesia, and Japan. The Iraqi state-controlled press might not have been particularly complimentary about Americans. But it paled compared to the North Korean press' call to "turn the citadel of imperialists into a sea of fire." Or its dictator's promise to "smash U.S. nuclear maniacs" in a "holy war" if they didn't back off.

There was absolutely no mixed message in the signals that came from North Korea's man in charge of liaisons with the UN's International Atomic Energy Agency. As the Associated Press reported, Mr. Son Mun San promised that his plutonium reprocessing plant stood in a state of "readiness." That sounded like an unadulterated "make my day" message to me. Surprisingly, Pyongyang's unambiguous bellicosity was interpreted in the U.S. as a "mixed message." That the U.S. chose to dilute a pure threat with favorable interpretations should occasion no surprise. Show a bully a fist and he will usually retreat, preferring to put a face-saving spin on the affair rather than follow through on the threat.

Which brings me to the multicult cards. Mr. Bush enlisted New Mexico's Governor and former Clintonite, Bill Richardson, to hold meetings with the North Korean Deputy UN Ambassador. Diversity Dick put the conflict down to cultural differences, claiming that North Koreans simply "don't negotiate like we do. They don't have our same mentality." There's an element of truth to this. Whereas the North Koreans were genuinely hopping mad at the perceived threat from the U.S., not least being plunked on the axis of evil, Saddam and the Iraqi people were truly terrified. Saddam's actions proved it. He had, after all, allowed UN inspectors to transform Iraq into a sophisticated crime scene.

Asian self-control being what it is, when the usually inhibited Asians froth at the mouth, beware! Arab effusive demonstrativeness being what it is, when Saddam, the habitual blowhard, toned down his truculence, it should have been taken as a sign of resignation. That is if sincere diplomacy was ever the administration's objective, which, of course, it wasn't.

Soon another American conceit reared its head. A million (doubtless hungry) North Koreans marched on that nation's capital, many chanting promises of "revenge with blood" for any country that violated their sovereignty. Just as Americans imagined the Iraqi people were panting for an occupying force to liberate them from Saddam, they doubtless believe North Koreans, at their core, are hunkering for a delivery of U.S.-style democracy. American sentimentality, childishness, and insularity simply don't admit of a strong national pride in so wretched a people as the Iraqis or the North Koreans. However oppressed, people would sooner deal with their homey Hun than submit to a foreign force, even if it comes bearing minute-made democracy.

107. 'JUST WAR' FOR DUMMIES

March 12, 2003

Without let, the United States continued to bully its way to war, in the process, bribing one opponent—Turkey—with American taxpayers' funds and thus attempting to suppress and subvert a democratic vote passed in a democratic congress; threatening another—Russia—with the loss of oil "rights" in a conquered Iraq; and generally dictating the terms of debate, including to frame as a moral failure any opposition in the Security Council to an invasion of a prostrate Iraq.

Amidst this chilling swagger, one thing became clear: The Russians got it. The Germans got it. The French got it. The Canadians got it, and many British and European people got it. Even

Hollywood, in its invincible ignorance, was able to grasp why the war Washington and Whitehall were about to wage was unjust.

What does this say about most of the nation's pundits, who never stopped licking their chops for war? What does it say about those who supported conquering and occupying a sovereign member of the international community? They've lost their moral and intellectual moorings. They're even dumber, and certainly far more politically corrupted and co-opted, than the likes of the bug-eyed bovine Susan Sarandon.

Iraq had not attacked in 12 years and was not poised to attack the U.S. or its neighbors. To attack Iraq was to launch a purely offensive, non-defensive war. This flouts the Christian duty to do no harm to one's neighbors. It flouts the Jewish teachings, which instruct Jews to robustly and actively seek justice. It flouts "Just War Theory," developed by great Christian minds like St. Thomas Aquinas and St. Augustine. It flouts the libertarian axiom, which prohibits aggression against non-aggressors.

And it flouts what the Founding Fathers provided.

A limited, constitutional republican government, by definition, does not, cannot, and ought not pursue what Mr. Bush is after, and what paleoconservative Gladden J. Pappin called "a sort of twenty-first-century Manifest Destiny." The fact that it does, can, and is intent on spreading global democracy by death and destruction indicates how limitless, unconstitutional, and dictatorial American government truly is.

I'm no pacifist. While I don't condone the lingering American presence in Afghanistan, and while I doubt the abilities of the U.S. military to contain al-Qaida there, I supported going after bin Laden's group in that country. That was a legitimate act of retaliation and defense, accommodated within St. Augustine's teachings, whereby a just war is one "that avenges wrongs, when a nation or state has to be punished, for refusing to make amends for the wrongs inflicted by its subjects."

Al-Qaida was responsible for the murder of 3,000 Americans. The Taliban openly succored the organization and its masterminding leadership. Mr. Bush had asked the hosting Taliban to surrender bin Laden and his gang. The Taliban refused, insisting on defending their murderous guests.

The impending attack on Iraq also flunked the criterion for a preemptive war, facilitated in St. Augustine's idea of the "just cause," whereby it's permissible to attack someone who would otherwise shortly and imminently attack you.

The Israeli Six-Day War is a good example of a legitimate preemptive war. (Although, to be accurate, Jordan initiated the first strike.) Before Israel proceeded to deal them a debilitating blow, Egypt, Syria, and Lebanon had divided their labor in stepping up raids into Israel's territory, shelling her farms and villages, amassing troops on her borders, signing a pact, kicking UN monitors out of the Sinai, and blockading Israel's main shipping route to Asia.

Notwithstanding Colin Powell's multimedia presentation of circumstantial and speculative bunkum, there was no evidence that Iraq was positioned to pounce as Lebanon, Jordan and Egypt were; nor that Iraq recently posed a "real and imminent" danger to the U.S. or her neighbors. The Bush administration continued, however, to mount a blitz of Goebbels-worthy misinformation in order to discredit the thorough job the inspectors were doing.

In the 2,000 kilometers he crisscrossed in three weeks of searching for nuclear development activities, in the 75 facilities examined, in 218 nuclear inspections at 141 sites, including 21 newly discovered sites, Hans Blix's colleague, Dr. Mohammed ElBaradei, met with an "overall deterioration" and disrepair in Iraqi infrastructure. There was no trace of North Korean or Iranian-style firing up of production. In his account, ElBaradei did make polite mention of an investigation into reports (spread by the U.S.) regarding Iraq's uranium transactions: They were "not authentic," he wrote. The American power-worshipping chattering classes (and networks) had concealed that the reports were forgeries!

Blix's own cautious report details no evidence of "mobile production units" for weapons of mass destruction. The units Colin Powell warned of turned out to be mobile food-testing laboratories.

Iraq's improving, although still less than optimal, cooperation was certainly not a legitimate cause for war.

As a counterweight to "Just War Theory," which places excess faith in the motives of public authorities, Americans have the Founding Fathers.

In his pre-war National Press Conference, however, Bush showed he hadn't a clue what was and what was not constitutional. After claiming his job was to protect America, and that this was the essence of his crusade, Bush immediately contradicted himself: "There's a lot more at stake than just American security... freedom is at stake," he said, going on to indicate his plan to "deal with" totalitarianism wherever it presents itself.

James Madison predicted this craven propensity: "The Constitution supposes what the history of all governments demonstrates, that the executive is the branch of power most interested in war, and most prone to it," he wrote to Thomas Jefferson in 1798.

Duly, the founders vested war powers not with the executive but with Congress! The framers entrusted the declaration of war to the legislature so as to avoid what we've seen play out. What the Founding Fathers could not have foretold, given their own scruples, is the cowardly abnegation by this legislature. This Congress, like many before it, simply surrendered authority to the president, *sans* debate, thus forsaking the people.

108. THE JEWISH CONNECTION

March 19, 2003

Patrick J. Buchanan issued a passionate "J'accuse" against the neoconservative "cabal" in the Bush team. His persuasive polemic in *The American Conservative* identified the clique as consisting of Jews whose loyalties lie first with Israel and Ariel Sharon. He charges that they have taken over the White House with the intention of launching "a series of wars that are not in America's interests," and "would be a tragedy and a disaster for this republic," but which would be of infinite benefit to Israel.

I don't blame Mr. Buchanan for being frazzled and hence less than logical.

Buchanan is one of the few American patriots left among the "nattering nabobs." He is a thorn in the side of the swarm of "neoconservatives and their pseudo-conservative allies—Messers Limbaugh, O'Reilly," and Savage—with whom Mr. Buchanan is forced to joust. In his latest offering in *Chronicles*, paleoconservative Thomas Fleming captures the essence of these gabbing gorgons:

"Their patriotism is on par with their moral conscience... They want our boys and girls to die for their political schemes." [Although you will seldom find an invertebrate neoconservative in combat.] "They are always in favor of bombing, embargoing, and boycotting anyone they disagree with. The fact that as many as half a million Iraqi children have died as a direct result of the embargo on Iraq that they support is all the fault of Saddam Hussein."

Mr. Buchanan is up against yahoos whose lax morals and boundless ignorance about "the world outside their petty urban hells" is matched only by their deadpan lack of charm.

In his opposition to this war, Mr. Buchanan might over-emphasize American national interests to the exclusion of "Just War" principles. But his steadfast "to hell with empire" isolationism bespeaks a respect for the sovereignty of nation-states, and for the founders' long-lost republic, which prohibits the *Pax Americana* project and the attendant unparalleled American adventurism currently underway.

I don't blame Mr. Buchanan for being righteously furious with neoconservatives and their vulgar front men and women. He, however, is seeing causal connections where none exist. What makes Jewish misguidedness more pronounced than gentile misconception is that Jews seem to rise to the top in many fields and professions, politics included. That there are many Jews in neoconservative seats of power is dismaying, but it's of no particular significance, other than to reflect Jewish upward mobility.

Similarly, Jews are overrepresented in anti-war circles, among whom are George Soros, Robert Reich, Todd Gitlin, and Michael Lerner, to name but a few. The late Senator Paul Wellstone of Minnesota was—and Carl Levin of Michigan is—an outspoken Jewish anti-war politician. And Jewish members of Congress and the Senate were well represented in voting No on the War Resolution authorizing the President to undertake a unilateral preemptive war against Iraq. *Commentary* is indeed the Jewish neocon megaphone, but then there are Jewish magazines like *Tikkun* and *Forward*; they adopt an anti-war stance.

The Jewish neoconservatives in and close to the administration—Paul Wolfowitz, Richard Perle, Douglas Feith, David Wurmser, and Elliot Abrams—are more than matched in ideological fervor and influence by their gentile counterparts: Donald Rumsfeld, Colin Powell, John Ashcroft, Andrew Card, Dick Cheney, George W. Bush, Karl Rove, John Bolton, James Woolsey, and Condoleezza Rice.

Why Buchanan finds the king's Jewish neocon advisors more sinister than his gentile neocon conferees is unclear. I suspect that, being a Republican at heart, Buchanan would rather not blame his party and president for their treacherous—but chosen—direction. I suspect it's easier to believe candidate Bush didn't lie when he promised to adopt a humble foreign policy, but, rather, was mesmerized by Jewish mambas.

The truth is harder to swallow.

Nonetheless, and for what it's worth at this late stage, this administration came to power with a well-formulated scheme for a post-Hussein Iraq and much more. By the early summer of 2001, Bush had assembled the neocon team, not the other way round. The plan to go global was in place well before September 11. It can be found in the "Project for the New American Century," written by a group of prominent global interventionists now in—or close—to the administration, and issued in September 2000. Bush began to plan for global pre-eminence as soon as he was crowned.

The blueprint for empire is way bigger than any petty plot to protect Israeli interests. If anything, Israel will also become the object of subjugation in the eventual scheme of things. The U.S., not Israel, has a military presence in roughly 130 nations. The Project delineates how, in the quest to straddle the globe like a colossus, the U.S. would secure a much larger military presence across the world. To this end, establishing a precedent for acting unilaterally is also a revealing feature of the report.

Neoconservatives have a vision that lends itself to—and blesses—power-hungry, messianic mania. Bush was not snookered into this by a Jewish coterie. Bush's romp with neoconservatives began with his quest to be the king of the world. Mr. Buchanan's slide into extenuation is forgivable, but he needs to face reality: King George is wicked in his own right.

109. ON PIMPS AND 'PRESSTITUTES'

April 16, 2003

The Faustian bargain hundreds of embedded journalists struck with the military involved capitulating to an elaborate set of limits and conditions. Embedded with the military turned out to be a euphemism for in bed with the military, which is how a truly shameful episode in American television journalism shaped up. For journalistic jingoism, it was hard to find a better example than the coverage of the high-tech media extravaganza known as "Operation Iraqi Freedom." What made the supposed American champions of objectivity so much more obnoxious is that they paraded flagrant bias as gritty and honest reporting.

Embeds, for instance, were supervised by the military in the same way Saddam once assigned minders to accompany western journalists. Even so, American television networks went beyond the call of duty in giving unquestioning credence to the home team.

As farsighted as Washington has been in controlling and shaping the emerging information—not least through the embed program—the degree to which the networks transformed into shills for the administration must have exceeded its wildest expectations. (Come to think of it, the dearth of hard-edged questions from the press in general at the U.S. Central Command's briefings would have done any dictator proud.)

The monolithic quality of the reporting/cheerleading coming from the networks was and still is proof of the slutty sell-out. Practically all network embeds focused exclusively on the Pentagon's version of who did what, when, and how. Logistics usurped real issues; spectacle replaced substance, as the viewer was subjected to a perspective as monochromatic as the green of the night vision optics.

In their coverage, the networks also evinced a thorough assimilation of the Pentagon's power words. With the deployment of bluster like, "Breaking Baghdad," "Decapitation," and "Shock and Awe," a morally repugnant zeal was the order of the day.

Journalistically, the word "embedded" has bad connotations. Still, reporters who slept with their sources were treated as paragons of truth, while those who refused such cohabitation, and didn't join the embed program were labeled "unilaterals." The more independent perspective was thus tagged as one-sided. The networks were complicit in this linguistic co-optation.

Some of the issues that ought to have been highlighted and weren't:

There was a compelling tale in the obscene power discrepancy between the dilapidated Iraqi military and the American military might. Instead, when network reporters obliged viewers with proof of "huge caches of Iraqi weapons," their cameras would invariably zero in on ancient AK47s and rusty tubs of bullets. Jarring disagreement between verbal description and image was par for the course in the coverage.

Surely the peculiar specter of the "coalition forces" feigning shock and indignation at Iraq's lack of commitment to the Geneva Convention was worthy of media commentary? Isn't the nation that has been aggressed against justified in deploying all methods to repel the invader? Would anyone, including our truth-seeking reporters, have flinched if, in 1990, Kuwaitis had gone all out against the invading Iraqis? If my home were broken into, and if I ruthlessly eliminated the burglar, even when he assured me he was there to ultimately improve my lot, would I be without logical warrant? Or as a 33-year-old Iraqi Shiite told the *Los Angeles Times*: "Do you allow someone to enter your home and force you out of it?" Iraq had been invaded, yet the Pocahontas Partners were complaining bitterly about the Iraqis' disrespected for the Convention.

I'm still waiting to hear why it is that the U.S. decides which nations are sovereign and hence immune from invasion, and which are not and can be invaded, their leaders hunted down and killed. Incapable of posing the kind of questions that come with elemental intellectual curiosity, journalists thus remained poker-faced when Central Command issued a corny list of the most-wanted figures in Iraq in the form of a set of playing cards.

The stories that should have been told and weren't?

I learned about 12-year-old Ali Ismail Abbas from the Canadian Broadcasting Corporation (CBC). Most of my information about Iraqi civilian casualties came from the CBC. Abbas lost both his arms when an American missile smashed into his home, killing both his parents. Sixty percent of his body was covered with burns that turned septic. The hospital director at the Saddam General said there were hundreds like Ali, killed, orphaned or maimed. Their faces are not seen on American networks.

Reporting hearsay as truth and failing to verify stories has also been part of the networks' war effort. A Geiger counter that went off in the inexpert hands of a marine was broadcast as possible evidence of weapons-grade plutonium. Every bottle of Cipro tablets became a likely precursor to an anthrax factory. Anchormen and women somberly seconded these "finds," seldom bothering to issue retractions for misinforming the viewing public.

Periodic reality checks came from the CBC: "So far, soldiers have found gas masks, chemical suits and some white powder. None of it has turned out to be the biological or chemical weapons they are looking for."

Knowing what we know about Saddam Hussein, it's probably safe to say that if he had an arsenal, he would have used it. Since he didn't use his lethal stash in the face of "decapitation," it's reasonable to conclude that, either he didn't have weapons of mass destruction (WMD) or, if he had them, he was an extremely responsible tyrant. Both conclusions incriminate Bush.

In the unlikely event that it will fail to convincingly coordinate the planting of evidence of WMD in Iraq, the Pentagon, aided by the "parrot press," has begun to prime the American audiences (no other population would swallow the bait) with a new twist. The Associated Press recently reported that, according to the Pentagon, the looters may have removed the evidence. Even better: The Syrians spirited the weapons away. Better still: Onward to Syria!

110. WARTIME SOCIALISM

April 30, 2003

"It is often sadly remarked," wrote Henry Hazlitt, the distinguished free market writer, "that the bad economists present their errors to the public better than the good economists present their truths." This, ventured Hazlitt, comes about because the bad economists are presenting half-truths. A consummate gentleman, Hazlitt did not explicitly spell out that propagating half-truths still makes one a wholesale liar. Or that these economists owe their perpetual popularity to the intellectual legitimacy they provide to the plundering class, the politicians.

For what politician would not warmly welcome an economist who, with the aid of indecipherable econometrics, legitimizes immoral power and property grabs? This is why the anti-free market central planning advocated by the late John Maynard Keynes has been embraced with renewed verve by George Bush. Like any good

Keynesian, Bush sees big government—huge public works—and big deficits (especially during depressions), not as a bane but as a blessing, to be embraced as the key to economic boom.

Hazlitt (drawing on Frederic Bastiat, the 19th century French economist and statesman) further hammered home that "the art of economics consists in looking not merely at the immediate but at the longer effects of any act or policy; it consists in tracing the consequences of that policy not merely for one group but for all groups."

When the Hazlitt prescription is followed, it becomes abundantly clear why a war, especially a gratuitous one, always destroys individually owned real assets and capital. And why, in the short term, the war against Iraq will benefit some at the expense of others; in the long run, it will benefit none.

Keynesians, however, stand by the absurdity that war is good for the economy. And while you won't find these economists suggesting that, in order to create jobs in their own communities, people should set fire to their homes, and so help spur economic activity among local builders, landscapers, plumbers, and electricians, the very same "experts" have no qualms touting the economic benefits that accrue from taking a wrecking ball to an entire country.

According to figures provided by Yale professor William Nordhaus and the Council of Foreign Relations, the eventual costs of the war on Iraq will be roughly $1.2 trillion. Mr. Bush, however, proudly presides over a budget deficit, the official upbeat estimate of which is $455 billion. Since this figure doesn't include off-budget spending, and since estimates of the preliminary costs of the war run to $200 billion, the deficit is more likely to be upward of $600 billion.

And since there's no free lunch, who is going to pay for the debauchery?

The finances for the war, of course, will come from the private economy. For every dollar the government spends, a dollar is suctioned from you and me. For every new smiling military recruit sitting pretty with a home, a porch, and a pension, some poor sod will join the army of (nine million) unemployed.

Given its debt, the U.S. government is fast becoming a bad risk as a borrower. To finance the war, then, it'll have to steal over and above the usual call of duty. Unlike "The Shrub" currently in power, Ronald Reagan understood a thing or two. He said this: "The truth is that inflation is caused by government. It's caused by government spending more than it takes in, and it will go away just as soon as government stops doing that."

More precisely, inflation is an increase in the money supply by the government. Having adopted deficit spending as an article of faith, Bush will call on the Federal Reserve and the printing press to print money to pay the costs of the war. The endemic price hikes and economic distortions that'll follow are but a by-product of this legalized counterfeiting.

Reports of freshly minted dollars making their way from the Federal Reserve Bank to millions of Iraqis, now on the U.S. payroll, suggest that the money market is already being flooded. The first counterfeit down payment on the war will soon be wending its way into the coffers of the selected war contractors and their employees.

So why is this so bad? Doesn't more paper money enrich us all?

No, it doesn't. Real wealth is created only by the production and consumption not of paper money, but of products. An abundance of goods, not money income, is what makes for an increase in wealth. When the initial $1 billion worth of new money is given to corporate cronies like Kellogg Brown & Root, the construction arm of Cheney's Halliburton, and the Bechtel Corporation, it will immediately spur an artificially created demand, causing their suppliers to raise their prices. It'll take time, but the new money will generate price hikes throughout the economy.

Rest assured though that Bechtel's George Schultz, the former Secretary of State, who is also the chairman of the Committee for the Liberation of Iraq, will get his honey well before you taste any, unless, of course, you work for said company or for the Parsons

Corp, or the Louis Berger Group, or any other of the corporations involved in war profiteering.

Rest assured too that another Bechtel senior vice president by the name of Jack Sheehan, who, according to the British *Observer*, is also "a retired general who sits on the Defense Policy Board which advises the Pentagon," will enjoy a fat cheque well before the general price increases caused by all the new money affect his purchasing power. Jack will get to spend the new wads before counterfeit coinage spreads across the economy, causing prices to rise.

By the time you and I, politically unconnected suckers that we are, experience a meager rise in money income (but not in tangible wealth), rising prices will have obliterated the tiny gain.

If civil society is the sphere in which people accomplish things by engaging in productive, peaceful, and voluntary exchanges, the state is the sphere where domination is achieved legally by force and destruction. And of late, the state has been encroaching on ever-larger portions of civil society. Under Bush, the shift of resources from the productive, private sector to the inherently unproductive bureaucracy and military-industrial complex hasn't been equaled in decades.

At the same time, the wasteful, wealth-destroying political and military might involved in exporting democracy is nudging Americans into cultivating a comparative—even an absolute—advantage in violence and force, at the risk of losing their edge in productive innovation.

Last but not least, the process of forcibly creating a demand for certain wartime products and shifting production away from others also skews a consumer-driven production pattern. Since there are no freebies, those working for this centrally planned command economy will benefit while others foot the bill.

111. MURDER BY MAJORITY

April 23, 2003

Remember the little Iraqi boy with the charred torso, whose arms were blown away by an American dumb bomb? Not that the news-cable operators would know it, but Baghdad's hospitals, such that they are, are full of similar small children. Still, the networks have only just awakened to the optics of Ali; Ali has become the face of "collateral damage." As such, he is the recipient of a very twisted message from American group thinkers. And who better to deliver the message to the docile boy than a CNN anchorwoman who has probably never had an independent thought in her carefully coifed head?

While conducting an interview with the boy's befuddled physician, the vapid woman repetitively inquired as to whether Ali had been told why he had been "disarmed." The boy should be "helped" to understand that it was for a Greater Good that he has two bleeding stumps for arms, the woman doggedly insisted.

The American collectivist calculus is as coarse as that.

The math that goes into winning hearts and minds for an unprovoked, unjust war was even better encapsulated by Victor Davis Hanson, author of *Carnage and Culture: Landmark Battles in the Rise of Western Power*. Hanson correctly forecast that the civilian deaths would be in the low thousands. He told writer Michelle Goldberg of *Salon* that for him, the arithmetic was easy. "If you ask, 'Do you really want to free Iraq at the price of 500,000 dead?' people will say, 'Of course not.' If you ask, 'Do you want to free Iraq at the price of 2,000 or 3,000?' more people would say yes."

This is how it works in the diseased system of democracy. Make no mistake; the president and his Revolutionary Assembly have gone by the polls. The Reign of Terror during the French Revolution was also executed by popular demand. Assembly-line guillotining was voted on by the leadership, which, much like Bush and his grisly henchmen, claimed to represent the Common Will.

Repulsed by majority rule, the American Founding Fathers sought to prevent a descent into democracy, but failed. Our own Revolutionary Assembly now gets to not-so-delicately calibrate who gives up his arms for which political expedients, and how many thousands like Ali luck out.

There are some minor snags, but democracies accommodate them just dandily. While all Americans have no option but to fund the Administration's adventures, American soldiers, at least, are not conscripted against their will. They *voluntarily* undertook to level a small desert nation that had done them no harm.

On the other hand, Ali and other dead and disfigured Iraqis are *involuntary* conscripts—they get to partake of the wonders of American democracy only indirectly. Having been deprived of majority decision making in their own country, the mob in a far-away land has more than compensated them, by deciding their fate. And by golly what a splendid job this mob has done.

Ali will never be a policeman and will never get to feel the woman he loves, but he can rest assured that a distant democratic nation had his welfare in mind, a distant democratic nation that would never allow its leaders to sacrifice 2,000 or 3,000 unwitting American civilians for the so-called Common Good.

The Iraq Body Count, a project that arose because no official agency has committed to providing an account of the cost of this aggression to civilian lives, confirms that the minimum number of collateral disposables is, at the time of writing, 1,878, and the maximum 2,325. (It has since risen to 7918 and 9749 respectively.) The Project doesn't take into account tens of thousands of Iraqi soldiers who were forced to fight because of unprovoked American aggression.

The fighting has almost ceased, but not the death toll. Children are maimed or killed daily by cluster bomblets that litter their neighborhoods. Ali Mustapha, age four, for instance, was blinded when he picked up a cluster bomb near his Baghdad home and it blew up in his face. Iraqis are supposed to pick up the shards of their broken lives, but how can they in a country that has been destroyed, pummeled to the ground. Many neighborhoods are in ruins. The "coalition" disabled water purification plants, the electric grid, and the sewerage services, leaving most residents in Baghdad to battle disease and hunger while fending off bandits.

To survive, the vast majority of Iraqis relied on a steady supply of aid. At the rate the UN is re-establishing it since the end of fighting, it will be a very long time, if ever, before pre-war levels of aid are delivered once again. Most of Baghdad's economic activity has come to a halt. Hospitals and clinics are closed or inoperable. Staff that isn't afraid to return to work labors without power, water, medicines or food to save hundreds of people.

But even Americans understand that you cannot operate a respirator or perform surgery without electricity or generators; that you cannot save people in the absence of disinfectants, medicines, anesthetics, and oxygen.

Balderdash about liberation and democracy notwithstanding, even the insular American public can understand that Iraqis whose lungs are airless, whose hearts are not beating, and whose eyes and limbs are missing are not free and will never be free.

Murder with the majority's approval is still murder.

112. RATIONALIZE WITH LIES

June 25, 2003

Some rather creative *post hoc* arguments are being concocted to justify the unnecessary war the United States waged on a sovereign nation that had not attacked us, was no threat to us, and was certainly no match for us.

One after-the-fact rationalization has it that because, at some point in history, the UN, the French, the Germans, and "everyone else" may have believed or stated that Saddam Hussein possessed weapons of mass destruction (WMD), their current objections to the war Bush waged are unjustified. We were only adhering to a common consensus about Saddam's WMD, the War Party now whines.

This worse-than-asinine reasoning leaves out that *saying* something is not the same as *doing* something. To say that Saddam may have had WMD is quite different from advocating war based on those assumptions. It's one thing to assume in error; quite another to launch a war in which thousands would die based on mere assumptions, however widely shared. It was not the anti-war-on-Iraq camp that intended to launch a war based on the sketchy information it had. The crucial difference between the Bush camp and its opponents lies in the actions the former took.

Those who insisted Saddam had WMD and said war was the only way were certainly not hedging their words or their actions.

Second, it matters a great deal when during the last decade someone said Saddam was in possession of impermissible weapons. "Everyone—the French, the Germans and the UN—agreed Saddam Hussein had WMD" is the battle cry from Fox News' Sean Hannity. Hannity's ahistorical bawling ignores that to have made the claim in 1991 is not the same as saying so in 2003, by which time Iraq had so obviously been cowed into compliance and was crawling with inspectors.

Naturally, at certain times during Iraq's belligerent history, opponents of this war would have agreed Saddam had a weapons program. But by 1998, sensible people realized that Operation Desert Storm, followed by seven years of inspections, made the possibility of reconstituting such a program remote. The Defense Intelligence Agency reached the same conclusion in September 2002, writing that, "A substantial amount of Iraq's chemical warfare agents, precursors, munitions, and production equipment were destroyed between 1991 and 1998." President Jacques Chirac said as much to both Bush and Blair, who pretended not to hear.

More significantly, the anti-war-on-Iraq camp, the most principled of whom were on the conservative and libertarian Right, agreed that there was no imminent danger from Iraq. As this column wrote in the Toronto *Globe and Mail* on September 19, 2002, "Iraq is a Third World nation, whose military prowess is now a fifth of what it was when hobbled during the Gulf War. It has no navy or air force. It is not a threat to American national security." Considering this self-evident reality, war was the last, not first, resort.

Michael Novak, a Catholic scholar of religion from the American Enterprise Institute, advances a different after-the-fact justification. The burden of proving Iraq had or didn't have WMD rested not on the administration, but on Iraq, he absurdly claims.

First, the burden of proof is on he who proposes the existence of something, not on he who claims that it does not exist. (For this point I am indebted to Dr. J. Stierman.)

Second, Novak's rickety reasoning, if one can call it reasoning, omits the one crucial variable—aggression. When initiating war against a nation which is not being aggressive and doesn't want war, the onus is on the aggressor, not the aggressed against, to justify his actions, at least according to the conventional morality espoused by the pope, Novak's formidable spiritual leader.

Novak is correct to say that Iraq was supposed to disarm or else. But his statement begs the question: he assumes that Iraq didn't disarm. How does he know that? The Iraqis claimed they did. That nothing terribly incriminating has hitherto been found in Iraq suggests that Iraq was complying with its obligations at the time it was invaded. The country had been thrown open for inspection and a report, which may turn out to be one of the few truthful documents circulating at the time, was issued by the Iraqis attesting to their compliance. But by then, it was too late. Nothing could loosen Bush's viselike grip on his victims.

Novak and his cohort are taking pains to lower the threshold of what constitutes WMD, so that when the administration plants or uncovers a couple of dozen drums of inactive, old goop, minus the necessary dispersing systems, "Boobus Americanus" will easily accept these as the real reason for the war. Unless told by their "truthful" leaders, Americans have little need to apprise themselves of anything, not least that many military experts don't even consider weapons other than nuclear to be WMD. Or that the few pitiable manned and unmanned aerial vehicles (UAV) found in Iraq have a range that would make getting to Tel-Aviv the stuff of an *Arabian Nights* miracle. A flying carpet was more likely to reach an American metropolis than an Iraqi UAV.

The justification of last resort now animating the nation, thanks to the propagandists, is counteracted by the Future of Freedom Foundation's Sheldon Richman: "There is no warrant in the U.S. Constitution for the president of the United States to launch a war in order to liberate people from a brutal government." Unless, of course, you join liberals in adopting the odious doctrine of a "living Constitution," as conservatives have clearly done.

Surprisingly, *National Review's* editors admit that the presence of WMD in Iraq was "the decisive argument in the pre-war debate." They have attempted, in vain, to balance on the rickety WMD scaffolding they helped erect prior to the war; even expressing embarrassment over the president's reflexive, ongoing lies about already locating WMD. (Yes, as the few remaining honest experts were admitting that the two burned-out trucks were not where the Iraqi *Einsatzgrüppen* plotted mayhem, Bush was telling the troops that these were without a doubt "mobile biological weapons facilities," a lie he repeated to Vladimir Putin.) The minicon NR scribblers have at least rejected as bogus the belated humanitarian *casus belli*.

113. BUSH'S 16 WORDS MISS THE BIG PICTURE

July 16, 2003

The chattering classes are doing what they do best, and that is to shed darkness wherever they go. This column informed readers about the Niger lie in March 2003, after Muhammad ElBaradei, the International Atomic Energy Agency's chief, unceremoniously and politely called the allegation that Saddam Hussein had sought significant quantities of uranium from Africa "inauthentic." It'll take the mainstream media a few years to work out, but many in the administration (not least Condoleezza Rice and Dick Cheney) had been sitting on this intelligence since February 2002, when a diplomat called Joe Wilson was sent to Niger by the CIA and the State Department to ferret it out.

Members of the media aren't capable of much more than fragmenting and atomizing information. Integrating facts into a conceptual understanding is certainly not what Howard Fineman does. Fineman is Chris Matthews' anointed analyst, and the brain trust on MSNBC's *Hardball*. To disguise his pedestrian politicking, Fineman discussed who, at what time in the afternoon, as well as when in the estrus cycle of the next door cow, did an official put the infamous 16 words about nukes and Niger on the president's desk. That ought to make a nation already bogged down in concrete bits of disconnected data see the forest for the trees, wouldn't you say?

Reducing this administration's single-minded will to war to an erroneous 16 words ignores the big picture. First came the decision to go to war. The misbegotten illegality that was this administration's case for war followed once the decision to go to war had already been made. The administration's war wasn't about a few pieces that did not gel in an otherwise coherent framework; it wasn't about an Iraq that was poised to attack the U.S. with germs and chemicals rather than with nukes; it was about a resigned, hungry, economic pariah that was a sitting duck for the power-hungry American colossus.

By all means, dissect and analyze what, in September 2002, I called the "lattice of lies" leveled at Iraq: the uranium from Africa, the aluminum tubes from Timbuktu, the invisible "meetings" with al-Qaida in Prague, an al-Qaida training camp that existed under Kurdish—not Iraqi—control, as well as the alleged weaponized chemical and biological stockpiles and their attendant delivery systems that inspectors doubted were there and which never materialized.

But then assemble the pieces and synthesize the information, will you? Do what the critical mind must do. The rational individual, wedded to reality, reason, and objective, non-partisan truth saw

Bush's sub-intelligent case for war for what it was. He saw Bush as the poster boy for "the degeneracy of manner and morals" which James Madison warned war would bring—the same "bring 'em on" grin one can also observe on the face of a demented patient with end-stage syphilis. The rational individual saw all this, and understood that when Madison spoke of "war as the true nurse of executive aggrandizement," he was speaking of the disposition of this dictator.

Hold the CIA responsible for giving in to the War Party's pressure, if you will. But recognize that the CIA was only obeying the wishes of its masters. The CIA had attempted to resist. Witness the early statements by Vince Cannistraro, former counterterrorism chief, who scoffed at the concoction of an al-Qaida-Iraq connection. Having come under fire after September 11, the agency gave in to White House pressure to politicize and shape the lackluster information.

Unforgivable? Yes. But consider who the intelligence community takes its cues from. Perhaps New Jersey's poet laureate Amiri Baraka had a point when he wondered, "Who know [sic] what kind of Skeeza is a Condoleezza." The National Security Adviser has since September 11 been rocking the intelligence community with her allergy to the truth. As if her Saddam-seeded nuclear-winter forecasts were not bad enough, on September 8, 2002, Rice told CNN's Wolf Blitzer that, "We do know that there have been shipments into Iraq of aluminum tubes that really are only suited to nuclear weapons programs." "That's just a lie," an appalled David Albright of the Institution for Science and International Security told the *New Republic*.

In her latest damage control interview with Blitzer, Rice continued to insist that Saddam Hussein was threatening his neighbors when the president pounced, and, as justification for the war, she still makes reference to Saddam's effort to pursue a nuclear program in ... 1991, and to the burying of old centrifuge parts prior to the first Gulf War. Rice, of course, continues to deny the Niger forgery.

Clearly, Whitehall and Washington will not willingly give up their dark secrets. With few exceptions, such as U.S. Sen. Robert Byrd; Congressional Progressive Caucus co-chair Dennis Kucinich; John Conyers, the ranking Democrat on the House Judiciary Committee; and Bob Graham of Florida, the utterly disposable and detestable Democrats have been only too pleased to aid and abet this (heritable) executive dictatorship.

And the media will continue to do what their collective intelligence permits: focus only on the one lie, thus making the lattice more impenetrable.

114. BRING 'EM HOME, MR. BUSH

September 11, 2003

The Iraq quagmire and its ever-mutating justifications show that George W. Bush is oblivious to a basic principle of his own conservative ideology: Top-down central planning—economic or political—is doomed to fail.

In the process of pursuing some sort of neoconservative "Manifest Destiny," President Bush has junked the American Constitution—it gave him no authority to "promote" global freedom, democracy or nation-building with blood and treasure not his own.

In his latest address to the nation, Mr. Bush spoke of more sacrifice (not his own) and promised to "do what is necessary . . . spend what is necessary to achieve this essential victory in the war on terror ... to promote freedom and to make our own nation more secure."

To people who are *compos mentis*, it is obvious that these abstractions are not advanced by leveling one country (Iraq), and driving another (the U.S.) to the economic precipice. Where does it say that defending the homeland must translate into bringing about "the triumph of democracy and tolerance in Iraq, in Afghanistan and beyond," as Mr. Bush said in his address? Security and peace are served better by circling the wagons at home.

The President's overheated rhetoric about the Middle East becoming a place of "progress and peace"; his prophetic visions of "tyrants falling and resentment giving way to hope, as men and women in every culture reject the ideologies of terror, and turn to the pursuits of peace"—this is the political equivalent of speaking in tongues. At best, it's ahistoric. Yet the American people are lapping it up.

The kind of faith Americans seem to have in the ruling crusts has dulled the outcry at the President's $87-billion "emergency-funding request" in lieu of the adventures in "Iraq, Afghanistan and elsewhere" through next year, an amount greater than the world gives annually in foreign aid for all countries.

Initially, the Bush administration had pegged the costs of the war at $65 billion, total. Recall, Iraqi oil revenues were going to pay for this unconstitutional exercise. Like other little pesky details (the missing WMD come to mind), the administration has neglected to mention that, because of the ongoing sabotage and erratic power supply (courtesy of the invaders), oil revenue will barely reach $7 billion.

The war in Iraq, destined to be shouldered entirely by the American people, is costing an estimated $5 billion a month, and Mr. Bush has shown no compunction about taking the nation from black to red. Spending levels across the board are roughly 24 percent higher than when Bill Clinton left office. This so-called conservative President has yet to veto one spending bill. We now have a deficit of approximately $500 billion (without war costs).

This means we're into Keynesian deficit spending—the government is borrowing and inflating the money supply to fund its profligacy, a practice that will accelerate the depreciation of the dollar, and may even lead to the horror of hyperinflation. While Mr. Bush was making a commotion about returning plunder to the people in the form of a tax cut, he was focused just as keenly on increasing the ceiling on a whopping $6.8 trillion national debt.

At a time when there is an army of nine million unemployed Americans (and these are officially finessed figures), Americans are expected to place a couple of countries on the payroll. A large portion of the new budget will go toward funding expensive and expansive bureaucracies. The *New York Times* reported that the civilian side of the occupation is expected to cost $30 billion over the next year. Once ensconced, these fiefdoms become self-perpetuating, interminable and parasitical, forming a permanent drain on the private economy and the American taxpayer.

The warfare state is more costly than the welfare state, and just as intractable.

The truth is, we are bogged down in Iraq. The 140,000 troops now on the ground are going nowhere. There are only 21,000 non-American troops; at most, we can expect an additional 15,000 more by next year. Meanwhile, 289 Americans are dead.* This includes the 148 who've died since the President declared victory. Nobody in office is willing to render the Iraqi death count.

The truth is that the U.S. is desperate. Yet it continues to conduct itself with insolence, prompting one senior Western envoy to ponder "whether the world is ready to pick the United States up off the floor and dust [it] off."

For those of us who believe the lessons lie in rejecting what the U.S. has become, and reviving the legacy of this great nation's founders, there's no better time to quote the memorable but oh-so-ironic 1821 words of secretary of state John Quincy Adams: "America goes not abroad in search of monsters to destroy. She is the well-wisher of the freedom and independence of all. She is the champion and vindicator only of her own."

Mr. Bush's "bring 'em on" bravado has been a disaster. The time has come for some bring-'em-home humility.

---

*Second-edition update: Casualty numbers are 4296 as of May 16, 2009. Since Obama's inauguration, 68 American soldiers have perished. The number of Iraqis dead: upward of 100,000 civilians.

115. BETRAYING BRAVE BOYS

March 26, 2003

War makes the memories of the boys I knew and who are no longer come flooding back.

I grew up in Israel, and lived through the 1967 Six-Day War, the devastating 1973 Yom Kippur War, the tragic incursion into Lebanon, and all the hostilities in-between. I left Israel partly because life there was just too painful.

In those days, it was war with the Arab states. Israel and the Arab states that surround her have not been to war for a long time. When a war is prosecuted in your backyard, you avoid it like the plague. Perhaps this is why Americans go to war so casually; they do it on someone else's turf.

Secretary of Defense Donald Rumsfeld had said that precision strikes were being lobbed "with great humanity." (A strange word to use about bombs sent directly into Baghdad.) His words made me remember precisely where I was in 1967, when the sirens sounded.

We lived in a place similar to, but not quite like, a Kibbutz. It was safe for a child to wander about along the paths, as I was doing at the time.

A man grabbed me and carried me down to the underground shelter. The border with Jordan was close by back then, and we could hear the artillery. Someone switched on the radio. We tuned into the infamous Broadcast from Damascus, according to which the Jews were being thrown into the sea. I was very frightened, as the people of Baghdad must have been when the "humane attacks" on their city commenced.

When the war was over, 759 men were dead and about 3,000 had been wounded. Arab casualties came to about 15,000. A nation's Remembrance Days become more gut wrenching when war is up close and personal. These agonizing days are devoted to the men who are gone. Those who return dazed and confused are often forgotten.

Thanks to both his legendary wit and lack of coordination, my own father was only ever consigned to a role as jester and coffee maker for the engineering corps with which he was stationed. But I'd overhear a lot of whispering about maimed buddies and missing digits.

The Yom Kippur War Israel nearly lost. Israeli intelligence failed miserably. As is usually the case, young men paid the price—a few hundred of them were stranded on the borders with no backup. They defended their posts heroically before being gruesomely slaughtered. Many were dismembered.

When that war ended, Remembrance Day swelled to include another 2,523 casualties—about one-tenth of one percent of the population was dead. Thousands more were wounded. The casualty estimates for Egypt and Syria were 16,000.

These days, I think a lot about Avshalom. The Avshalom I knew was as beautiful as his biblical namesake, King David's son. Avshalom had dimples to die for, big brown eyes, and blond, sun-streaked curls. The vision of him, shirtless, on a red Ferguson tractor, as he ploughed the fields of the kibbutz, was very fetching.

Avshalom was 19 or 20 years old when he died. Like all Israeli boys, he was conscripted and he fell in some or other maneuver. My class lost another boy. There may have been others since, but I lost touch.

This much I know: Israelis loathe war. Living with such obscene carnage was bearable only when the alternative was conquest and national death. When the people learned the truth about the Lebanon War—that it was a grand offensive hatched by leadership—and when the boys kept dying, Israelis—Left and Right—flooded the streets. They formed human chains from Tel-Aviv to Haifa to stop the madness.

When this grandiose war on Iraq began, the polls showed that Americans had a stomach for sacrificing up to 1,000 youngsters. How was this possible?

Dare I say low opportunity costs? The average American doesn't associate the war with prohibitive costs to himself. Few of us know anyone who is in harm's way. Thanks to the armchair warriors' propaganda, Americans will not associate loss of jobs, a weak dollar, unstable financial markets, taxes, and deficits with the war. On the surface, and for now, our lives remain unaltered. With few visible costs to foot, what's the big deal?

Perhaps if Americans were unable to go about their daily lives, like Iraqis, or Israelis, or Egyptians, or Syrians or Lebanese, or Palestinians during the wars in that region; perhaps if every American personally knew an Avshalom—maybe then they wouldn't be as eager to send men to kill and be killed.

Make no mistake, our soldiers are brave. But is our "nation" brave? What I learned growing up in a war-torn region is this: A courageous nation fights only because it must; a cowardly one fights because it can.

Index

Beethoven, Ludwig, van, 229
Bernal, Martin, 258
Berry, Halle, 216, 217
Bill of Rights, 26, 57, 61–62, 184
bin Laden, Osama, 117, 188, 268, 269, 307, 311, 316, 317
Black, Conrad, 91
Blair, Tony, 25–28, 199, 331
Blix, Hans, 317
Block, Walter, 76, 87, 109
Blogging, 167–68
Bloom, Allan, 180
Bolton, John, 320
Bon Jovi, 80
Bono, 86–88, 97
"Boobus Americanus", 332
Borjas, George, 303
Bowman, Marilyn, 180, 244–46
Boys
  feminization of, 191
  medicating of, 248
Brand Bullies, 80, 104
Brimelow, Peter, 261, 262, 292, 293, 302, 303
Britain, 25–28, 37, 201, 222
Brooklyn Museum of Art, 222
Brussels, 86

Buchanan, Patrick J., 292, 299, 300, 303, 318–21
Buckley, W.F., 49
Budget, 4, 64, 65, 111, 196, 266, 325, 338
Bullying, 1, 104, 127, 179, 180, 181
Bureau of Citizenship and Immigration Services, 266, 291
Bureau of Economic Analysis, 65
Bureau of Labor Statistics, 295
Bush, George W., 3, 4, 8, 17, 25, 26, 34, 39, 40, 42, 46, 48, 49, 52, 59, 65, 66, 67, 87, 88, 96, 99, 118, 124, 121–24, 142, 153, 186, 237, 265, 267, 272, 277, 291, 306, 308–14, 316–18, 318, 320–27, 328, 330–33, 335, 336–38
Business cycles, 17–19
Butzer, Karl, 263

C
Calhoun, John C., 24
California, 95, 109–12, 162, 307
Caligula, 49
Campaign contributions, 6
Camus, Albert, 234

Thompson, Myron, 60
Thompson, Tommy, 146
Three Mile Island, 99
Thurmond, Strom, 7–9
Tikkun, 320
Time preference rates, 89
Toogood, Madelyne
    Gorman, 170–72
Tragedy of the commons,
    72
Triangulation, 124, 287
Tripp, Linda, 216
Trotskyist, 38, 49
Truman, Harry S., 8
Tucker, Jeff, 42
Turner, B.L., 263
Twelve Step, 130

U
Uncle Sam, 46
"Unilateral" journalists, 322
United Nations, 27, 52, 69,
    70, 86, 99, 103, 150,
    268, 281, 330
    Convention on the Rights
        of the Child, 185
    Drug Convention, 154
    inspectors, 308–10, 312,
        314, 317, 331, 334
    International Atomic
        Energy Agency, 314
    Relief and Works
        Agency, 53, 286
    Security Council, 315

World Summit on
    Sustainable
    Development, 13–17,
    70
University of Michigan,
    121–24
University of Virginia, 60
Upson, Sandra, 159
Uranium, 310, 311, 333,
    334
    transactions, Iraq's, 317
U.S. Supreme Court. *See*
    Supreme Court of the
    United States
USA Patriot Act, 273–75
USSR. *See* Soviet Union

V
The Vagina Monologues, 166
van Gogh, Vincent, 206
Van Halen, Eddie, 224, 225
Vaughan, Stevie Ray, 224
Vehicles. *See under*
    Environmentalism
VH1, 268, 269
Vick, Michael, 28–32
Virginia Statute for
    Religious Freedom, 60
Voltaire, 30, 263

W
Wahhabism, 186–88
Waksal, Samuel, 73–78
Wal-Mart, 83
War, 98, 101, 243

www.ingramcontent.com/pod-product-compliance
Lightning Source LLC
Chambersburg PA
CBHW020602270326
41927CB00005B/132